The SECRET

KNOWLEDGE

of WATER

The SECRET

KNOWLEDGE

of WATER

DISCOVERING THE ESSENCE OF THE AMERICAN DESERT

CRAIG CHILDS

SASQUATCH BOOKS
SEATTLE

Printed in the United States of America
Distributed in Canada by Raincoast Books, Ltd.
04 03 02 01 00   5 4 3 2 1

Cover and interior design: Kate Basart
Cover photograph: Gary Ladd
Interior illustrations: Regan Choi
Copy editor: Don Graydon

Library of Congress Cataloging in Publication Data

Childs, Craig Leland
    The secret knowledge of water : discovering the essence of the American
desert / Craig Childs.
            p.   cm.
Includes index.
ISBN 1-57061-159-9 (alk. paper)
    1. Southwest, New—Description and travel. 2. Deserts—Southwest,
New. 3. Water—Southwest, New. 4. Water, Southwest, New—Psychological
aspects. 5. Natural history—Southwest, New. 6. Childs, Craig Leland—
Journeys—Southwest, New. I. Title.

F787 .C47 2000
553.7'0979—dc21   99-057283

Sasquatch Books
615 Second Avenue
Seattle, Washington 98104
(206) 467-4300
www.SasquatchBooks.com
books@SasquatchBooks.com

In memory of Josh Ruder,

who was taken by the water

CONTENTS

ACKNOWLEDGMENTS

Without the inspiration, hard work, and friendship of Walt Anderson, few of these words would have come to paper. I have been humbled by his knowledge and propelled by his enthusiasm.

I am also indebted to my editor, Gary Luke, for asking gentle, necessary questions, drawing this story into the light. There have been many other people who have made this work possible, countless researchers who have added to the body of knowledge from which I have drawn. Among them, I especially thank Ellen Wohl, Bob Webb, Dennis Kubly, Father Charles Polzer, W. L. Minckley, Gale Monson, and Gayle Hartmann. I also thank the Nature Conservancy's Muleshoe Ranch and Cabeza Prieta National Wildlife Refuge for allowing me to perform research on their lands. Finally, thank you to my father, who was born in the desert and, during the floods and storms recorded in this book, died in the desert. Thank you for making certain that my eyes were always wide open.

FIRST WATERS

MY MOTHER WAS BORN BESIDE A SPRING IN THE HIGH desert, just north of where West Texas and Mexico meet along the Rio Grande. Born three months premature, she was kept alive in an incubator heated with household lightbulbs. An eyedropper was used for feeding. The water from the spring bathed and filled her body, tightening each of her cells. It filled the hollow of her bones. Years later, as the water passed from mother to child like fine hair or blue eyes, I grew up thinking that water and the desert were the same.

Beyond the spring grew piñon and juniper trees, their wood grossly twisted from years of drought, while here, where my mother was born, cress and moss grew from the spring. A weeping willow, imported from an unfamiliar place, dusted the surface with seeds. I traveled there once, walking up and pushing away the downy willow seeds with the edge of my hand. I dipped two film canisters below the surface. I capped these, walked back to my truck, and drove away before a stranger could appear from the nearby house to run me off the property.

I figured that the water might come in handy someday. If my mother ever grew ill and her death was near, I would bring this water to her. The spring had kept many people alive before her. It was an essential stopover for Spanish explorers in the seventeenth and eighteenth centuries and for whomever traveled the desert for the previous millennia. I would slip its water between her lips, tilting her head up with my palm. Her body might recognize it, the way salmon make sudden turns to follow obscure creeks, the way dragonflies work back to the one water hole held between desert mesas.

An early memory of the low Sonoran Desert where I was born is of my mother walking me out on a trail. I remember three things, each a snapshot without motion or sound. The first is lush, green cottonwood trees billowing like clouds against the stark backdrop of cliffs and boulders. The second is tadpoles worrying the mud in a water hole just about dry. Each tadpole, like the eye of a raven, waited black and moist against the sun. The third is water streaming over carved rock into a pool clear as window glass. These three images are what defined the desert for me. At an early age it was obvious to me that water was the element of consequence, the root of everything out here. Even to say the word *Sonoran* required my lips to form as if I were about to take a drink, and the tone of the word hovered in the air the same as *agua* or *water*.

The desert surface is carved into canyons, arroyos, cañoncitos, ravines, narrows, washes, and chasms. The anatomy of this place has no other profession but the moving of water. When you walk out here, you walk the places where water has gone—the canyons, the low places, and the pour-offs—because travel is too difficult against the grain of gullies or up in the rough rock outcrops.

At the time that I gathered my mother's spring water, I was out of work, beginning a series of monthlong foot treks through each of the North American deserts, starting here in the Chihuahuan, a desert that in winter sounds like fields of rattlesnakes with dried seedpods of yucca ticking in the wind. In the coming months I pressed myself into the desert, the land of my familiarity. When I pressed hard enough, water came out.

As I traveled from this west Texas spring, I saw water issuing from each piece of desert, and every turn I made pushed me into water. In the desert below the Chisos Mountains near the Mexican border, and just south of my mother's spring, I found small creeks flowing during the night, then drying and disappearing come daylight. When night fell again, the creeks flowed once more with small fish appearing like driven spirits out of what had been nothing but dry stones. Diving water beetles suddenly flashed alive in the new water. I witnessed these events like miracles.

It was a season of unusual water. March rains had gone heavy, flooding the desert. I was in my early twenties and had been in the desert enough, but hadn't seen this. I had not seen water leaking from fissures in rocks, ferns uncoiling in the shade of cacti, or rivers plunging along canyons I always knew to be dry. In the desert, water in any amount is a tincture, so holy that it will burn through your heart when you see it. To see it erupting from the ground was impossible.

On this cross-country journey I slept beside a flash flood at the mouth of a slot canyon in Utah. The next morning I climbed into the canyon where the last of the flood's earnest, red water coursed along the floor. I dipped my hand to gather the floodwater, then brought my hand back up. I put the thick water to my lips and it stung with the sour taste of dead animals and fresh mud.

There are two easy ways to die in the desert: thirst or drowning. This place is stained with such ironies, a tension set between the need to find water and the need to get away from it. The floods that come with the least warning arrive at the hottest time of the year, when the last thing on a person's mind is too much water. It is everything here. It shimmers and rises and consumes and offers and drops completely away, changing everything. I watch it move and can't help but want to walk straight into it. To be taken. To be purified by its oblivion. To never come back.

This Utah canyon's interior had been swept into sensuous, conical chambers. Down the walls the light of day bent until the place became as dark as an avocado bruise, me below wading through leftover floodwater. The entire passage was a flood path. Water had moved through here fifty feet deep the night before. The image of a flood in such a narrow canyon is terrifying, where a human body is twisted so hard that bones pop apart. Boots are ripped off, found downstream still tightly laced. Fingers snap off like twigs. I walked through with this memory, the canyon still and quiet around me.

I stopped. I heard people talking. I turned my head and waited to make sure of this. For at least a week I had seen no one else. This sounded like a group. As I reached the next turn, I could hear a fair number of people, maybe as many as ten; an overburdened backpacking group or worse, a hiking club. Speech against such slender walls tends to echo like spilled coins, but the enclosure was still too loud with running water for me to distinguish exact words. I could hear inflections well enough. Questions, then answers. I could nearly tell the age of people by the tone. I heard a woman in her forties.

It annoyed me that they spoke so loudly and freely in here. I thought I would startle them as I rounded their corner. I hoped so. They would fall silent upon seeing me, a man from out of the desert, fingers bandaged from cuts, eyes deliberately wild. When I waded around their corner I stopped. Water funneled down the canyon's cleavage. I stood knee-deep in the pool, sunlight landing in small daggers. There was no one.

I became aware of my breathing. The weight of my hands. The voices continued. Right here, in front of me, around me. Now they were so clear I could see the point where they began. The canyon crimped into a sliver ten feet up from the pool. Out of that sliver, water fell from darkened hallways. Within rooms I could not see, the stream plunged, poured, filled, and overflowed, addressing the canyon with innumerable tones, which then folded into echoes sounding so much like human voices that I had no category for them. I walked forward, approaching the slim waterfall. I reached my hand out and slipped it inside. Red water came down my fingers and laced my forearm like blood.

⌒

This book was written nearly a decade after I heard the voices. I focused a solid two years on the search for desert water, and my journey is written here. My pursuit was not of the edges of water, but the center of it. Not to be traveling through, but to be arriving. In the time this book came together my life was shoved back and forth between dramatic forms of water until I considered myself blessed, then overly blessed, then terrified.

In a part of the world inundated in water politics, I chose to look elsewhere than the dams and compromised rivers and skeletal canals leading to Phoenix, Los Angeles, and Las Vegas. It was desert water I was looking for, the water that is actually out there, that has been out there for thousands of years. The water holes, springs, rare creeks, and floods. I searched among stones in the wilderness, relying on disparate pieces of information: obscure research papers, my own recollections, stories told to me by old men, a 300-year-old desert map prepared by a Jesuit missionary.

Years before I wrote this book, in the bottom of the dark canyon, I stood in a shroud of voices. They spun up the canyon walls, radiating through the dusky interior, and I realized that part of my life was here, something I would have to seek with full attention, dictated by the water from my mother's spring sent from her body into mine. The voices were part of a complex language, a language that formed audible words as water tumbled over rocks, and one that carved sentences and stories into the stone walls that it passed. I would grow older with this language, tracing its meanings like working back through genealogy. I would study its parts, how different types of canyons varied their conversations. When there was no fluid, as was most often the case, with my hands on the water-carved walls I would read the language like some sort of seer. If you want to study water, you do not go to the Amazon or to Seattle. You come here, to the driest land. Nowhere else is it drawn to such a point. In the desert, water is unedited, perfect.

Part One

EPHEMERAL
WATER

Water, stories, the body,
all the things we do, are mediums
that hide and show what's hidden.
Study them,
and enjoy this being washed
with a secret we sometimes know,
and then not.

—Rumi, thirteenth century

The desert looks hideous. Burned-out cores of volcanoes, hundred-mile basins with floors mirrored in mirage, and terse, studded mountains. You would be a fool to believe water is here. But I have seen water holes. Back there, among boulders too hot to touch in the sun, thousands of gallons, blue eyes on the land. Or just enough in a hole for one swallow and then gone.

They cannot be located by verdant islands of greenery visible from miles away, or traced as clouds pass over to spill rain. They are random, hidden, and ironic.

During open-desert cattle drives, livestock sometimes suddenly turn and, with nostrils flared big as oranges, march in some random direction, undaunted by slaps and shouts from horseback riders. Hours or maybe a day later, far off course from the cattle drive, they reach water, pawing into its banks and inhaling it. Coyotes have been reported to trot over twenty miles straight to a water hole, deviating only to sleep or hunt rabbits. Omens and rumors are constant in the desert. It is all a matter of learning how to read them, and when to commit to walking straight across desolation to reach the right place.

Merely from traveling out here, needing to drink, I have earned some degree of knowledge. I've inserted this into my bag of instincts, able now to crouch on a piece of barren rimrock looking five miles out and say there, on the far point, on that open plain of sandstone, there will be water holes. It is a party trick, impressing companion travelers. A knowledge of geography, geology, shapes. But I've still been left puzzled. A hundred holes dry and one full to the edge. No water for three days, then a galaxy of water holes.

Common knowledge of water means nothing in these regions—the lowest reaches of Arizona, California, or Mexico, or the baked stone rims of the Four Corners. That it flows downhill, that it is cool to the lips, that you can splash it across your face and still have plenty to drink, must all be forgotten. Sometimes I catch the smell at night, a greenish scent without a return address. It wanders by. Some lost plug of rain in an old hole wetting the air just enough to perk my nose. Then gone.

Imagine thirty miles of rock and coarse sand, and a steady, clean light from the sun. You are walking east perhaps, driven by a rumor that water is out there, but you are not certain exactly where. It is one hole maybe four feet wide in a desert that is fractally endless. Abrupt mountains stand in your way and you must choose whether to search the mountains, sharp with rock and nearly absent of vegetation, or the dizzying trails of sand-filled washes below. Inadvertently you bite your tongue, seeking moisture. Say you find the water hole. It is surrounded by art-work of cultures here long before: complex, undecipherable etch-ings on boulders. You drink, mouth to the surface, and it tastes like the foamy sweat of the earth. It enters your blood, preventing your organs from shriveling like the raisins that they are in the leather pouch of your body.

Now say that the hole is dry, or you do not find it, and you have walked thirty miles only to place into your mouth a pinch of sand damp from the night before. The sand is a desperate act, and you die a few hours farther with grit on your swollen tongue. You leave your bones there, in the place where your last fragile thoughts drifted away.

There are great, natural cisterns out in the desert, marvelous contraptions of rock, but each is buried within miles of difficult land. They are revealed gradually, through patient inquiry, through stories told over hundreds of years. Yes, they may be worth dying for, because anytime I find the water holes, they stand out like emeralds in the sand.

1. MAPS OF WATER HOLES

Cabeza Prieta, Arizona
February–March

THE DESERT BREATHED AND THEN WENT SILENT AT THE first mention of nightfall, a kind of quiet that comes only at the edge of the earth. The last small winds broke apart, rolling down unrelated washes like pearls off a snapped necklace. Then came stars. And a crescent moon. And a desert strung in every direction, iridescent indigo in the west where the sun had just set, black in the east.

I walked west, toward an escarpment on the horizon barely into Arizona from the Mexican border. In evening silhouettes, these sere, isolated mountains had the look of tall ships strewn about the desert. Between were gulfs of open land furrowed with slight washes. Within the washes were the dimpled tracks of black-tailed jackrabbits and kangaroo rats, and within them the curled parchment of bursage leaves left by a wind gone somewhere else.

Across the flats I heard only the hushing sound of my boots through sand, then the sharper sound of my boots through the

7

broken granite above the washes. The hum of one of the stray breezes through thousands of saguaro cactus needles. The sound of creosote leaves scratching the brim of my hat. At night it is best to walk through the desert with a hat held in the hand, pushed forward to block the thorns and sharp spines of occasional unseen plants. Almost everything alive out here is armored with some barb, spike, or poison quill. From the years that I did not carry my hat, the back of my right hand is scarred as if it had been offered to a furious cat.

Tonight the moon, a waxing crescent thin as an eyelash, would not give enough light for shadows. I used it as a reference, walking directly toward it, carrying on my back all of the gear needed to resupply a base camp fifteen miles out, and the gear to supply the lesser camps beyond that. I had come to map water holes, working on a project for the U.S. Fish and Wildlife Service. The agency wanted to know what kind of water hid among these mountains, in some of the driest land in the Western Hemisphere. There are years when rain never falls, and sometimes the water holes contain nothing but rainwater that is twelve or sixteen months old, if they hold anything at all.

To find the water, I took thirty-seven days to traverse a single mountain range, hunting in its cracks and canyons. I carried simple measuring tools along with a device that communicates with satellites to record latitude and longitude of whatever water I found, perhaps a quart of evaporating rainwater in a rock depression. With my coordinates recorded, I placed small red marks on the map, showing one water hole, then the next.

This survey area was chosen not for any special characteristics, or a promise of water, but because it looked as arid and embattled as any of the mountains out here. Now and then I would return to my truck, which was parked beside a wash, off a long-winded road made of sand. There I would refill my supplies and cache them in the desert beyond. As I found water from the outlying natural cisterns, I was able to drink and extend deeper into the range, until I had recorded lifelines of water holes leading from my base camp into nowhere.

The final product of this work would go to the files of Cabeza Prieta National Wildlife Refuge. The refuge is managed primarily for desert bighorn sheep that supposedly thrive on these quarts. There are those people who worry for the sheep, who believe water should be shipped into the desert during early-summer droughts so that the sheep can maintain an "optimum" population, so that they can fill their range. There are also those who believe that after ten thousand years of seeking water, sheep do not require our aid.

While out walking through these canyons, below summits sharp as ice picks, I have heard sheep clattering among rocks but have rarely been able to get close enough to see their eyes. I have lifted their discarded bones and horns, turned them in my hand, and studied their tracks near water holes. One morning I watched a group of four rams carefully pick through steep talus. I waited above, crouched shirtless in shade, observing their choices, how their hooves negotiated each small rock. I tried to decipher their boldness and indecision, learning how an animal must behave in this landscape. The fourth ram, the youngest, waited until the others were out of sight before making its own mistakes, then backtracking. This made me smile, made me rest easier.

My personal reasons for mapping water holes here had little to do with bighorn sheep. I came to put a story back together and recover parts that had been lost. The story, when it was complete, would have told of secret water in a desperately ragged place, would have shown the route to safely cross from one end of Cabeza Prieta to the other. I wanted to understand water in a land this dry. Within the 860,000 acres of this refuge, only one spring exists. It is a bare, dripping spring, yet is enough to have bestowed the entire mountain range in which it sits with the name *Agua Dulce*. Sweet Water.

The desert cities have their cement aqueducts to siphon distant rivers, and holes are drilled into ten-thousand-year-old banks of groundwater. Familiarity with scattered water holes has become obsolete, left only for the bighorn sheep. Words are now missing from the story of ephemeral waters, severing critical pieces of information. Many people have died while crossing this desert, regardless of their reasons for being here. They died because the story was forgotten.

This country is not idle. The mountains are bitterly seared. Rising a couple thousand feet off the floor, they are offset by swaths of bulged, rolling desert, called *bajadas*, that take days to cross. As I walked on this night of the crescent moon, the bajada unfurled to the horizons to the north and south. Here and there it was intercepted by farther mountains, each an island, or a chain, or a misshapen monstrosity bursting straight from the ground.

On long night walks like this, brushing through plants and walking up and down against the grain of dry, north-flowing washes, I told myself stories, recounting whatever I remembered about the place. Stories gave the land definition at night, as the mountains vanished around me. Sometimes I would speak the stories out loud to break the loneliness. A particular one came from a site about eight miles straight ahead of me. An archaeologist making a sweep of the area found among assemblages of prehistoric potsherds two .45-caliber Colt cartridges, manufactured by the Winchester Repeating Arms Company. They had probably been discharged onto the ground in the early 1900s. The two cartridges had been rammed together, making a small, enclosed capsule. Inside this capsule was a note that read, "Was it worth it?"

So I invented scenarios, tried to imagine what the message meant. Death or desperation or gold that was never found or somebody like myself pushing the edges of the desert only to be confronted with this question in the end.

Just south of these two cartridges, in six hundred square miles of lava flows, cinder cones, and dune seas, ten forty-pound boulders were found butted against one another to form a perfect southeast-to-northwest line. It is not possible to tell if it was constructed hundreds or thousands of years ago, but it was done, for whatever reason, by strenuous human labor. I told myself stories about this. Perhaps they levered the boulders with wooden saguaro ribs tied together, rolling them from miles away. For what?

Cabeza Prieta

To appease certain gods? To reinvent the mountains? To invite the rain with a signal that could be seen from the clouds?

In another place each small rock on the ground had been cleared, revealing the pale belly of earth in a line six feet wide and seven hundred feet long without deviation. There are other, more ornate sites: geometric designs hundreds of feet in length, with mazes and inner circles that can be seen as a whole only from an airplane. I have seen in one of these stone clearings the life-size and accurate image of a horse, probably a sixteenth-century Spanish horse as seen by an indigenous artist, while around it ran a web of exposed lines radiating into the landscape.

In the mountain range ahead of me, a Spanish missionary of the Franciscan order came through in the 1700s, querying local inhabitants about the mounds of horns and bones from bighorn sheep he found erected near the water holes. He was talking to the people called the Hia C'ed O'odham, known as the Sand People by the Spanish. Without offering further explanation, the people gave him a simple answer. The horns and bones had been placed to keep the wind from leaving the country.

Stories everywhere. This is the place where people came to hold on to the wind. It is where they brought expectations that were rammed into rifle shells. In the coming dark, the desert grew richer with stories. And I became more alone. I knew of a small group of archaeologists with a work site about a four- or five-day walk southwest of here. Probably a few illegal immigrants were coming up from the border, but not through here, where people die from exposure and thirst. So I figured I was the only person for thirty to eighty miles in any direction. This left a kind of openness and remoteness that made merely breathing feel obscene. A friend once traveled with me here and as we walked the perimeter of one of these ranges, he said the vastness reminded him of the Arctic, up by the Brooks Range where great basins of tundra lie between distant and imposing mountains, where there is no human artifact. I nodded at the time, realizing a sensation I had not yet been able to place. Humans are absent here because they die. One document records the death of four hundred people here by 1900, many of whom were traveling from Mexico to the California goldfields. More have died since. Within view of several distant mountains, a family had been memorialized by black pieces of basalt arranged to form the numeral 8, telling how many family members perished. Sixty-five graves surround one of the better-known watering sites, presumably from the times that the holes went dry. Most victims died of dehydration and exposure, but occasional reports concerned those who drowned, too weak from thirst to climb out of the deep stone water holes into which they had plunged.

There are more recent deaths, those of illegal immigrants from Mexico, who come seeking jobs picking watermelons or cleaning houses. These people walk out in small groups, some of them from the tropics, never having seen the desert. They hire a person, a *coyote,* who deposits them across the border and points the way to Interstate 8. Each carries a gallon plastic milk jug filled with water, which in the summer lasts a few hours. The walk takes many days and they live maybe until the afternoon of the second or third day, their tracks of discarded belongings and empty milk jugs signaling insanity. Some of their milk jugs are, in fact, found half-full beside their bodies, skin taut to bursting. This story repeats itself every year.

As in stories I have heard from Mount Everest, where bodies of climbers are dispersed among glaciers, bodies here are turned to bones and spread across the sand and gravel and in the rocks.

The bones are uncounted and unburied, scattered like offerings. It is perhaps these bones, rather than those of bighorns, that now prevent the wind from leaving the country.

Coming close to the horizon, the moon appeared to move quickly. As it fell into the mountains of Cabeza Prieta, it described ridges as splintered as dry wood broken over a knee. For a moment, all that remained in the sky was the watermark stain of the moon's dark side. Then it set, leaving this hysterical swarm of stars. I chose certain constellations and followed them, my hat still extended in my hand.

There were good places to sleep. There were open flats where the ground curved slightly, barren of most plants. I could lie on one of these flats with my eyes open, the earth presenting me to the sky as if I were a newborn or a sacrifice. I chose instead a narrow wash, one barely depressed so that the wind had to bend down to find me. I protected myself beneath a creosote bush on ripples of wash sand. This is where I slept, in a country littered with arcane rock symbols, and death, and rumors of water.

First I followed bees. This was three weeks ago, when I arrived at a six-hundred-foot block of white granite floating on the desert like an iceberg. I slumped into its shade and craned my head up, hearing a drone of bees above. The sound told of an unusual congregation, so I scrambled up the smooth shield of rock. The bees led into a crack where they busied themselves in and out. I had already taken my shirt off in the heat, so as they commuted from the hole the bees thudded into my bare back and chest.

For seven days now I had found no water. Everything I had was carried on my back or left cached in caves. I had begun to doubt my choice of research sites, spending days where nothing was to be found but rock and ocotillo and bighorn scat. In this bee hole I could see a reflection within a rectangular crevice: a smooth, shaded mirror vibrating slightly against the wing beats of several hundred bees. The color quieted me. It was like a purple dusk sky suddenly masking the hot white I had been walking through all morning. I bunched my shoulders and squeezed in as far as I could, reaching my hand back until my fingers touched water. Circles spread over the barely lit surface. The circles fell back on themselves.

This was not the kind of water that could make war on the desert. It was a secret, a softly spoken word that the surrounding desert could not hear. If the sun ever found it, it would be gone in days. This was an artifact of the last rain, which had sheeted over the face of this isolated mountain and just happened to catch in this dark place where a block of stone had fallen, leaving a hole like the pulling of a tooth. Bees had come because it was the only water in their range. They distended their abdomens with water and carried it back to cool and moisten their hive.

I unraveled a tape measure and slowly passed it through the bees, then reached down to scratch numbers on a notepad. Bees landed on my forearm. They explored my fingers, with their legs catching in my hairs. This hole, I calculated, contained twenty-two and a half gallons of rainwater; it was about three feet long, a foot wide, and a tapering foot deep. Crustaceans called ostracods, each small as a dill seed, cruised the floor, their presence suggesting a longer life to this pool than I might have thought. Weeks rather than days. Bees started bottlenecking against my body, troubled by my movements, making me nervous, so I pulled my head backward into the light.

This particular island of granite, so heavy and white with quartz that it was hard to look at in the middle of the day, became a regular stop, a landmark to let me know how far it was to the mountains to the west. Halfway points are more important than the destination with these kinds of distances. On the morning after the crescent moon I paused to take measurements and drink a cup of water from the bee hole. It had only a slight, earthy taste of rock. As I drank I could feel the water fill the inside of my body as if I were an empty jar. There was no water on my back. Everything had been stored at my base camp, where I would arrive before sunset. I felt as if I were treading in the middle of the Pacific Ocean, no land in sight. I would stop now and then just to test the feeling, to say out loud that I had no water with me and see how that felt. It was a peculiar combination of arrogance and vulnerability. With this drink, I climbed down and walked farther.

Distances are meaningless here. Walking toward this western mountain range seemed, for most of the day, to be a futile task. But by afternoon the range, which had kept still since morning, began to shift. What was a single ridge unfolded into a backdrop of different mountains. The hazy blue of far objects became a variety of colors. Smaller mountains came and went, rags of granite that took no note of my passage. A mountain range that had looked like crumpled paper on the horizon now occupied most of the view, then opened into canyons, coming around me as I walked inside. Chasms spread up from the desert floor. The smooth bajada behind me was put away, and the world became a ring of quartz cathedrals, steeples playing all over the sky.

The somewhat barren land of the bajada was replaced at the foot of the range with groves of ironwood and paloverde trees, vines of devil's claw skulking among fallen mesquite branches, saguaros clumped together like old men waiting for a bus, and massive, spidery ocotillos with arms sprawling at the air. The desert here became arboreal with what little moisture drains from the mountains during a storm.

I reached my cache, a small cave sealed with dried elephant tree limbs and a tarp. Everything in this cave had been deposited over a period of several weeks during my passes-by in search of water holes, as I dropped off extra supplies and water for when I would later need them. I withdrew objects slowly, watching for scorpions. I grabbed the canvas water bag and it collapsed between my fingers, empty. Rodents had gotten in. Chewed a hole in the bottom, letting the water spill into the hole, soaking sand, then drying. They had not disturbed the food or the notes in plastic bags. They took my water.

Thirst, I remembered, is mostly a psychological pain, at first. It can drive you insane so that you die of something other than dehydration. Falling or getting trapped on a cliff or walking in the wrong direction. I remembered this and steadied my mind. I methodically unloaded new food supplies into the cache, took five days' worth of what I needed, and sealed the thing up, walking south now without water. I was still treading in the ocean. Still couldn't see land.

Weeks earlier, I had recorded a hole several miles away, and in my notes it was marked as Dry 001, meaning that it was the first of a series of dry holes. Because of what I remembered of its shape, a certain moistness to the sand in its floor, curtains of dry algae, and its position along the bottom of a constricted canyon, I thought it might someday hold water. There had been signs of a coyote digging in its sand. Light rain had come once since I had last seen it. Perhaps light rain twenty miles away meant heavy rain over the hole.

I rose through canyons where nolinas grew fifteen feet tall, each with slender, exotic trunks like those of palm trees and a crown of grasslike leaves. Canyon walls worked into odd shapes like nests of bones—finely curved ribs, sockets, and skulls. I climbed through these, coming over a pass and dropping down the other side into a wash. I bit lightly on my tongue, finding it dry.

When the wash tightened into bedrock I found Dry 001. It held about sixteen gallons of clear water. I stood for a moment in front of it, trying not to act desperate or crazily excited. I simply stared at the water, letting my hands list to my sides. I drank, taking water from just beneath the surface, then made notes and measurements, spanning a tape measure across the surface and then to the bottom. The hole was the shape of a cone, so I calculated the volume based on the volume of a cone. Not too accurate, but good enough. The name for a water hole like this is *tinaja*, Spanish for "earthen jar," a description I have always liked. A person who constructs or sells water jars is a *tinajero*. The English word often used as a parallel is *tank*, not nearly as rich or descriptive a term.

I gathered a couple of gallons from the tinaja. A gift. I tried to take this with my head down, and I worried that my disinterested taking of measurements might not be the proper response to something giving me life. I paused there thinking of how I should act, what words I should use. Nothing came. The desert is full of simple acts with indescribable significance. I merely rose and left, a thief of water.

Just after nightfall I dropped gear at a place where the contrast of dark basalt boulders on the pale quartz surface looked like raisins drying on linen. An ocotillo reaching its arms all over the sky made me think of a black octopus gathering stars. I sat beneath it, staring.

Being here alone had a sharpened edge to it. The edge came at night, whenever I stopped and sat among rocks. I had no stove, only nuts, raisins, and chocolate, so I did not have the ritual of preparing a meal. I reached out and spread my hand to measure spaces between stars. The magnifying glass of the atmosphere pried constellations apart at the horizon and then made them smaller as they rose. For a sense of comfort and familiarity, I arranged each of my belongings, placing my knife on a rock beside my headlamp, the water on my right, notebook on my left. I again spread my hand into the air to see how the stars had changed.

An ecologist working in this desert once looked straight at me and with a quiet voice told me to be careful. "I don't know what it is about the place," she said, "but there are hoodoos out there." She then started telling me stories I did not want to hear. One researcher had her vehicle burn to the ground, with a total loss of equipment and records. It burned for no reason. *Hoodoos* is an odd word for a uniformed federal scientist to be using, as if warning me of ghosts. But the word stayed with me.

So far the only odd event had been that my truck was broken into near a fifty-mile-long sand road. The break-in was a sign of desperation from people who kicked out a window and went past all my valuables to the food, clothes, and water. Anything else would have weighed them down, lessening their chances of getting out of here. Nearby, I came upon their vehicle—a beat-up Camaro from Mexico—with one tire shredded and the rest bogged so far down in sand, up past the doors, that the occupants had had to crawl out through the windows. Empty plastic milk jugs lay in the back.

At the same time as this break-in, a body of a backpacker was found southeast of here. The man had been missing for nearly half a year. With the proper permits and equipment, he had arrived to hike into the Agua Dulce Range. I surmised that he got out of his car and was seduced by the vacuous bajadas, kept walking until he collapsed from thirst. For the people working at the refuge headquarters, the time that the body went undiscovered was like a door left open, making it hard to concentrate. The body was found, the door closed. But other doors are still open all over, banging in the wind.

Out here I hesitated to tell myself stories about such things as hoodoos or found bodies. I preferred to study the stars rather than wonder why I would wake suddenly at night. An aerial bombing range surrounds the refuge, and daily I found unexploded missiles stabbed into the ground. Occasionally jet fighters came barreling in and out, chasing each other's tail, raking behind them a wall of noise. I have been told of pilots mowing down endangered Sonoran pronghorn with machine guns. From the cockpit of a jet fighter you might imagine that nothing down here could get you. One pilot was dropped into the refuge for rescue training. Sitting alone on the bajada in his flight suit, he said he felt fine. Night came. Then, he said, his world was not so easy. He could not sleep as he sat alone on a hump of granite. Maybe, with how quiet it gets at night, he could hear all the banging doors.

⁓

In this small pack, the one to be taken beyond the first and second supply caches, was room for just enough gear: small tools of measurement, something to sleep in, dry food, notebook, a pen and pencil, first-aid supplies, and a headlamp. A set of folded papers fit neatly down the side. These papers were not important items that might save my life or keep me comfortable at night, but under the midday shade of ironwood or paloverde trees, I unfolded them in the sand and read. They consisted of copied memoirs from a Jesuit missionary who had been sent here from Spain in 1683. Among the memoirs was a reproduction of the missionary's map, which is what first interested me in Father Eusebio Kino, a man I remembered from Arizona History classes in high school. He was the first person to record on paper the location of water holes in the Sonoran Desert.

Handmade Jesuit maps of the sixteenth and seventeenth centuries were of a meticulous, artful quality, detailing places previously unknown to European cartographers and explorers. Kino's work was one of these puzzle pieces, and it was in fact one of the best maps of the New World at the time. He recorded latitudes by astrolabe, holding the instrument against stars and the horizon. As I studied, I was taken by his accuracy. His map is a square, centered on the delta of the Colorado River, incorporating parts of the Sonoran coast and of Baja, where Kino had explored in 1683 under the title of royal cosmographer. It is the first map to show California not as an island but as a continuous segment of North America, a supposition borne out by Kino's overland travels. At the time, the survey of larger landmasses was commonly done from ships along coastlines. Kino chose to do his work on foot and by horseback. He had to cross Cabeza Prieta in order to do this.

On his map this vast interior country, unmarked by missions or any sort of township or *ranchería*, bore only the names *La*

Tinaja, Agua Escondida, and *Aguaje de la Luna.* Three watering sites. Just above 32 degrees latitude sat Aguaje de la Luna (Watering Place of the Moon) and Agua Escondida (Hidden Water). Below 32½ degrees was La Tinaja (The Jar). He called the holes at La Tinaja *pilas,* meaning baptismal fonts.

On February 22, 1702, Kino and his party were held back by heavy rains that overtopped local tinajas, causing them to cascade from one to the next. Even knowing that they were not constructed by human hands, he described these as "very sightly rocks which appeared to be very fine tanks made by hand and with very great art."

Kino's gentle language reflects the tone of his explorations. His was not the bloodbath journey common to his contemporaries in the New World. He did not sever feet from the youth of villages or pluck eyeballs from old men who refused to beg for their lives. His concern for gold seemed no greater than his concern for granite. Slavery would have only befuddled his interests, and he petitioned the Spanish government to allow him to convert Native Americans without requiring that these new converts commit the following twenty years to labor on estates or at mines, as was the law. He led cattle into the desert so that if he came upon any encampment of people, he would have something to offer.

Even the military personnel who joined him were not brought for reasons of war. Kino wanted secular witnesses who could return to explain that these people of the desert were not monstrous savages who, as the Spanish believed, ate their own children, but were human beings of a composed nature. The Spanish, for the most part, did not understand the desert, did not understand that people could survive without going mad.

During his twenty-four-year residence in the desert, Kino made more than fifty journeys, what he called *entradas*, each varying between one hundred and one thousand miles. Although he was a markedly skilled cartographer, technology was not yet available for the field recording of longitudes. So his maps do not pinpoint his route exactly, and there is debate as to where certain tinajas lie. His travels through Cabeza Prieta were done east to west and then west to east, setting a line roughly corresponding to what is now called *El Camino del Diablo*, the Road of the Devil. The line follows the water holes.

Of personal items along this route, Kino carried in leather saddle bags only essentials: gear for survival; an astrolabe for mapping; a black cassock, typical of the Jesuit faith, which extended from his shoulders to his feet; field notes; a small telescope; metal knife blades or trinkets—glass beads, ceramic pieces, or rosaries—which could be offered as gifts if he should encounter anyone; and, finally, devotional necessities (while crossing the desert, mass was performed for twenty minutes each morning, which would have required a gourd for wine, a host chalice, water, and bread). For reasons of faith or obligation he constantly wore a vow cross made of brass, inlaid with a wooden crucified figure.

Of all the people who have died here, none were under Kino's watch. None of his people wandered off lost in search of water, never to return—a record that was due partly to the knowledge of Native Americans who joined his travels and partly to Kino's refined sense of landscape. There were apparently times when neither Kino nor his companions knew where the next water would lie, and they relied on each other to find it. Kino watched closely. He recorded each detail.

I imagine those who now die here are intent on getting across rather than intent on finding water. The only way to get across is to have the sole intention of finding water. This was made apparent by Kino's constant mention of water in his notes.

The dead are most often found on the rolling bajadas and even lower, where the desert spreads itself flat, as if they thought that somehow they would find salvation at the lowest points, where gravity always carries water and leaves it. They would crawl under the spade-shaped shadows of brittlebush and the speckled shadows of creosote, or cooler paloverde, and there would suffer slow, delusional ends. The mountains must have looked too forbidding, too far away, too much like struggle and fear waiting on the horizon. They are also the only places that carry reliable water here. Kino always routed his entradas through these mountains when the easier way would have been to go around.

Once rainwater pours into the calligraphy of low, sandy washes, it is gone. Water is all up there, in the crags and chasms of the mountain ranges where containers have been carved from the rock like secret vases and ollas. The ranges along El Camino del Diablo are particularly poor at holding water, their granite too coarse to form neat bowls and the canyons too steep to allow the water to pause in a hole as it races down. Of deserts I had walked through, this was the most covert with its water. Still, Kino found and named some of the most remarkable sources. His small telescope was often employed in the scanning of distant mountains. He could not see water, but he could see the angle of rock, the abundance or absence of shadows. Steep, dark canyons speak of water, and they can be studied sometimes from thirty miles away. Whether they actually hold water or not is a different question. He had to go there to find out.

His first arrival at Aguaje de la Luna, in 1702, came under concern that water would not be found at all. It was just past midnight when the party entered a deep gorge and, with an accompaniment of a full moon, scrambled upward. Stock animals, unable to maneuver through the steep boulders, were left behind. These peregrine travelers entered a mountain range that stretched like a parched spine, a place now called Sierra Pinta. The moonlight must have made the granite look even more like bone, softening its edges, removing aberrant colors. Among the sharpened processes of this spine, they chose this particular route, perhaps because of its deeper shadows. Nearly halfway up a gorge, drenched in moonlight, they came upon a tinaja containing nearly two thousand gallons of water. It is one of only two tinajas in the range. Kino named it for the moonlight. On his third arrival at Aguaje de la Luna, when he was in his late fifties, Kino cleared a trail for his animals out of these boulders, beating apart rocks by hand to reach the water.

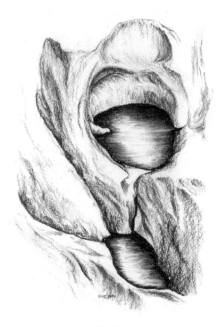

Tinajas

My original, childhood vision of what Kino looked like, a squat Friar Tuck kind of man with a jovial, plump-faced grin, was replaced by the image of a lean, muscular man who set his body against work that needed to be done. He would rarely wear his black cassock on these entradas—reserving it for formal encounters—and so wore ordinary clothes of the period. He wore far less regalia than his military escorts. Under the sun of the desert, on these great expanses between ranges, he looked like an ordinary man bearing no weapons, no helmet, and no robe of faith. Only a small vow cross hung against his chest. And each morning he dropped to his knees in the sand, performing his humbling ritual, his holy water gathered from a tinaja.

Walking for so long in a place few others travel, I have come across my own footprints, a bit formless in the grainy sand and gravel after days or weeks of wind. I have followed myself, investigating my own rituals. Up an arroyo, out to a creosote bush where I peed, along a gauntlet of sprawling ocotillo looking for dried flowers. I found the marks of my shoulder blades where I had slept, and a fallen, rotten saguaro that I had severed open with a knife to see what was inside, its black, spilled innards now dried like syrup on a table. With my finger I have studied the depth of my tracks, finding where I had given or taken weight, where I had barely paused to turn my head. If there had been much of a pause, I looked up to scan the horizon I would have viewed, looking for what I had looked for, imagining who I was when the prints had been left. I found where coyotes had crossed my path and sniffed at my heels.

When I came to the canyon that holds the largest tinaja, set deeply back into the range, I intersected my own tracks four times. A busy location for me. Each set of tracks marked a return for water at a place I could rely upon for months. I stopped in today to fill up, walking along stacks of boulders, past a rib cage of a bighorn sheep toppled to the side in sand, the same rib cage I had seen unmoved each time before. The canyon narrowed into a resistant rock, a hardened volcanic slurry that turned soft in its eroded shapes. The narrows burrowed down so that the walls became curved rather than sharp, squeezing until they revealed a disk of water fifteen feet across.

Two thousand fifty-three gallons of rainwater. This was the one that could last through a summer when everything else, even the water in the surrounding mountains, had gone out. The pool sank into a greenish chest of shadows, showing the way through hollows in the rock floor. It was almost blinding to see so much water. Look across this mountain range—in fact, look over the whole of Cabeza Prieta and the surrounding ranges: the Kofas, the Trigos, the Gilas, the Cargo Muchachos, the Ajos, Growlers, Craters, Childs, Granites, Mohawks, Pintas—and the thought of water will sting the back of your neck. It is out there, but to actually find it, to find *this* tinaja, is overpowering, like coming across blood on snow. I spread my fingers so that my palm floated on the surface. Shadows of my fingers cast through the fine mist of microscopic organisms. Waiting in the canyon above was an archipelago of tinajas, adding up to forty-five hundred gallons. Each tinaja hung gently over dry plunges from one to the next.

This was not an oasis in the classic sense. There were no palms, no broad leaves big as a hand, no lush grasses. It was raw and exposed, rock and water, making it appear not extravagant but completely implausible. I filled my bags, then crawled down on my stomach to drink straight from the hole. The back of my calves baked in the sun. A couple of red spotted toads glued themselves to the dampness surrounding the tinaja. *Toads,* out here. Seventy miles from the nearest reasonable, permanent water source, which is Quitobaquito Springs in Organ Pipe Cactus National Monument to the east.

Water fleas of the genus *Daphnia* dangled just beneath the surface, hardly visible to the naked eye. Under a hand lens *Daphnia* is as fine and crystalline as an ornament of blown glass, its body almost invisible except for the faint shadows of internal organs. When I've taken a powerful microscope to this water, it has appeared as if full of broken slivers of glass, countless fragile organisms. With the sun on the backs of my legs, I cupped these organisms in my hand, staring with the lens. Shapes like these should not be here, not in the desert, not something so delicate. Only at a tinaja could there be such a display of incongruity.

Rock contoured around the water's surface as if hands had rubbed the clay of this earthen jar, just as Kino had described. No sharp angles existed in the rock. Curves were as smooth as where the neck meets the shoulder, as where the arch of the foot sways off the heel. Everything else in Cabeza Prieta bears the cross lines of busted granite, the landscape looking like a heart ripped from the body, something out of violence, made in a fist. The mountains are heaved upward, pinnacles thrown to the sky so that boulders topple over themselves. Down at this very point, where the fingers of mountains have drawn together, the shape turns ceramic. Within the shape, as if invited to come, is water.

I once came up a canyon a few miles southwest of here, scaling shadows and the sculpted brows of granite. The word *water, agua,* rested on the lips of these rocks, waiting to be spoken. Finally it was said in a curved, shaded bowl beneath a dry waterfall—a broad, clear pool cupped against the rock. The sand and small rocks below glowed with colors like animals in a tidal pool. I had known that I would find water there. The shape of polished stone told me so.

A tinaja is so specific in its shape that any alteration changes even the condition of the water. Nearly each time I have seen human improvement attempted at a tinaja, the water has been bankrupted. The bowl of a tinaja is steep at the upstream side and shallow at the downstream, which pouts outward like the lip of a pitcher. This gently sloped exit, a happenstance of hydrology and erosion, ensures that organic debris is flushed out with heavy rains. Cement dams have been constructed to increase the holding capacity of some tinajas, with the intention of supplying more water to bighorn sheep. What happens instead is that organic material on the floor swirls around during a flood, unable to top the impoundment. The tinaja rots. The water becomes the color of decayed fruit. Under a microscope it is little more than a jungle of single-celled algae, no sign of the glasslike baubles.

In some cement dams, not only is the flow of organic material cut off, but also flood-driven rocks and boulders are stalled. I found a dam built in February 1948, spanning a 32-foot-wide section of canyon that once proved excellent at garnering water into holes. After fifty years it had long since filled to its nine-foot-tall rim with rock debris, impounding twenty-three hundred cubic feet of rock instead of water. A former refuge manager for Cabeza Prieta told me that at one improved tank he had to go out with a shovel after each heavy rain, digging sand out of the hole.

⌒

Of the water-hole maps I have seen, the one that most intrigues me is one left on the ground, out in the open, completely different in style from what Father Kino produced in 1705. Rather than something recorded on paper, by hands, with filigree handwriting, this was set by feet below the mountains in a style more fitting to the era of rock art than of Jesuits. It consists of subtle trails, too wide and intentional to have been left by wildlife. Sunlight was too bright, washing them from view, so I looked for them at night. Vaguely milky in moonlight, the trails showed as faint as breath on a cold day.

Kino never mentioned these lines in the desert, but I'm sure he saw them, or at least involuntarily followed them. They take the easiest routes, curving where they hug high points on the bajada, aiming toward particular canyons or mountains. I've come down one of these trails at night and stopped where another entered from a different angle, leading away into darkness to some other starting point tens of miles farther like a country road striking off.

The trails were formed by the passing of countless feet, which sorted each small stone to its flattest profile. These prehistoric routes are not consciously constructed. They are instead recordings left out of habit, out of slow repetition, obviously of some antiquity because many pass through three-hundred-year-old saguaros without flinching. Other markings tell of use within the past hundred years: I found a series of small stones spelling out the word WATER, with an arrow pointing toward a canyon where there was indeed a large tinaja. The trail beside this message was older than the word. It was probably older than the English language.

I talked with Gayle Hartmann, one of the archaeologists who did work at the Tinajas Altas camp west of Cabeza Prieta. Her impression of the people who had left these trails was that they were in constant motion, a demand put on them by the land. "You can't park yourself at any tinaja and expect to survive very long," she said. "You're going to quickly eat up everything around you. These people were in small groups and moved around through broad areas with a really intimate understanding of what was available at what times of the year." She described great journeys these people had taken. It was documented even up to three hundred years ago that people regularly walked hundreds of miles from near Tucson to the ocean. Shortly after the time of these great walks, Anglos and Mexicans were dying in droves just trying to cross modest portions of the same route. The moral is that if you know the land and its maps, you might live.

Closer to large tinajas the trails converge like strands of a spiderweb coming to the center, and within a few miles of water, broken pieces of pottery tend to appear alongside. Mostly the pieces are plain: thick-rimmed, ochre ceramics called Colorado River buff ware. Clay vessels would have been hauled back and forth until finally a carrier stumbled. The stumbles added up in places so that over hundreds upon hundreds of years pottery became evenly scattered, in some places pieces on top of pieces. Along with the pottery a small number of shells might be found, brought from far oceans probably for adornment, wealth, or ceremony. Along one of these trails I picked up part of a shallow-water cockleshell, its delicate hinges still intact after being carried hundreds of miles from the Sea of Cortés.

I started calling these trails *waterlines*. Waterlines are the opposite of canals, moving people to water rather than water to people. This bestows a formidable significance on the origin itself, the tinaja, because that is where you must go. *Must*. It comes and goes over the year, or over the days, while the location always remains the same. You can put your finger down and say *here*. Of all this land, all this dryness, all of these mountains heaped upon mountains, *here*.

With full water bags tamped into my pack, I walked away

from this largest tinaja. The field of surrounding boulders was a litter of black basalt, shiny the way coal becomes when rubbed with a cloth. In the sun all day, certain angles of these rocks burn flesh at the slightest touch. They hold their heat well into the night. They also hold drawings. Walking through, I could see the drawings around me as if heaps of strange artwork had been toppled out of a dump truck. These were lines and inset curves, each carved by hand, the hands of the same people who left the waterlines. On some boulders every possible facet had been marked, like the tattooed face of a Maori fisherman. Some petroglyphs swayed to the underside of a boulder, coming out on the opposite face, leaving half of the art down where scorpions wait out their days.

That there were no familiar symbols, no animals, dated these to a style common three or four thousand years ago. But the age of rock art here is unknown. One archaeologist suggested to me that it might be no older than four hundred years, or as old as four thousand, explaining that because of the rigors of survival in Cabeza Prieta, people maintained whatever rituals had kept their culture alive for thousands of years—ways of gathering food, finding water, or leaving signs on rock. Mostly these signs were carved webs and rays and intersecting lines. It was a sort of geometry that made the place look like a chalkboard left unclean after a math class. These people rarely addressed the larger or more prominent boulders, choosing instead the more numerous commonplace boulders, as if in a gesture of humility.

Directly between the etched boulders and the string of tinajas was an alcove. The back wall of this alcove showed a faint handprint made with dots of ashen paint, probably hundreds if not thousands of years old. It was the last piece of artwork after the boulder field of rock art, where waterlines approached from all directions and met the tinaja. It was the X on the map. It said, *Here, you have arrived. Drink.*

⌒

In the morning I crossed a place called Cabeza Prieta Pass and turned north. At each of the passes and notches I found pottery, enough in some cases that I could bend over and piece together a portion of a jar. I followed corridors of peaks and valleys, stepping down into washes, crushing the leaves of desert lavender between my fingers so that I could set the smell loose. I wiped the scent across the base of my throat and over the skin between my wrist and palm.

Walking into one of the interior ranges, held within a larger range, I found a place where the walls muscled apart, revealing a nucleus basin suspended within one of the mountains. Inside of this I followed the rounds of boulders and the trunks of fallen nolinas. In a small parabola of rock sat a little more than a tenth of a gallon of water. I came to my knees and placed hands on both sides. Even being so small—less than a foot across and one and a half inches deep—it housed a community of mosquito larvae, midge larvae known as chironomids, and gelatinous flatworms. I smelled it instead of tasting it. Not enough water for even a sip. It carried the scent of life, the smell of something green. How this had endured the past weeks of sun was not clear. It had never been much larger than this, so slight that if I dropped a nickel into the dish, the change in volume would be visible. Easily it could be dismissed, stepped over without notice. The rest of the world has water: lakes and streams and faucets and drinking fountains and swimming pools. The rest of the world is insatiable. Here, a tenth of a gallon is as striking as acid, yet I could inhale that amount through my lips and in two seconds it would be gone.

I once spent twenty days north of here in the Kofa Mountains. There I would come to a tinaja and strip off my clothes, sinking into it and letting the shock of cold in the desert rise through my spine, into the sky. Every chance I got I doused myself in these waters. This happened every few days. Now, in Cabeza Prieta, I felt like a parched ascetic. Salt ringed my eyes. Brittle trails of blood decorated my calf muscles. The prosperity of the Kofas had been replaced by rarity in Cabeza Prieta.

I dabbed the surface of this tiny pool with a finger as I had done to each one, not out of conscious choice but involuntarily to keep from weeping, to do anything so that I could touch this water. I touched only with my fingers because I remembered the Tohono O'odham people who live east of here, and how it is their customary belief that water is not to be taken boastfully. It is important to listen to people who have been in the desert for some time. To ask for too much water is to invite disaster. Only in a place like this would you bow your head and humbly request just the water you need and no more. Only here would you walk away from water when thirsty, but not thirsty enough.

Forty feet up the canyon from the tenth of a gallon I found two gallons, then another gallon. I left them in place, taking no water on the chance I would find something farther. Which I did: four tinajas of thirty-four gallons to the north.

⌒

With so many people dying from dehydration and exposure in this region, in 1917 the United States Congress appropriated $10,000 to send surveyors into southeast California and southwest Arizona

to map watering sites. Breaking into teams of two, each with camping supplies, a plane table for mapping, and a Ford automobile,
the U.S. Geological Survey crew scattered through sixty thousand
square miles of desert looking for water. Kirk Bryan, head of the
field program, kept notes on their finds.

Beyond the center of the Cabeza Prieta Range by ten miles, he
described a place called Coyote Water, where water can be
obtained by digging about four feet into the sand of a particular
arroyo. South of Coyote Water, Bryan reached Tinajas Altas, one
of the more reliable sources. He arrived in October 1917, taking
note of nearly seventy nearby graves as he passed. His notes on
Tinajas Altas are indicative of how he approached each water
hole, taking down as many details as might be needed for those
coming behind him:

> Water will be found in a series of tanks in a very steep
> stream channel or dry falls 500 feet west of sign [which
> was placed by the team]. The lowest tank is commonly
> full of sand, and water will be found by digging in sand.
> The second and third tanks are best reached by turning
> left (south), where a steel cable will be found, up which it
> is easy to climb the smooth rock face. The upper tanks are
> difficult to reach, and it can perhaps best be done by tak-
> ing trail to right and climbing to "window" and then
> going down to canyon above falls. The water lasts all year,
> but the lower tanks are sometimes exhausted by travelers.
> If so, climb to upper tanks and pour water down channel
> to fill lower ones. The water is palatable but there are usu-
> ally dead bees in it. Occasionally mountain sheep slip and
> fall into the tanks and contaminate the water.

The teams erected 305 water signs, each one anchored into the ground with two redwood blocks. They were made of 18-gauge steel, white background with dark blue letters offering names, distances, and directions to watering places. Standing alone on a trail or a rarely used road, these signs were classic, with arrows pointing off to seemingly nowhere, which in certain cases could only enhance a sense of despair.

GARLIC SPRINGS 24M

As a warning, Bryan said that the traveler here "must drink what is available, and the permanent inhabitant is so hardened to water contaminated with mineral salts or organic matter that he accepts without question water which elsewhere would be considered unfit for human consumption."

A series of maps emerged from the fieldwork. The one I took interest in was titled "Relief Map of the Western Part of the Papago Country, Arizona, Showing Desert Watering Places." When I came across this document, it was stiff with the feel of a starched collar, neatly creased from having been folded, unseen for seventy years. Mountains were shaded in a grainy brown, as if from a clear evening light from the northwest. Small red triangles marked the tinajas.

My own record of water holes was preposterously focused compared with Bryan's. By the end of my time here, I would have found fifty-two individual water holes, but most were too small to capture the attention of those at the refuge headquarters, and they would not last long enough to maintain bighorn sheep populations. In all I had found about fifty-five hundred gallons of water. This mountain range, parched as table salt, has water.

Contrary to every impression you gather from looking across this country, there is a way to survive.

Each evening in the field I would regard my own map. The water holes I had marked with a black pen corresponded to a notebook where I recorded the longitude and latitude, the aspect, gradient, and dimensions of each hole, a rough inventory of invertebrates, the size of the watershed, the type of rock and its texture; then there were sundry notes on, for instance, the taste of the water or whether bighorn sheep had been there recently or not. These notes were my map of water holes.

I once left Cabeza Prieta in the middle of my research to travel to an archive in Tempe, Arizona. There I asked to see a book of maps published in the late 1800s. I was presented with an object that stood about three feet tall, its cover tied closed with three strings sutured into the book itself. Too heavy and cumbersome to carry with one hand, it had to be hauled to a reading table with both of my arms supporting it from below, as I would carry a tray of fragile dishes. The maps in this book had been drawn during a survey by the United States and Mexico International Boundary Commission. A party from the commission, four men traveling from Sonoyta, Mexico, to their post in Yuma, Arizona, had once reported their encounters with emigrants who were struggling from a lack of water. Writing in his personal journal, one of the crew left this passage:

> Some men had died from thirst, and others were nearly exhausted. Among those we passed between the Colorado [River] and the "Tinajas Altas," was a party composed of one woman and three men, on foot, a pack-horse in wretched condition carrying their all. The

men had given up from pure exhaustion and laid down to die; but the woman, animated by love and sympathy, had plodded on over the long road until she reached water, then clambering up the side of the mountain to the highest tinaja, she filled her bota [a sort of leather flask], and scarcely stopping to take rest, started back to resuscitate her dying companions. When we met them she was striding along in advance of the men, animating them by her example.

I untied each of the binding strings, and the Boundary Commission book, published in 1882, opened like a vault. There were no explanations inside. No tales of travel or intriguing encounters. Any language used was official, in both Spanish and English. The book was meant to convey only topography and a bold line marking the border between two countries. I ran my finger along this border, turning broad, heavy pages from New Mexico into Arizona, looking for the edge of Cabeza Prieta.

There, on the correct page, I recognized the shape of topographic lines, how they made impressions of mountains I had walked across. Within these lines were black dots and, beside each dot, the word *tinaja*. There were no other words nearby, no descriptive terms or names of landmarks. I studied these sites for several minutes. I recognized the water holes, could see them in my mind: where they sat in a canyon, what their water looked like tucked into the shade of smooth rock, the ripe taste they carried after months of no rain.

I closed the book, placed my hands on the solid cover, and realized then that I had been wrong. The story of water that I had been trying to repair had not been lost. It had never even been interrupted. When I began this mapping project I believed that I was personally bridging a gap my culture had clumsily left open. We had not kept the story of water and its maps going. Now I saw that it was no accident or coincidence that these record keepers came into the desert and mapped its water so diligently. Every era produced its own map, sent its own people into the deeper desert to come back telling stories. The story is still intact, ritually retold in the maps, papers, leather-bound books, and the carvings on rock. Each generation is linked by the knowledge of this water.

I kept my hand on the book, feeling partly ashamed for underestimating the people of this land, yet filled with a sense of completeness. The finding of water turns out to be intrinsic, stored in our desires that push us out looking even in the most hostile of places. We never forgot to move the story ahead.

In a month's time Father Kino would have crossed hundreds of miles, and Kirk Bryan's crew would have erected signs around numerous mountain ranges. In the same period I wound tighter and tighter circles into this single mountain range. The circles, growing smaller and more detailed, felt almost obsessive and I took careful notes to remind myself of what I had seen, that there was more than just these stones beneath my feet.

Several hours before sunset I climbed high, using a canyon that cut straight up the center of a mountain chain. When the canyon ended, I scrambled up the edge, then topped out at a thin razorback of granite. The inside of the backside of nowhere. I spread my arms for balance and looked across the world. Usually I would remain in the canyons hunting water, where I would sleep, but I wanted to come up and see. I wanted to breathe. The washes, marked by bands of greenery, made fine loomwork, their strands descending from the knots of mountains, spreading across the curve of the earth. I stood two thousand feet straight over the desert floor, my hands open to the sky.

To the south, in the low, early evening light, I could see the ellipse shadows of sand dunes in Mexico, how they curved like cusps of crescent moons. Rows of mountains encrypted themselves into each other, one behind the next, too many to count. There were mountains I had not even known existed, occupying the earth to every edge. Winds came up from both sides, pressing my body. They carried smells. Desert lavender. Creosote.

Below somewhere were El Camino del Diablo and Aguaje de la Luna. So many curious names and mysterious deaths out here. These are stories, and they say something about the place, the same way water tells of the shape of an object as it passes. But the stories are not the place. All of the names and the deaths and the bones piled up to keep the wind from leaving the country are our replies to this landscape. These are the comments we've made as we have been confronted with the mountains and the long stretches below. Long before we made any of these remarks, there was water. There was this single definition to the land, which eventually formed the words on our lips as we traveled here, which told us which way to go to get across. My stories about this water are only my telling of the shape as I pass by.

Like following a circus tightrope, I walked this long, slender ridge. It swayed in front of me, sometimes too sharpened for walking, forcing me down on one side with my fingertips jammed into the cracks, then back to the top where I walked with one foot directly in front of the last. The sun went low. Shadows tilted to the east, marking every tower of rock. The desert turned to fire, hot cadmium reflecting off even the blackest of rock. Then it turned quiet. Shadows had everything. The wind stopped.

In the last light I found a clearing about the width of my shoulders along the axis of the ridge. It had been scraped flat by the hooves of a bighorn sheep, cleared of sharper stones so an animal could fold its legs and lie here with its belly against the ground. A rough bed at the top of Cabeza Prieta. Clusters of hard, dry sheep droppings had been pushed to the edges, shoved out of the way so I could see the outline of the sheep's resting body. I tossed a few rocks down, listened to them clatter until I could no longer hear them. I unloaded my gear onto this slim clearing, then sat with my knees drawn to my chest. A handful of peanuts and raisins. A long drink of water. My back damp and cool with sweat. I watched the desert disappear into the night. Then the stars took everything.

2. WATER THAT WAITS

AN ACCOUNT OF WATER WAS ONCE BROUGHT BACK FROM a region of sand dunes in the Gobi Desert. In the first decade of the twentieth century a woman had gone in search of an extensive lake, called the Lake of the Crescent Moon, rumored to be deep within the dunes. Working as a missionary, she spent time traveling the region, inquiring into the lake as she went about. She was told that it was in the Desert of Lob, beyond many crests of dunes. The directions became more specific as she came closer, until she left the town of Tunhwang and walked four miles into the dunes to find this exiled body of water. She described her feet slipping in the sand and how, exhausted, she scaled the last dune to peer over the top to see water below.

Swales and crests of sand loomed five hundred feet above the lake, casting shadows across its untroubled water. She had no explanation for this anomaly. It was perhaps thousands of years of rainwater gathered on a buried hardpan of rock. Or it was the one spring where dunes fed their sparsely gathered precipitation. She wrote, "Small, crescent-shaped and sapphire blue, it lay in the narrow space dividing us from the next range like a jewel in folds of warm-tinted sand." The image haunted me; I have always thought it to be true—an enigmatic, ultimate source of water. There are such places.

The ulterior store of water—not just a place to drink, but a jewel like the lake in the sand dunes—was an elusive image, formed in my mind but extremely difficult to locate. Some people had suggested to me that if such a lake was out there, it was already known, cordoned off, confined to a national monument or a state park. But I had been out searching for water for so many years in places unknown, finding bits and pieces, that I came to believe it would be there. I tried not to be a clown about my belief in some great, unaccounted water source. I traveled efficiently, keeping tidy camps, walking at night when necessary, and looking for water only because I had to. Always in hopes.

In this place, west of the Four Corners and Navajo Mountain, along the Arizona-Utah border where the Great Basin Desert comes south, I had found no water at all. The heels of my boots dug into the peach-colored sand of Navajo sandstone. I sat with my back pressed against a rock wall, my body seeking shade, scooting another inch tighter as the sun moved in. Every once in a while I stuck my hand forward to feel sunlight playing down like a clean, odorless poison. The September sky was as curved and blue as a robin's egg, a color and shape that implied scant moisture in the air and a far walk to the horizon. My partner, a broad-shouldered man named Tom Vimont, breathed heavily in the shade ten feet away. His eyes were closed, his jaw slack against the sand. Morning. We had already walked as far as we could in the last cool between darkness and 10 A.M. Now the day had begun. Heat was everywhere. When the sun crawled onto my boots I could feel it through the leather. In my toes. I stood and hoisted my backpack. Tom opened one of his eyes.

"I'm going," I said.

"Okay."

"I'll be at the next ridge. The white one with those boulders fallen on the west side." I pointed out there. He did not look. I told him I would wait for him in that next shade.

"Whatever," he said. "You go get lost in the heat. I'll find your bones when it cools off." He closed the one eye.

When not alone, I usually travel with one other person and we share few words during the day. I carefully choose the people I join for these walks, making certain they are not too abrasive or loud, or they carefully choose me. Tom is of a different quality, vocal and prankish. I travel with him because he rousts me from my quietness. He dances naked on rocks shouting obscenities to the sky, not caring if God hates him. He was once a mountaineering instructor. He sang in a punk rock band, was hired as an exotic dancer. When he was fifteen, as he so often enjoys saying, he got his girlfriend pregnant and stole a car, drove off with her to get married on the other side of the continent. I travel with him because when I say I'm heading into a piece of desert I know nothing about on the off chance of finding water, he grins and asks *When do we leave?*

Leaving Tom half asleep in the shade, I walked into the heat. From a distance, this is an inconspicuous land. It is a tilt rising gently to a high ridge at the roof of the formation called Navajo sandstone. It looks barren, uneventful. I had seen it a number of times from twenty or thirty miles away and never considered

Waterpocket at sunset

walking in this direction, always having been bound for more
spectacular country. But on the voluptuous stone of the Colorado
Plateau nothing is ever as it appears. There is constant potential.
The desert is not dried up and empty as if it might blow away like
the seeds of brittle grass. It is the bones of the earth brought to
daylight, half stuck out of the ground so that winds and flash
floods constantly reveal more. Just as it is beneath our own flesh,
the bones are the sturdiest, most lasting parts. With their hollowed sockets and deliberate lines, they set a foundation upon
which the flesh of forests, mountains, and oceans might accumu-
late. Only here, the flesh is gone, the last of it turned to dune sand.

The convolutions grew as I walked. Forms of carved rock rose
above me. Colors shifted between the red of salmon and a cream
white, highlighting changes in the shapes of rocks. Navajo sandstone in particular wears into the most sensuous of shapes. It
erodes into moons and the backs of whales, across which I walked.

I had studied a master's thesis by a man who did his field research somewhere in this area, a man who had spent time searching the rounded top of the Navajo. I was told he was ambitious with his travels in the desert, and that his skin had hardened against the sun. He had been studying habits of the crustacean species *Triops*, a creature an inch or so long, looking like a cross between a horseshoe crab, a trilobite, and a catfish. It is the oldest living animal on the planet, perfectly matching fossils from 180 million years ago, each part of its anatomy unchanged since then. It is an aquatic species, unable to survive on dry ground or even mildly damp ground. It must have some deep pocket of gathered rainwater that lasts weeks or months. I figured that there had to be a fair number of these pockets to support enough *Triops* for a master's thesis. Between the woman who found the clear lake in the sand dunes and this man who had found *Triops* on blistering sandstone, the place with water must exist.

Tom and I were both carrying whatever amount of water seemed prudent. I don't like to haul more than a couple of quarts at a time. A gallon is enough for one day of drinking, but that is too much weight, eight and a third pounds. Water would need to be found by nightfall. I flooded the air ahead of me with faith that radiated away, then disappeared in the dryness like a hot afternoon breeze that cannot stir a leaf.

Water created life the way it creates creeks or springs. It did this, I think, so it could get into places it could not otherwise reach, so that I would act as a vehicle carrying it into the desert. As living beings, we consider ourselves to be independent with our fingers, arms, and voices. Unlike alpine creeks, we are not all tied together, so we imagine that we each behave with free will. We can tie our own shoelaces and write poetry. But especially as I drink the last of my water, I believe that we are subjects of the planet's hydrologic process, too proud to write ourselves into textbooks along with clouds, rivers, and morning dew. When I walk cross-country, I am nothing but the beast carrying water to its next stop.

Sit in a car on a cold night and you will fog the windows with the water you carry. Touch your tongue or the surface of your eye and you will find water. Stop drinking liquids and see how difficult it is to maintain a coherent thought, and then, days later, how difficult it is to remain among the living. Specialized equipment has been designed to find a person behind a cement wall by bouncing 900-megahertz waves through the wall and off the liquid in the human body, as if we were all water-filled balloons unable to hide our cargo.

We are not as ephemeral as clouds. We cannot dissipate at the first downtrend in humidity, then expect to re-form elsewhere, so we have developed legs to walk us to the shade and hands with which we can construct faucets and swimming pools. Like any stage of the hydrologic process, we have our own peculiarities, our organs making us nothing more than water pools or springs of bizarre shape, filled with pulsing tubes and chambers.

Within my body I escorted well over a hundred pounds of water into the sand and rock on this day. Another four pounds were in my pack, for drinking. I carried this water across the supple shapes of small dunes and along the better footing of stone slabs. Whenever I scraped against a rock too hard, out leaked blood, nothing but glorified water. Tipped saucers of rock leaned upward and I dropped off their backsides, walking around clusters of shoulder-height juniper trees screwing out of cracks in the rock. Two ravens crossed. Their wings sounded like cardboard whooshed through the air.

I removed my pack and turned up through the boulders at the far ridge. At the top I pulled out binoculars and could see Tom, who had begun to move, groping through his gear a mile away. I watched his candid gestures, how he threw his head back to drink. Ahead I saw farther ridges, and beyond them a massive dune of sand rising five hundred feet to where it slept against a higher ridge.

About a hundred yards east of where I had just walked, freckles of water-filled pockets extended over a sandstone plain. I squinted, then started counting. They looked like fallen pieces of sky, so delicious that dry seeds would split open just to know of their presence. Each sat in the open as if lounging, unaware of the aridity surrounding it, mocking the sun. They had been beached here by thunderstorms, slowly hissing into nothing beneath the sky. I counted twenty. Maybe twenty-five when I included glints of reflected light from behind rock swells. These were sizable rainwater depressions, some of them the largest pockets I had ever seen in sandstone, thirty feet across.

In the Sonoran Desert they are called tinajas. Here on the Colorado Plateau they are waterpockets, generally different in structure than a tinaja, usually pocked across open plains of sandstone instead of in the line of a drainage. As it sits for different seasons over thousands of years, gathered water carves its own hole in the easily eroded sandstone. The longer the hole has been there, the deeper it becomes, the more water it holds. Hydrogen bonds in the rainwater pry sand grains from the rock, deepening the hole.

I jumped down from the ridge, grabbed my pack, and stumbled along the slope to intercept Tom. I shouted once, shouted the word *water,* and pointed east. My voice came back from every direction.

Tom motioned to his ears. Couldn't understand.

We met at a ravine and he waited in the shade of a piñon for me to catch my breath. I told him that there were at least twenty-five of them. We would have walked right past them. *I'll show you, follow me.* Down into the white sandstone, where it mingled slightly with red, we followed sand, then exposed rock. This opened to a rolling dance floor. On the floor was water. It had gathered from rain, but was substantial and would stay for some time. At a quick guess, I figured about fourteen thousand gallons rested in the rock before us. If water had created life in order to reach odd places, it created waterpockets in order to stay there.

I walked among the pools forgetting Tom was with me, letting me stride ahead. I did not watch each pool. I let them pass, feeling the prosperity of not having to bow and drink at each one. Some were thin and snakelike, others shaped like a woman sleeping on her side. There were crescents and deep envelopes, none of them feeding plants. They were all in bare rock, each one supporting *Triops* shrimp as well as a flood of clam shrimp and fairy shrimp. I swallowed my saliva, my throat dry. I stopped at one of the deeper pools. It sat twenty-five feet wide.

Tom stepped beside me. He did not wait. He stripped off his clothes quickly. Naked at the edge of the water, he posed theatrically with his hands praying to the sky. He is a big man, looks like he could crush rocks with his fingers. He glanced at me, grinned, and entered the water.

I stripped and followed. There could have been discussion about us damaging the ecology of the hole. There was not. Even though filter-feeding organisms might profit from our flailing and stirring of sediment, I would never profess our presence to be a benefit. But it was hot outside, and there was water.

When I entered, I did not jump. I slipped in at one end until only my face remained above the surface, my body seizing for a moment and then relaxing. It was not the coldness of the water that brought the quick seizure, but the absoluteness of the transition between desert and here. The shift was not slow or buffered. The only boundary was this perfect lens of blue, matching the cloudless sky for every value of color. The water turned smooth after a minute. My arms and legs hovered half-cocked, the way they do for sleeping astronauts. My face floated on this liquid mirror, surrounded on all sides by hot plates of sandstone tilted at the sky. I lifted a toe to penetrate the surface, watching rings drift outward, their movement opening a passageway from an inconceivable world.

Tom crawled onto the rock, his body doused, draining water back to the pocket. Water ran the depression of his spine, off his face, from between his fingers and toes. He rolled onto his back and the heat worked into his skin from both the rock below and the sun above. He closed his eyes. His mouth opened. In a groan, he said *Yes*.

Leaving Tom half-asleep on the rocks, his body surrounded by a thin, evaporating sheet of water, I took a notebook and skirted the pools barefoot, counting them, figuring which had what combination of crustaceans. Each seethed with life. The shrimp grazed on smaller organisms from the floors or from the open water, undulating their appendages so that every liter was guaranteed a good going-over. The deepest pocket, its floor hidden from daylight, belched *Triops* from the darkness below. Some had only fairy shrimp, which patrolled the water like schools of squid, trailing their teeming shadows over the round floors. These were slender and transparent of body, showing rhythmic sways of feathered appendages, which both propelled them and gathered oxygen. Other pools specialized in clam shrimp, with bodies similar to those of fairy shrimp, but seated in a bivalve shell thin as onion skin.

The *Triops* were by far the largest and most aggressive compared to the milquetoast fairy and clam shrimp. Their undersides, decorated with appendages of a slightly blue tint, gave them the appearance of crafted Japanese fans. They quarreled like cats whenever encountering one another, sometimes killing and consuming neighbors, hauling their bodies away. They scraped the floor with urgency, tracing the shapes of question marks as they arced through the water.

The species looks ominous with its shield for a carapace and two poppy-seed eyes seated next to each other, a fleshy, pronged tail ringed like that of a rat, and wired sensory organs splayed off the front. In my palm they slung their bodies with electrified twitches, trying to return to the water. Once returned, they got back about their business without pause, showing a distinct lack of memory. Still, I was hesitant to touch them, fearing whatever mechanism they had developed to defend themselves against seafaring dinosaurs. Creatures like sharks or scorpions or dragonflies are often considered to be some of the oldest on the planet, but they represent only an old style, an old type of organism. Their bodies have changed in the hundreds of millions of years while *Triops* has not. It is the same now as when it left fossils of itself.

Theoretically, the one thing that placed *Triops* into these holes was the evolution of predatory, suction-feeding fish about 300 million years ago. The only defense these crustaceans had was to move out of the oceans and into these loose affiliations of water holes, surviving by following the rise and fall of various climates, moving from one temporary water hole to the next across the planet, waiting out dry times in the form of eggs parched as dust.

Desert water holes produce the oddest of non sequiturs. In Cabeza Prieta, at the Mexican border, the eight-inch-long Colorado River toad, *Bufo alvarius*, has been found in a number of tinajas. Some of these toads, so large that their skin is folded, robelike, were found in tinajas 140 miles from the Colorado River. Along that straight line happens to be the driest land of North America.

How does the toad or a *Triops* make the trek to some small pool of water? A list was once compiled recording items known to have been unexpectedly delivered by the sky, mentioning spores, pollen grains, algae, diatoms, various microscopic single- and multiple-celled organisms, rotifers, living mites, pieces of dried algal mat, mussels weighing up to two ounces, fish, salamanders, frogs, turtles, and rats. If it seems unlikely that aquatic animals can be regularly transported to their water holes by wind, keep in mind that among these falling turtles and rats, there have been nearly a hundred accounts of fish raining from the skies.

Just before eight o'clock on the morning of October 23, 1947, fish numbering in the hundreds fell upon the streets, houses, and walking commuters of Marksville, Louisiana. Several people were struck directly by falling fish, most of which were either frozen or at least very cold. Their temperature suggested a recent ride through high clouds, meaning they were probably sucked out of a lake by an atmospheric disturbance, something that in the desert is commonly called a dust devil.

A biological investigator from the Department of Wildlife happened to be eating breakfast in a Marksville restaurant when the waitress told him about the thudding sounds outside. He immediately moved to the streets, where he collected samples of largemouth bass (one of them being nine and a quarter inches long) and various species of sunfish, pronouncing them to be "absolutely fresh, and . . . fit for human consumption."

More than likely, however, organisms deposited in waterpockets by wind would be smaller than fish or *Triops*. They would be algae and microscopic diatoms the size of ground glass. Desert rains are particularly rich with minuscule aquatic organisms, richer than mountain rains even, pulling down a dusty atmosphere of creatures, then directing them to waterpockets as they flow over the ground.

Still, wind and rain are not particularly efficient at relocating animals. The fish of Marksville did not benefit from the random rolling of atmospheric dice. They were, instead, ready for eating.

Hitching a ride with an animal heading to water offers far better chances. In 1930 a researcher sent a letter to an associate, mentioning, "When examining the contents of a frog's rectum yesterday in the course of our lab work I noticed several living ostracods." An ostracod, commonly called a seed shrimp, is a water-hole crustacean much smaller than *Triops*. The creatures either had been living permanently in the frog's rectum or, more likely, were passing through.

Although a *Triops* or a Colorado River toad the size of a softball cannot be comfortably passed by most rectums, their eggs can. When domestic mallards were fed dust from a desert playa bed that had been dry for several months, the ducks defecated the eggs of fourteen crustacean species including *Triops*. Some of these were brought to hatching within twelve hours.

As a more seemly way of travel, these same species also gather on the outsides of animals. A single dragonfly was once meticulously cleaned and found to be carrying twelve viable samples of unicellular algae, eight samples of filamentous blue-green algae, a rotifer (a microscopic aquatic organism), and fourteen other small aquatic creatures. One wasp produced nineteen species of animals and plants from around its wings and legs.

None of these dispersal methods are especially quick or predictable. The result is that species in water holes, the ones that can't get up and fly away, do not move around very often. They become genetically isolated over thousands, and then millions, of years. In 1992, after nearly all of the temporary vernal pools of California were destroyed by human development, researchers went out to catalog those still intact. Of the sixty-seven species of crustaceans found in the remaining pools, thirty had never been documented anywhere on the planet. People had to suddenly set about inventing names. A quarter of these newly found species were each found in its own pool among the fifty-eight pools studied, meaning there is not much motion between one pool and the next. What was lost in the hundreds of destroyed pools is unknown. Extinctions from ephemeral pools have probably been occurring at massive levels, banishing numerous species that have never been seen or even imagined by humans.

A study of such magnitude has not been performed on these Navajo waterpockets, so diversity between each pool is contained in the genes of these creatures and not in our papers and studies. Already I had noticed a number of different species among both fairy and clam shrimp. Walking barefoot, I had recorded twenty-eight waterpockets in the white sandstone. Some had floors of clean rock, some mud. There were floors dotted with swollen cacti that had blown in, floors of juniper berries, and floors of sand. Some of the water had the faint red-wine color of tannic acid from nearby junipers, while some were olive green and others absolutely clear.

These pockets led me farther east, where the dance floor ended, rising into a series of tall, narrow fins. Once I reached the fins, the skin of my feet growing sore against the heat and the kernels of rock, everything changed. I stepped up one of the backbones and looked down into a sea of waterpockets. I stood for a second. Then I crouched. There were over a hundred waterpockets below me.

This I had never seen. Nothing like this. The rock formations themselves were remarkable, having the configuration of egg crates with round water holes seated in the pits. I walked across the connected high points, looking down thirty or forty feet into smooth white craters on all sides where water had gathered. Each depression was entirely sealed from those around. I had to go back and get my boots. From there I kept counting, but I soon had trouble remembering where I had gone and where I had not. The fins and their cauldrons were beyond measurement. I put away my notebook at 138 waterpockets.

The only thing that could have adequately prepared me for this was to have walked in Cabeza Prieta. Following bighorn sheep off the Mexican border, my first discovery had been a bee-infested crack with twenty-two and a half gallons of water, my fingers trembling just to touch it, which allowed me to now see the garishness of this fortune on the roof of Navajo sandstone. Within a few hours today I had seen over seventy thousand gallons in water holes. This would have been unthinkable in Cabeza Prieta.

Tom joined me at the cauldrons before sunset. We left our clothes at a lip near one of the deeper holes. There we climbed in and sank our bodies. The sky became a confined circle. We spread our palms on the smooth stone as *Triops* bumped into our backs and burrowed beneath our feet.

We climbed out and, naked in the copper light, walked the narrow bridges, casting shadows of our bodies on the next fins over. The land, with all of its turns and holes and cryptic back rooms, rose up and swallowed us.

We returned at night and I lingered at the dance-floor pockets, near our small camp. Stars of a moonless sky reflected from the water so that the sky looked as if it had shattered and fallen messy across the earth. I was able to map the Milky Way by walking a circle around one of the pockets. A few hours before sunrise, a thunderstorm took the sky, rumbling and churning to the south. I woke and moved to the water, where I sat with knees against my chest. The pockets threw back the electric-white flare of lightning, the desert thumping with thunder. I waited for rain, to watch water run into the holes. Instead the storm broke in two, swerving to the east and west, offering only drizzle here. As the storm moved north I watched lightning crack the water's surface.

Eventually I returned to my own camp, which consisted of a sheet and a ground pad. Crickets got back to their Morse code after the passing storm. I lay on top of the sheet and fell asleep, my body peppered with light rain.

In the morning we packed and left, walking east. I had originally wanted to stay for days at these waterpockets, but the territory was vast. We had food for only four days and neither of us knew anything about the territory. First we crossed the cauldrons, stopping to stare into the pits. Then we descended a narrow canyon, pushing through crowded junipers and the prodding limbs of rabbitbrush into a broad wash that separated the last region from a taller cluster of fins ahead. In the wash were sand dunes fortified with bunches of Indian ricegrass that kept the valley bottom from blowing down to bedrock. Our footprints sank and caved in on themselves as we plodded to the next escarpment of sandstone, the canyon shaping around us as if we were being swirled up into a dust devil.

This took us several hundred feet above the floor of the wash, leading to the tallest of fins. From there we looked down into numerous vaults of water. Our packs hit the ground. We scattered, walking lines of stone that laced over these new pockets, even deeper than those before. There were more at this location, many inset by fifty and sixty feet, leading into tiered holes stacked one above the next. Some were so deeply inset that rims heaped up like excess clay on a potter's wheel. In the few pockets that held no water, sand had collected. On the sand grew juniper, ricegrass, foxtail, purple asters, yellow spiny daisies, scrub oak, broom snakeweed, and prickly pear, each garden its own particular arrangement. The rest had water. Cones and bowls and tubs of water.

I kept shouting over to Tom that this was beyond the realm of reason. He shouted back words of disbelief, then disappeared into one of the holes, his voice coming out as if from a barrel.

One of the early government surveyors of the canyon Southwest, Major John Wesley Powell, told of water like this. Giving vague directions, he wrote that one day in September 1870, he was traveling along the foot of the Vermilion Cliffs, having found little water other than briny springs. The next day he climbed a cliff to a "billowy sea of sand-dunes" where he found canyons wrestling into a tilted mesa top. "On the slope of this ridge," he wrote, "facing the mesa, there is a massive homogeneous sandstone, and the waters, gathering on the brink of the ridge and rolling down this slope, have carried innumerable channels; and, as they tumble down precipitously in many places, they dig out deep pot-holes, many of them holding a hundred or a thousand barrels of water. Among these holes we camped, finding a little bunch grass among the sand-dunes for our animals. We called this spot Thousand Wells."

An etching by Thomas Moran and W. J. Linton accompanied Powell's description. The etching showed two Indians, one on hands and knees to drink from the largest of a series of oval pools.

This spot Tom and I had reached was Powell's Thousand Wells. It could be no other place. Even with the vagueness of Powell's directions, it matched. We decided to stay on task. We turned to the southeast, which took us from the waterpockets and sent us to lifting tables of sandstone. Quickly, I entered the mode of desert walking as my breathing became metered, my thoughts simplifying into bare bones. A straight-faced walk. Hot. Still air. I picked up small rocks or the bones of animals, then set them back without having formulated a thought more profound than *bone* or *rock*. I could hear the crunch of Tom's boots on the ground a quarter mile behind. I saw the way he moved, how he had accepted the desert, how his thoughts had centered as he sought routes over bulges and boulders.

As soon as I felt at ease, taking on the rhythm of walking in heat, I came to water again. This was in slanted, loose shelves of red sandstone where I would never look for water. Deep red sandstone is not as pure or as tightly packed as white sandstone, and never seems to hold water as well. The position of the rock, the angle of the bedding planes, was all wrong. I could not even find a drainage that would have filled it. The only way to get in was from the sky. My comments of impossibility became instantly hysterical as I waved my hands in the air before this pool, forty feet across, the largest we had seen. This whole region was absurd.

We removed clothing in a fashion that was becoming routine, leaving our own brand of piles: socks stuffed in boots, my notebook out of reach of wet hands, his clothes in more of a pile and mine more in a line. We sank into water the depth of our shoulders. Instantly we became playful, embarrassingly so as we made the water slosh back and forth unnecessarily until it tipped out one end. Then we walked, drenched, on the surrounding rocks. The sound of slapping water, the deep swallows made only by large masses of liquid, was almost too much to bear. I stood at the edge of the waterpocket, where much of the desert dropped off below, showing pockets of even greater size, and lifted my arms straight into the sky. Beads came down my body. This was abundance.

We walked to higher country, spending hours working toward a stretched dome of red sandstone. The tables steepened in the last mile to this highest point where the uplift broke its back, falling twelve hundred feet to a chasm below. The cliff was as smooth as lake ice. A rock could be dropped and it would not once touch the wall. Just beside the edge, as if lifted onto a pedestal, was a waterpocket. I told Tom that what we were witnessing here made everything I had ever seen inadequate. Tom laughed at me, said that I always say that. We go to places for particular reasons, he said. We came here for opulence.

I had not been counting religiously, but we had now passed between four and five hundred waterpockets. Maybe 300,000 gallons of rainwater. My careful counting of waterpockets the day before felt like a prank on myself.

As we slipped into the hole, our arms draping across its rims as if over the back of a couch, I said to Tom, "This has been years. I knew it would be here. If I looked long enough I would find it. I've been trying for years. *Years.*"

Skirting a pool that measured about one hundred feet in length, we could see a prickly pear cactus lurking in the depths. It was surrounded by *Triops* and a cloud of fairy shrimp. The cactus had not fallen in. It had grown there prior to the water, indicating that years of drought must have preceded this water. When this pool is dust, it must retain the seeds of aquatic life for however long it takes a cactus to grow.

To survive, these aquatic-desert organisms have taken an evolutionary course that rejects mechanisms of survival used by most everything else. Bypassing all accepted notions of life, they cope with extremely long periods of drought that would kill every jackrabbit and human out here. They shrivel up until they are dry as cotton balls, releasing all of their water, entering a state known as *anhydrobiosis*. *Life without water.* Basically, they die, but with the loophole of being able to come back to life.

Anhydrobiosis is dehydrated life—life shrunk down to its most primary aspects. No energy is spent on what would normally be considered to be living. The participants become sealed containers against the world, cells turning from living structures into reinforcement material. Sensitive organs are tucked away into specialized membranes, like wine glasses wrapped in newspaper for a move. Molecules, mostly a disaccharide called trehalose, are

produced to shore up the shriveling internal structures. The organism's insides become crystalline, a material very similar to the
liquid crystal in digital watches. A dehydrating roundworm converts a quarter of its body weight into this trehalose material
before going completely dry, coiling into a compact circle and
reducing its surface area to a hardened bulb about 7 percent of
the original size.

If an anhydrobiotic organism regularly lasts for three weeks
from egg to death, it does not matter if one hundred years of
drought are placed in the middle of the life cycle. It will still live
for three weeks, the extra hundred years being nothing but a
pause on the biological clock.

Abandoned in dry water holes, these barren animals can be
exposed to heavy doses of X-rays, gamma rays, neutrons, proton
beams, high-energy electrons, and ultraviolet radiation with no ill
effects. Embryonic cysts of an ephemeral pool crustacean were
actually dangled outside of the space shuttle, exposed directly to
the cold and radiation of outer space, and were later brought
back to earth and added to water, where they came to life within
minutes. The universe could be accidentally colonized by such
creatures. In a sadistic array of experiments, adult tardigrades,
known also as water bears, were once kept for eight days in a
vacuum, transferred into helium gas at room temperature for
three days, and then exposed for several hours to nearly -450
degrees Fahrenheit. Placed in water at room temperature, they
returned to life, no questions asked.

Perhaps the most telling experiment is that anhydrobiotic
cysts of crustaceans are packaged and sold to children. Often they
are sold as "sea monkeys," presented on packages with the
females wearing pink bows in their sensory organs, and families

of smiling crustaceans reclining in underwater living rooms (the wife wearing an apron, the husband smoking a pipe). At a toy store I once bought an envelope of *Triops* eggs (Desert Dan brand); the print on the back informed me that they would live twenty to seventy days, "unless, of course, they are eaten alive by their cannibal siblings."

The packaging read:

TRIOPS

From The Age Of

DINOSAURS

Watch

Their

AMAZING

AQUA-BATICS

They're

ALIVE!

Just Add Water

They Hatch In

24 HOURS

EVERYTHING YOU NEED TO GROW INSTANT PETS

I put them in a cup, and within twenty-four hours small objects could be seen scuttling across the bottom. No false advertising. I instantly had pets. And they were, indeed, from the age of the dinosaurs, as Desert Dan had professed. The aquabatics would come later as they began eating one another.

What truly separates these dehydrated organisms from every other living thing is that they have no metabolism. Even scientists who contend that all life requires a metabolism admit that anhydrobiotes must exist at the minutest fraction of the speed of normally

Water hole shrimp eggs

metabolizing specimens. If this were a human, the heart would beat three times every year. But there does not appear to be even a slow heartbeat in anhydrobiotes. Using radiochemical assay, researchers have not been able to detect enzyme activity in any "live" organisms below 8 percent water content by body weight. There appear to be no working parts in these organisms: they are as dead as rocks. If a Mars lander were to be given a scoop of dust from a dry water hole and allowed to run all of the spores and shrimp eggs and desiccated adults of various species through its battery of life-finding tests, it would conclude that no life was ever present.

The question then arises as to what actually defines life. The crustaceans in limbo are not dead. Yet a viable egg of a desert toad cannot be differentiated from a nonviable egg until water is added and the egg either hatches or does nothing. Death and life in this case are structurally identical. One scientist, especially preoccupied with this topic, slipped out the words "cosmic metabolism," but quickly dismissed this as a notion with little meaning in the biological context of metabolism. In the case of these creatures waiting for the next desert rain, he commented, life is more a quality than it is a quantity. It cannot be defined or measured by our tools, but it is there, perhaps more philosophical than detectable. The basic constituents of life are not at all what we had scientifically imagined.

How long can these creatures actually last before the arrival of rain? Shrimp such as *Triops* last for decades, at the least. They have never been kept longer than thirty years, while evidence suggests that they may survive for centuries. Again, at the least. Because adaptations are similar, they can be compared to seeds awaiting germination. Although data are not firmly proven, a seed of an arctic lupine from the Yukon was viable after 10,000 years. A dormant seed from Danish soil was viable after a proven 850 years. An example that seems most fitting comes from a *Canna compacta* seed that was recovered from an archaeological site in Argentina. The specimen was found enclosed in a walnut shell, which was part of a rattle necklace excavated from a tomb. After lying dormant in this tomb for 600 years, the dry seed was removed and placed in soil. Unfazed by this long period of quiescence, the plant produced a healthy root system and within ten days presented its first leaves. Reaching a height of six and a half feet, it flowered, finally showing itself to be a particular species belonging to the ginger order, Zingiberales. It fertilized itself and produced seeds that fell from the flower in proper sequence. It came just like that, simple as waking in the morning.

Because the rigors of the dry, almost lifeless period are more taxing than the wet times, the actual shapes of creatures-in-waiting are more visually complex as anhydrobiotes than as productive adults. Animals thought to be of the same species were found to be completely different when the structures of their anhydrobiotic cysts were studied.

There is always an artful construction to these waiting organisms, revealing an interior genius within nature. Seen through an electron microscope, anhydrobiotic cysts are a gallery of architectural styles. The closer the view, the more complex they become, with passageways and pillars and sponge platforms enclosing arrays of spikes and welded orbs, each of these shapes designed for some unknown, peculiar function. In many ways, they are similar to pollen grains or snowflakes, their composition symmetrical, intricate, and enigmatically individual. Sealed against complete drought, a fairy shrimp, *Chirocephalus salinus*, surrounds itself with pastrylike structures, each raised from the surface and arranged into pentagons. A clam shrimp cyst bears the topography of a rib cage curved into itself to form a sphere. *Tanymastix stagnalis* is a flying saucer with a pouting equator, its surface as dimpled as that of a basketball. Complicated and unrepeated between species, the shapes are nothing but a response to incredible adversity. Since the anhydrobiotic animal has no moving parts to defend or transport itself, it must make parts that work even when the animal is basically dead.

Biologically these waterpockets are the edge of the earth. To say that periods of drought present the only antagonism to life out here would be untrue. The entire cycle of wetting and drying refuses calendars and predictions, working the inhabitants so hard with instability that adaptations must be honed to the intricacy of fine lace. Pools dry and fill at irregular intervals, relying on mercurial thunderstorms, topping off in the winter, carrying three days of water in the summer, staying full for five months, then dry for two years straight.

Pool water will easily go from 60 to 95 degrees Fahrenheit between sunrise and afternoon. Then, during dry times, the barren surface, with its anhydrobiotic life poised for the next rain, will reach a summer high of 158 degrees. Daytime oxygen levels in the water jump by 88 percent, plummeting at sunset while, in the coming dark, acid levels rise by nearly a third.

An aquatic kingdom that turns its chemistry inside out between day and night, and exists every now and then in a scalding desert, invites not resilience as much as it does ingenuity. One observer visited an Arizona stock tank for each of the nineteen days that it held water after a heavy summer rain. Nearly twenty species of invertebrates and amphibians appeared during this time, and he took note of each. Predaceous beetles, *Eretes sticticus,* arrived as eggs after adults flew in from unknown water sources to lay them. They hatched into thousands of beetle larvae. Their development seemed to follow in perfect stride the slow vanquishing of the pool. On the nineteenth day, at 10:30 in the morning, the pool came very near to drying. En masse, the beetles, which had only recently reached their adult phase, suddenly produced an intense, high-pitched buzzing. Then, while the man stood watching, the entire group of beetles lifted into flight at once. The swarm set off to the southwest, disappearing at the horizon. Within one hour the pond went dry.

This kind of prophetic knowledge is not uncommon among dwellers of ephemeral waters. The adaptation is called *phenotypic plasticity,* meaning the ability to alter the body's shape in step with its environment. Toads and fairy shrimp and beetles will shrink and stretch their growth rates in precise cadences with the pool's life span. Development rates in water holes depend not on the original size of the pool but on how fast it is drying. Thus small pools do not necessarily produce small organisms. Rather, pools that dry quickly produce small organisms because the animals must develop rapidly, resulting in dwarfed adults. It is not the actual volume of water that is perceived, but how fast the volume is decreasing.

No one yet knows how this is perceived. After numerous studies, mostly involving mosquitoes, researchers have been left guessing, suggesting that the organisms distinguish the time or effort necessary to move from the top to the bottom of a pool, or that they gain cues from increased crowding. It could even be that they discern a changing volume of air in their tracheal systems during descent to the bottom of the pool. Whatever it is, these organisms know exactly how long their habitat will last. In the case of *Eretes sticticus*, it was down to the hour.

And once the pool dries, then where to? Like *E. sticticus*, the predaceous backswimmer *Notonecta* is able to leave the water and fly with wings it keeps sealed in a protective casing. To find the next water, it seeks polarized ultraviolet light reflected from smooth bodies of water, the same method used by water striders and dragonflies. Ultraviolet sensors are situated in the lower portions of its compound eyes. The backswimmer flies with its body tilted 15 degrees to the horizon, placing these UV sensors at a level that will strike polarized light off a flat surface at an optimum angle, initiating a dive-and-plunge response. Only a certain crossing of angles between its body and a polarized light source will send the backswimmer into a dive. It makes a pinging sound when hitting the flat hood of a darkly painted car mistaken for water.

A researcher in Arizona found that the best way to catch flying aquatic insects was to lay black plastic garbage bags on the ground just as a storm moves in. The insects tend to be out flying around storms, seeking new water, and the bags, like car hoods, reflect polarized ultraviolet light from a flat surface. The insects would plummet straight at the bags, which he had coated with glue. *Notonecta* did this to me once in Utah. These backswimmers began bombing me at sunset (when reflections from water are their most striking) until five of them had bull's-eyed into a cup of water in my hands. The mouth of the cup was only four inches across.

With life being tied into such knots and going through so much time, my own life had to be measured by completely different standards. Tom and I were lithe, short-lived creatures who would never know how to sleep for an entire hundred years. I kept scooping *Triops* from the water in cupped hands, holding them upside down, watching their fans run so quickly that, like a car wheel reaching a certain speed, they appeared to move backward. I did not do this to watch them as much as I did it just to touch them. This was a different strand of life from my own.

From the highest waterpockets we found the fast way down, skiing in our boots along the face of a sand dune, sand splashing the air from our soles. This was steep, hundreds of feet to the floor of a wide canyon. My path wrote cursive letters in the face, a clumsy language that would be erased by wind by tomorrow. Our habit was to walk from first light until dark, and tonight we slowed near sunset, coming into a deep well of pockets in the evening. One in particular caught Tom's attention. It was almost a perfect square, like a picture frame with richly wrought edges where water had left small erosional marks. Behind it was a long view, probably fifteen miles of desert seen between symmetrical colonnades of sandstone. He observed this pocket from several different vantages: first from directly above, then from a straight shot across the vista, then from a narrow cleft where he could sit on a ledge, and finally from just beside it.

We were both exhausted from the day, and the coming darkness caused our muscles to go limp. Our skin was burned from the sun. I joined him on the opposite side of the water and we stared at it for fifteen minutes. I rolled onto my back after a time and, seeing the first couple of stars, asked Tom if he wanted to swim.

He looked up, surprised to hear my voice. He spoke as if slowly coming awake. "No," he said. "No. I think I'm good right here."

The next day, on a broad shelf midway down a seven-hundred-foot cliff face, we found a long, narrow balcony of pockets hanging just at the edge. One pocket extended along the shelf and Tom stood high on a ledge, performing a headfirst dive into it. His feet plunged under last and he was gone. It was at least eight feet deep. I watched the pale image of his body arc below the surface like a shark. The image stayed in my mind, even after he broke the surface again and inhaled with a loud gasp. We swam in a pool nearly two hundred feet long, our arms tiring as we reached the opposite side. Half a million gallons out here, I figured, enough to fill an Olympic-size swimming pool. It was all contained within about two square miles of deeply ribbed and finned country, where we had been walking for three days, dawn to dusk. And this was just the water we saw.

We walked out at sunset, stopping once to gather a panful of water from a final pocket, shuttling it back to the shade where we prepared a meal of egg noodles and curry. From there, walking took us away from the water, down a canyon and into a region of sand dunes and blackbrush. There was no racing against the dark to get back to the truck. The night simply moved over us. Headlamps were never brought out. We walked on starlight, becoming groggy tired, talking with animation for thirty minutes, slogging silently for an hour, then exchanging bad jokes. We talked about what we would eat when we got out, how we would drive until finding a town with an all-night store. In our minds we were already gone.

Hours later, at one in the morning, we reached my truck and within three minutes of driving had it foundered oil-pan-deep in loose sand. Tires spun helplessly. When I walked around in this sand I thought of Colorado's April snow, how it sits on the ground like goose down. We got the truck out of one hole with swatches of carpet stuffed under the tires, only to make it three feet farther along the road, burying ourselves again. Eight times this happened. The region had reached out and grabbed us. It had drilled us into the sand, informing us that indeed we were still here. We had left in our minds to some all-night store where we could buy microwave burritos, and the desert said, Do not leave this place quite yet. Remember. Take the sand and sweet memory of water with you. Become thirsty and pained again before you go.

"We should put on our packs and start hiking out now," Tom offered. I knew he was delirious. He'd been the one pushing the truck from behind, while I wore on the four-wheel drive from the cab. "We should get to the road and find a bigger truck to get us out."

"No," I said. "That's crazy. Not tonight. We should sleep. We'll go out tomorrow."

We did not argue about it. We were too weary, so we went

ahead and rocked the truck out of that hole and into another one. Sand sailed into the air. Back tires dug themselves a grave. We stopped for a minute. The darkness made the world empty around us, the headlights vanishing into the sky from our hole in the sand. I shut off the engine and headlights, got out and sat on the ground, Tom standing beside me looking at the stars, praying perhaps. With its hind wheels laid deep, the truck tilted upward like a sinking rowboat in an ocean too big to get out of tonight.

Even as the scent of burning clutch dissipated, the air did not smell of water. The water was ephemeral in the greatest sense. Since we started walking tonight we encountered no sign of it, we did not find its scent. It got farther away, first by miles, then by distances that could not be mentally crossed. Now it was gone.

Part Two

WATER
THAT MOVES

The people who climbed up on Superstition Mountain huddled
together and watched the water coming up. With them there was a dog.
One night the dog spoke in plain words: "The water has come."

—Akimel O'odham story, Central Arizona

When I began hunting for water in small, isolated holes, I had wished for a tangible knowledge, a line of information I could personally own. Water holes come in their own packages, with their own distinct rules. I had taken notes carefully and made my own maps, quantifying whatever I could measure. *On the top of the Navajo sandstone at the end of the summer rains. In steep, narrow canyons of granite, not in the arroyos below.* To prove my knowledge, I wrote academic papers

on the positioning of water holes, spatial distribution, ways of
determining longevity, submitting these to scholarly reviewers for
a master's degree program I had applied to. My measurements of
water holes in Cabeza Prieta came out in stunning, colored
charts. Weeks of fieldwork from the wildlife refuge appeared in
fifteen pages of:

> **Pool #33 104 l (28 gallons)**
> *Coordinates:* N 32° 20' 15.1" W 113° 48' 36.4"
> *Elevation:* 1,650 ft
> *Depth (h)* = 0.18m
> *Average width (2r)* = 1.5m
> *Protection:* Protected
> *Local Catchment Area:* Large
> *Sediment:* Low
> Turbid
> *Invertebrates:* Mosquito larvae/pupae, chironomid larvae

Because of their simplicity, water holes are effortless to study.
They need only be found. Regardless of the mystery they imply, of
water hidden in impossibly dry places, they have discrete boundaries that take easily to a tape measure, a global positioning
device, or a Brunton compass. Moving water is different. Where
water holes are the ascetic monks, robed and silent in the desert,
moving water is the jester. For all of the jester's elusive leaps and

sudden appearances then disappearances, there is wisdom in the movements. In the desert there are places where canyons surgically incise underground aquifers, bringing ancient water into the sunlight. Entire rivers appear from the faces of cliffs. I could sit with water holes for the rest of my life, taking in their potent solitude, but there was more than this to learn from water. I traveled to find these other places.

As water began to move I again heard the voices. Water furrows itself into shapes as it runs, immediately telling stories out loud, decoding messages from stillness into momentum. An alphabetic string of symbols is left in sand and on rock faces after it passes. My papers and notes from ephemeral waters turned suddenly arcane and restrictive. The knowledge was no longer so simple to possess. It was not as innocent as *where* and *how much*. It was now asking questions of me.

I listened to the sounds, the liquid timbre in thin canyons, water running where there is no sound elsewhere, no water even if I walked for days. Vowels lifted from the purl. Whole words. Unintelligible garble, then words again. Water taught me that it was an organism itself, alive, not merely a landmark. At times I woke suddenly in the dark, sat straight up from my bag and reached to grab something—my knife, a headlamp, something. Even coming fully awake, I could not talk myself down. The voices in water are real, for whatever they might mean.

Parched land wrinkles to the horizon and in one place, a rock outcrop, a seep emits a drop every minute, a light tap on the rocks below. The drop is sacred. Doled in such apothecary increments, this scarce water is almost deafening, surrounded by total silence, by hot sand fine as confectioners' sugar. It is a single word, a mantra.

In places it gathers speed, finding pathways, turning from seeps to springs to streams to rivers. To be near such moving water in the desert is like being in a vacant concert hall with a solo cellist, like standing on tundra with a grizzly bear. You must listen. You must make eye contact. The water cannot be resisted. Drops become elaborate cadence. The flow becomes song. It burbles from the ground, tumbling down hallways of isolated canyons. Life bends into preposterous shapes to fit inside, plying the narrow thread between drought and flood. Orders are given: you must live a certain way, and do it swiftly, elegantly, because this is a desert, this water is only here, and then a hundred miles of nothing.

In the *Kama Sutra,* erotic sounds are said to come in seven categories: the *Himkāra,* a light, nasal sound; the *Stanita,* described as a "roll of thunder"; the hissing *Kūjita*; the weeping *Rudita*; the *Sūtkrita,* which is a gentle sigh; the painful cry of *Dutkrita*; and finally the *Phutkrita,* a violent burst of breath. I have heard all these in water, and then a hundred others, none of which have been offered titles besides *plunk, plash, swish,* or *splash.* I have heard the Phutkrita in the snapping of a tree limb during the sudden upwelling of a flood, and the Sūtkrita sigh as that same water slowly spun itself into a downstream eddy. Horse trainers have so many names for horse breeds and colors, and Arctic dwellers have entire dialects for the nature of snow, yet few names have been given specifically to the sounds of water. It may be that water is too commonplace. Since it must pass your lips every day, and you wash your hands with it as a habit, it might seem too pedestrian for study. If this is true, if water is so prosaic, come to the desert and listen to moving water. I have been held for days in a single place not because I needed the water, but because I had to listen.

The water comes from below. Low, exposed country uncovers subterranean streams, allowing them to surface, most often in the form of barely a trace of moisture at some inconsistency in the rock, sometimes as measurable water gathering in the shade, even more rarely as a newborn stream.

I once, for no memorable reason, hurled a single-bitted ax into my father's backyard in Phoenix. It cartwheeled through the air and squarely struck the ground, embedding itself blade-down. Clean water suddenly bulged from the earth. The first half-second was glorious. Water sprung to either side of the blade, the way the sea splits around a driving bow. Clean, pure water. I had tapped the interior of the planet. I had opened the desert. When water flows onto a dry place, something astounding is at work. Where, other than at the turn of a faucet handle, have you witnessed water actually *begin*? Where have you seen the leading edge? Even to chase car-wash water along a street curb, watching its soapy finger probe the concrete, has a peculiar enchantment. But seeing it burst from the planet was far above such common magic.

In the next half-second I realized I had severed my father's water line. A look of betrayal crossed my face, as if this was the least possible of the two options. I heard my father's *what the hellja do that for* voice from somewhere behind. Nonetheless, it was the original moment that captured me, not the hose clamps, new fittings, and wrenches that came after.

When I was younger, before the ax incident, my father took me to an Arizona canyon called Valentine. There he showed me a place just up from the floor where a rock about the size of a hand protected a small underground waterway. The rock itself was cushioned in green spongy moss, like a brick seated into velvet. He lifted it gingerly. Beneath was a tunnel of fine, red roots clutching a stream no wider than my wrist. It flowed straight through the ground as if we had cracked open a pipe to look inside. Its delicate sound of motion beneath the surface told of another world. The way a person learns to see pipes and storm drains running invisibly beneath streets, I began seeing threads of water moving beneath rocks.

My father used to talk about wild things a lot. He led me to believe that everything worthy out here was a secret, that other people were not to know, not to be present, all of it beyond humans (even for both of us, who were privately sneaking in for a peek). So this water, like the half-second of water I would eventually access with an ax, was perfect. It was true. To open a hole and let my eyes fall into the water the same instant as its first sunlight was the ultimate act. My father did not smile as he looked in with me. He was serious, as serious as I was. Even if he was only trying to convey a sense of importance, relaying to a curious child the meaning of reverence, even if he knew in his heart that a person could hardly be sustained on such secrets in this world of humans, I absolutely believed him. After this hidden spring, the only way I was going to be able to survive was by crawling on my belly looking for secrets.

We returned to the spring many times, lifting the rock as carefully as opening a music box, being sure to place it back just the right way upon leaving. We both kneeled, one after the next, to drink from the underground stream. As the water, slurped off the surface with a circle of mud and bits of moss pasted to my face, entered my throat, I did not fully realize what I had learned. In fact, I had not learned anything. I simply knew, however wrong I may still be, that everything must be perfect, like this secret, like the euphonious voice of moving water. Then we put the rock back and walked out of the canyon, my future decided.

3. SEEP

75-Mile Canyon, Grand Canyon
October

ON A SUMMER DAY I SPOKE WITH AN ARCHAEOLOGIST who had once worked in the Grand Canyon. We stood outside her home in the mountains near Flagstaff, both of us with our hands in our pockets, looking across a large meadow of grasses surrounded by stands of ponderosa pine. The sky was a clear blue dome without clouds, a kind of sharp blue that comes to the dry skies of the Southwest.

When I told her of my interest in water, she offered this story. Not many years earlier she had escorted a number of Native Americans down the 270-mile stretch of river that lies in the bottom of the Grand Canyon. Many of these people were tribal elders from a wide range of cultural backgrounds, each of them having some affiliation with the area. The tribes of Zuni, Hopi, Hualapai, and two Paiute groups were represented, stuffed into life vests, clinging to tie-down straps through the rapids. She brought them in order to reveal a number of archaeological sites that might have pertinence to their traditions, these often being sites she had found herself.

On the river they stopped at numerous side canyons, where they tied off the rafts and hiked up. While she pointed out various facets of what she had found, say, the shape of a granary's doorway or a type of painted pottery, the people distractedly glanced up-canyon as if wanting to keep walking. This continued from site to site until she found herself insulted by their rudeness. When she finally confronted them, the answer was clear. These sites, these haphazard, everyday remains of a lost culture, were dead. What they wanted to see were the springs.

They had been looking up-canyon because water sources were nestled up in the cliffs and caves at the far points of these canyons. Certain springs were well known, but only through stories or family names or by ceremonial kachinas, and they had never actually seen them. One person told her that the springs were entities. Such a descriptive word as *spirits* was not used. Nothing of great contextual merit was offered. The springs were simply alive. They were points where creation came to the surface and spilled out, where a hand could actually reach forward to feel the emergence. The importance of anything out here paled in comparison to the springs because this was the Grand Canyon, the place of springs, its desert interior riddled with running water.

There was an innocence in the woman's wish to show archaeological sites, to her belief that what was important was only the datable, stratified record of human events that could be questioned and classified, and that the more mysterious aspects were too sentimental for report. The woman understood her own innocence. They walked to the springs instead.

When I drove away from her home I did not turn on the radio

to search for stations. Instead I recalled the springs of the Grand Canyon. I went through each that I could remember after having spent, at one time or another, over two hundred days walking in the canyon. I had listened to water dripping down there. Where small springs gathered beneath ceilings of sandstone, the orchestration of water beads had halted my thoughts. My chest settled. My fingers spread against the ground. This water comes from cracks in the rocks, weaknesses between bedding planes, and in small seeps that fill a water bottle only after it has been propped below for an entire day. The original collecting place of this water is rain and snow on the surface—the high rims, days, years, or millennia ago, where it filtered down and became trapped in underground catacombs and paper-thin spaces before again emerging.

As I drove from the archaeologist's home, I remembered a Grand Canyon backpack trip the previous autumn where I stopped one morning to study a garden of seeps from beneath a rock shelf. A seep is differentiated from a spring because a spring will produce a liter of water in less than a minute, and a seep will take longer, sometimes days longer.

I slung my pack into a deep alcove and sat there for a time, listening to the gracious sounds of water tapping rhythms against the canyon floor. There seemed to be a pattern to the drips from each seep, a pattern I had heard before, wondering each time if there might be a sort of specific timing. I remained for a morning, pulling out a stopwatch, placing a notebook on my knee.

An assortment of young seepwillow with a garnish of twining snapdragons grew below, half of them uprooted and combed downstream by floods. I sat in a nest of these plants, listening to the *drip drop drop drip drop*. The sounds were predisposed, unaware of anything more important than their own syncopation.

They ran down breasts of moss, coming to single points before releasing, then landing in well-worn thimbles in the moss below. When I studied the spacing in time, I found that the seeps ran like clocks in a shop, each ticking and chiming at its own interval.

The quantity of water exposed here could not be compared to that in the holes of Thousand Wells on the Arizona-Utah border. Thousands of years would be required to capture this seep water and even come close to matching those waterpockets. But this water was of a different nature. It was alive and intricate, revealing that it is not the volume that finally matters, but how it is presented. The seep was in motion like glass trade beads passed between hands, able to convey, relay, and arrive in a new place, still moving on from there, into the moss, into the ground, below the floor of the canyon, reentering other springs to be released again elsewhere. Water holes stay put. Here I was witnessing a mission, seeing a snapshot of the seep's life. A few times I disregarded the stopwatch and moved in to examine the forming droplet, to study its pregnant bulge, how it swelled before falling and how within the swell I could see a mirrored globe reflecting everything around. I saw my own face, upside-down. I caught some drops on my fingertips, bringing them to my mouth, like placing rubies on my tongue.

Two hundred years ago water was considered to be a pure element, like gold, oxygen, or iron. But it is not a true element; its atomic structure can be easily broken into Hs and Os, a fact that startled many at the time of its discovery. It behaves so curiously, however, able to move unlike anything else we know of, that it is still unscientifically considered to be an element. It announces its presence everywhere that it shows, hardly able to blend invisibly into the incumbent granites and sandstones. It has a different set of laws, obeying them by threading between our fingers like liquid mercury and by flowing down our throats into our bodies, directly into our blood and our flesh, making us look quite different than granites and sandstones. I've often thought that a planet without water would be a dull, sad place. Most, if not all, water on this planet came from countless small comets thumping against the atmosphere (which continues at

Ferns on a cliff wall seep

about ten thousand comets or pieces of comets per day, enough to add a twenty-five-foot depth of water across the entire globe every half a million years). That it comes from space suggests why it is so peculiar and fascinating here on earth. It is a substance from far beyond our reach.

Oxygen and hydrogen atoms, H_2O, arrange themselves tetrahedrally in water the same way silicon and oxygen atoms form lattices in quartz crystals. When you throw water molecules at the ground, they land locked together, but hinged off one another so that they change shape to match whatever they touch. The molecules respond to the air the same way they respond to oil—

by shunning it and adhering to only themselves. Because water's positive and negative electrical poles are unable to bond with nonpolar air or oil molecules, water fortifies itself, fronting a wall of oxygen atoms while hydrogen atoms cling to nearby water molecules within. With hydrogen atoms pointing inward, bonding to the next oxygen atoms below, water basically turns its back on the world, showing a tight hind-side of oxygen, which accounts for water's tremendous surface tension and its ability to exist as a single body: a drop, a stream, or an ocean. Then, when separate pieces of water meet, they immediately bond into each other like painless surgery. Anything else—dirt, glass, or bone—breaks apart and stays that way.

The entire hydrologic cycle from atmosphere to ocean and back is a marathon line of nearly unabridged hydrogen bonds, a continual flow of awareness. To touch water, especially water out of a spring or seep, is to return to each origin, meeting the rains and the snowmelts and the cold interior of the planet, meeting, in fact, the comets machine-gunning against our atmosphere. I am surprised that when a hair dryer falls into a bathtub we are not all electrocuted.

Each drop I witnessed at this Grand Canyon seep relied on a mathematical arrangement, a balance between gravity and the attraction of atoms breaching when the drop fills to an exact point. I continued through the morning and into the day with the stopwatch, ticking numbers into my notebook beneath the rapping of water. I monitored one seep for half an hour. It dripped every four and a half seconds, and the space between drips never varied by more than a tenth of a second. Even when I came back in the afternoon, it was still every four and a half seconds.

Another seep released a bead of water every four minutes,

showing startling precision as each drip lingered for maybe an extra second, or fell three seconds early, but most often came exactly at four-minute intervals, not missing a second. I wondered if even the minor variations I recorded had something to do with me, that my breathing or the opening and closing of my eyes added just enough atmospheric weight to offset the timing. If there was an offset by one drip, it was answered at the next drip by an offset in the opposite direction. Then it returned to its pattern as if it had recalibrated itself.

I measured others; they each behaved the same. I wrote this in my notebook, charting rows and pages of numbers that grew so numerous they looked like a musical score. This is what math is for: when something beautiful, something magic, or the Big Whatever passes by, the only thing that can be accurately held when it is gone is numbers. These hours' worth of pen marks were to be taken out of the backcountry and turned into statistical units, diagrammed so that I could find each variation and pattern. Nothing especially scientific showed from my record, and the information did not imply any audacious order to the universe. It was only that I was mesmerized by the metronomic grace of this escaping water.

Driving from the archaeologist's home, I imagined that the indigenous people who first studied these Grand Canyon water sites had no need for stopwatches. They saw the seeps and springs and immediately knew they were alive in a way that could not be defined by simple languages. They understood what I first knew, before I prepared charts and broke numbers into statistical arrays. My intuition was simply that I would find order. The order implies process, some hand of god or breath of life or ratio of fissures and pressures within the rock. The process suggests that a spring is a route to a more fundamental mathematical or mystical rule. Whenever I find something so orderly, so hypnotically abstruse, I hunt around its backside for the thread connecting it to everything else. As water freezes, it grows into complex, symmetrical crystals, the same as its arrival in tides that can be calculated to the minute from one century to the next, the same as its seeping from the rock with the exactness of a clock. Time on this planet is counted out by water, the small second hands ticking away in the back of some desert canyon.

I drove from the dirt road onto the paved road, remembering the seep and its gentle, metered rain, and still did not turn on the radio.

4. THE SOURCE

Interior Grand Canyon
February

AS SOON AS THE WATER TOUCHED AIR, IT ROARED LIKE a violent god. An underground river struck sunlight, thundering from the face of a cliff. I could hear it a mile away, the sound lifting from an envelope of canyons, shuddering against boulders and eventually, from far enough away, turning to a distant, static hiss. The water came from somewhere inside the planet—no one knows the actual source. Experiments have been performed on these explosive springs at the north walls of the Grand Canyon, traceable radioactive isotopes scattered in the water of the country far above to see where they might emerge in the desert five thousand feet below. The isotopes have only van ished, drawn into puzzling underground passageways, taken to some remote spring and spilled onto the ground unrecorded.

I came to the floor of the Grand Canyon, following canyons and the side canyons of side canyons for three weeks. On this day I hiked toward the source of unusually clear water cascading like an alpine creek in the desert: water born from a distant, bolting spring. I reached its origin, which was a waterfall pouring straight from the rock, and stood just beyond where it struck the earth with such force I could feel an erratic heartbeat in the ground. The vision was incongruous: desert cliffs rising thousands of feet, bare and dry as chalkboards, and out of one, the emergence of water. It plunged hundreds of feet from the high face, pounding against several ledges, then rumbled into boulders with the strength of a river. What was more incongruous than the sight was the sound. This was a spring by definition, a tap into an underground water source, not bubbling and singing like the larger springs I had seen, but bellowing furiously at the air.

For fifteen minutes I climbed a series of narrow ledges until hugging the final wall, fingers crimped to the rock as this waterfall sprung three feet to my right. The falls dropped about forty stories beneath my feet. Just at the point of discharge, where water appeared from rock as if from the touch of Moses' staff, I could see an opening in the wall where dollops of flying water met their first bluish light.

There was madness to this. The water seemed desperate to get out, to be born, *wanting*. Mad with ignorance, too, it knew nothing of the outside world, completely pure at this very second. Just at the entrance came a deep, hollow sound, like a bow dragged across a string bass. It sounded frightening, as if I were too close to something I should be watching from a distance. To get inside of this spring and its cave I would have to enter through the waterfall, through the sound, wedge into that hole, and work against the push of water. My first thought was that I would instantly be blown out, sent sailing down with the falls. My second was that I would not be able to turn and exit the cave without losing my grip. I was already testing my body by hanging on this edge. Mist skated against me. The trembling of stone and water worked into my bones, into my face pressed to the wall. I clutched the rock for several minutes, ducking my head into my shoulders, wincing at the force. Wind leaked out of the hole, from around the edges. A wet, steady wind.

I inched closer, creeping to a thin spine of rock, reaching my right arm until it touched water, until it recoiled and tugged at the muscles in my chest. Moving this fast, the water felt like a stinging flood of pea gravel. I dropped my foot and worked my way to the next ledge below, backing away from the spring.

Returning to the base of the falls, I stared at threads of mist trailing into the sky, feeling the shivering of the ground. I studied the dry cliff, the mentally agonizing anomaly of a spring out of a wall. And what is behind this? What is in the dark, inside of the rock where the water has no idea of daylight?

I waited a year. Came back in February. The man with me was a friend, Keith Knadler, a tile setter and river guide out of southwestern New Mexico. We had both traveled the backcountry together and had, at different times, approached this one spring, both of us climbing to the same rock spine, plunging our hands into the flow. He is the one who first told me of this place. Now we brought the equipment necessary to enter the cave: wet suits, webbing for climbing, and metal chocks that could be slid into cracks as anchors.

We entered the Grand Canyon midday with heavy packs, finding a way through a deepening gorge off one of the northern rims. The Grand Canyon is arranged so that down the center flows a single river, about three hundred miles in length, and feeding in from every side along the river's length are six hundred more canyons, some twenty or fifty or one hundred miles long, then thousands of canyons feeding into those. We were coming down one of the thousands across difficult terrain without trails. Boulders stared up from the floor of our canyon, looking back to where they had started, maybe one hundred feet higher. Many were freshly shattered, plugged into the sand, or broken across each other. Everything above was poised for falling, leaving the bottom clogged. It was the scent of a crime scene, blood trails still wet, the powder of boulders yet to blow away. Packs were slung over the wreckage, handholds taken as we lowered crack by crack, short, agonizing leaps made with the weight of full packs driving tendons and small bones into our ankles. Keith was tall, lithe. He moved cleanly. I followed his feet and his hands, trying to take after him, to move without doubt. We vanished into this interior web of canyons on each other's trail.

During these first days of a weeklong trek to the waterfall, our eyes adjusted to the dimness, pupils wide to screen out engulfing shadows. In the canyon's dusk, every color shifted one notch toward the darker blue end of the spectrum, an effect I have seen elsewhere only at the ground level of Wall Street in Manhattan, where buildings crop the light of the sky until the value of each color—people's skin, sidewalks, and granite facades—is forced to the blue. At each sharp turn, where cliff walls caved into the floor, the boulders rioted. They threw both sharp edges and smooth, slick faces. These we climbed silently, as we found small holds, sliding our gear down, hoisting it up the other side. I had my boot on a hold no thicker than a matchstick, my right hand groping around, Keith about four feet straight above me, when I felt the weight of my pack. It tugged and I shot a glance over my shoulder into a dark pool directly below. I teetered for a second, gritting my teeth, feeling the edge of a fingernail split against the solid limestone. Without looking down, Keith said, quietly, almost so that I did not hear him, "You've got to *really* want it." He knew exactly where I was. He was talking about these handholds, and about climbing. I obeyed, taking the next hold as if there was no mistake, finding a strong grip above that one and pulling myself up, the pack heavy as a sack of iron. At the top we pushed away flood debris and slid down the opposite side into deep mud. Then, in a pen of boulders, we rested, sitting against the steel-cold limestone, backpacks slumped into one another to prop us up, our faces expressionless, arms poured limp into our laps.

The two sides of the Grand Canyon, the north and south divided by the Colorado River, have different spring water. Here on the north side, where the Kaibab Plateau flushes out large under-ground volumes, the taste of springs does not alter much from place to place. On the opposite side, below the South Rim, I have found that water tastes different at nearly every canyon. The earth there is tilted differently, changing the entire network of springs. Most South Rim water comes out slowly and tastes ancient, biting at the tongue like seawater. It is old water, having seeped twenty-five hundred feet into the ground to wait indefi-nitely in underground baths of minerals before leaking out. High calcium-magnesium bicarbonate concentrations are easily detected in the mouth, easy to spit out. The water on this side, beneath the North Rim, does not wait. The angle of rock formations sends it down rapidly, sometimes exploding it from the faces of cliffs.

One upshot of salty, laggard South Rim water is that it is not markedly radioactive. The water is old enough that it shows no sign of the decades of nuclear weapons testing. Unstable isotopes, embedded into the atomic structure of the water, cannot be filtered out as springs percolate through the ground. So the South Rim aquifer shows no trace of the nuclear age, having received its water long before people began tinkering with atomic bombs. Meanwhile, North Rim water is hot with tritium, as irradiated as most tap water and bottled water—not especially dangerous to human health, but notable on a Geiger counter.

This is not to say that all the springs on the sides of the Grand Canyon are rooted into only two distinct wells, one being salty and prehistoric, the other being fresh and radioactive. The underside of the Grand Canyon actually looks like a motherboard of circuitry with lines crossing from one region to the next, springs interlaced where they meet underground. Some springs will not alter their flows for a hundred years, while others nearby perk to each rainstorm and die with every drought. For the most part, though, springs on the north side carry young water, no more than forty years old. Springs to the south probably date back thousands or tens of thousands of years.

The main canyon below us took on its own springs as we hiked farther inside—North Rim springs that were clean, easy on the tongue. They welled out of bare rock, draining to the floor, eventually filling the canyon with a clear creek. This troubled our work. It sent us higher onto shelves. It filled our boots with water, causing us to skid and slosh.

If a hole is dug this deep anywhere on the planet, water will probably come out. The Grand Canyon is a hole over five thousand feet deep, nearly three hundred miles long, its side canyons severing aquifers left and right. This kind of hole opens underground floodgates in almost every canyon. No other desert in the

world has such a blatant
show of spring water.

Each day about 400 mil-
lion gallons of water spill
from rocks into the Grand
Canyon—enough, statisti-
cally, to supply several hours
of showers, irrigation, car
washes, toilet-flushing, lawn-
watering, and faucets left
running to the entire population of California. But
when engineers stand on
the high rims with drilling
rigs, even with so much
water beneath them, their
target is elusive. Caverns
and subterranean hairline
passages break and turn
around one another, some of

The waterfall

them filled with water, others abandoned and dry. So to find water,
it is best to come all the way to the bottom, to the interior desert
canyons where it appears. The cruel complexity of buried joints
and faults reveals itself in sweet, graceful gestures, having evaded
the poking of well drillers who go three thousand feet for water.

Most of the water used by humans in the Grand Canyon is
indeed drawn from these desert sources. In the central Grand
Canyon, a waterfall appears from a cave, a place called Roaring
Springs, turned into the public water supply for both North Rim
and South Rim developments. I traveled there ten months earlier,

to where power lines slung down thousands of feet, sweeping over cliffs to a pump station and helicopter pad. The mouth of the cave was penetrated by a pipe that rerouted much of the water down to the pump station.

The station processing the spring water held an assortment of hex wrenches, hard hats hung from pegs, grease guns, and hand-turned valve wheels big as car tires. Display boards flickered with lights and commands. The pump housing, which now contained the spring, had been constructed by Bethlehem Steel.

As I walked through the pump house, I found myself staring at a sign. It read:

DO NOT LOOSEN TWO-BOLT CLAMP BEFORE CLOSING LINE
SHUT-OFF VALVES AND DEFLATING CARTRIDGE

The sign seemed out of place because it said nothing of an underground river or the darkness within. I had arrived on a day when the pipeline broke open, so the pump had to be shut down. I hiked with the station operator, a man named Bruce Aiken, up the steep embankment to where Roaring Springs emerged from the cave and entered a series of pipes. He came to adjust the flow while the break was being repaired.

Surrounding the cave were stairs and platforms made of metal grates, sealed off with a locked gate and barbed wire. Straight into the mouth led a red, corroding pipe with a T-joint sending another pipe into an adjacent cave. A smaller pipe led a quarter-mile inside, used for water quality testing. My immediate thought was that, shoved into the cave, the pipes looked like some grotesque catheter.

I climbed the stairs behind Bruce as he unlocked the gate.

With rigid grating, all cave entrances had been closed around the pipes to keep bats out. Their guano might contaminate the water supply. As Bruce spent half an hour adjusting the valve handle, restarting the water to both rims, I opened one of the bat grates and peered into the darkness. The water moved steadily, its surface silken. I reached in and touched it.

I know of a single spring on the east side of the Grand Canyon that shoves 100,000 gallons a minute out of one hole into the desert. The Hopi of northern Arizona call this spring the *sipapu*. It is symbolized by the hole dug into the center of each of their ceremonial kivas, the hole from which they climbed into this world from the drowning dark of the last. It is nothing like a water hole that sits waiting in a rainwater depression. It is literally bursting, throwing itself from the hole. The affiliation the Hopi have claimed with this spring is not happenstance. It is the sipapu, *the place,* and is not mistaken for any other spring nearby, and no other tribe has claimed ownership to it. It could be said that the Hopis' emergence from the sipapu is merely unsubstantiated myth, but in the area of the spring archaeologists have consistently found prehistoric pottery that can be traced only to the Hopi culture.

Fourteen miles, twenty-nine canyons, and innumerable springs to the west of the sipapu is another noted spring. The Zuni, who now reside primarily in New Mexico, claim this as their emergence point. Springs here are so unique, so individual, that there is never cultural confusion between one and the next. Hydrologists have found that the reservoirs beneath these two ceremonial springs originate in entirely separate parts of Arizona. Their waters differ in age, in fact, by thousands of years.

We came to a spring that flushed probably ten gallons a minute to the canyon floor from a heavy garden of willow, columbine flowers, horsetails, seepwillow, cattails, and maidenhair ferns. It was young water, fair tasting. Scrambling into the vegetation, we hunted its source, relieved to be free of our packs, finding any excuse for a break. We spent fifteen minutes getting poked and scraped until reaching a dense mat of monkeyflowers. Pushing away the covering revealed a single, fist-size hole. Water swelled from inside.

It is always like this finding the source of water—a second of silence, the clandestine enchantment of encountering something small and sacred, then down on knees to see where it actually appears, how far inside I can reach. Without discussion I rolled up my sleeve and stuck my hand in. I looked up at Keith, who was waiting to see if something would happen. Nothing did. He nodded, so I stuck my forearm farther into this tunnel of roots thin as dental floss, following a passage straight down. I drew my forearm out, rolled my sleeve farther, and slipped back in, finding small pebbles held in suspension by the water's force. Then I pulled off my shirt and moved my entire arm in until I was flush to the earth, my hand prodding into the underworld.

Keith took his turn at it. He got his elbow down the hole, then jumped back, yanking his arm out with a panic. He studied his hand for a moment, as if he had burned it, but could not find the injury. He flexed his fingers. "I have this distinct memory," he said. "I was very young and I stuck my hand down a hole in my neighbor's backyard. I got down to my armpit and something grabbed me."

"Something?" I asked.

"Something, someone, I don't know. I can't really explain it."

"What kind of hole?"

"The kind of hole kids stick their hands into."

"Why did you stick your hand in it?"

"Because it was a hole."

I stood still, reviewing his words, looking for deeper meaning. There wasn't any. His logic was clear. The Hopis and the Zunis struggled to get out of the hole, climbing up to this world of light and air, while we struggle to get back in.

This spring was part of a larger network. A hundred yards downstream we found a massive deck of ferns out of which poured a shower. The ferns had gathered over time, collecting among their leaflets tons of blow sand, precipitated minerals, roots, rhizomes, twigs, leaves, and dead insects. The spring sank into this flying buttress and disseminated through it. Out the underside came streams of a spreading waterfall, pouring eight feet into the creek below. A forest of triangular leaves shivered against the droplets, hanging pillars of ferns sending streamers to the ground.

Keith and I stripped naked and stepped underneath, scratching at our flesh to clean off the sweat and mud, feeling the sting of wounds penetrated by fresh water. We scrubbed our scalps with fingernails and opened our mouths, letting them fill like bowls before swallowing.

The place sounded like a steady winter rain in western Washington, overflowing the roof gutters, slapping the garden stones all night long. But it had not rained in this part of Arizona for months. The desert could be seen beyond: ladders of prickly pear cactus hanging from rock ledges, and simple, dry daggers of agaves sending seed stalks to the air, blooming only once in a life that could last decades. There was blow sand out there that would slide like flour through fingers. The world beyond was slow and sere. Here it was sudden and quite alive. Our arms reached upward, into the rainstorm, brushing the luxurious undersides of maidenhair ferns, pulling rivulets down to our faces and chests and legs, turning our bodies into connection points, like spark plugs or lightning rods. We carried water.

The main canyon became ridiculously huge and dark. It led us through days of work, sometimes five straight hours of walking the pointed tips of boulders. We set camps under ledges and in gravel heaps left by floods.

On the fifth evening we had climbed from the main canyon and were now diving in and out of one canyon after the next, walking up one, down another along a washboard of chasms. We reached the narrowest slot so far and slept inside, on a lip where water spilled above and below us. I set my bag on a smooth back of sandstone, my left arm nearly in the water, feet pointed downstream. Water came around my right, too, leaving me on an island about four feet wide. We were only cutting across this particular side canyon, not needing to travel along it. Still, I kept looking down there, wanting to get inside, listening to the roaring siphon of water. Overhead was a view of the Pleiades and Hyades star clusters framed by the walls as if they had been cut out of the sky to be stuck onto a bulletin board.

I had studied the canyon closely during the last light of the day, while after dinner we walked its ledges without gear. Carved in a chocolate- and cranberry-colored sandstone, the canyon was darker than those of the blue-gray limestone. Sandstone resisted water differently, curving like child-bearing hips into a narrow abyss. My body wished to be inside. Not just my eyes with their cursory craving, but my flesh. Water ran into it, forming clamorous waterfalls that vanished around the next bend below.

Above were handprints. These made the canyon even more peculiar, more curious to me. They were left by the Anasazi, predecessors of the Hopi and Zuni, the pre-Columbian culture that first built kivas, and the hole to symbolize the emergence from the sipapu. Possibly the prints were eight hundred years old. Hidden among ledges, they had been painted on outcrops and within recesses hundreds of feet up from the floor. They were made of white paint sprayed against hands so that negative impressions remained, both of children and adults, all of the handprints with fingers spread as if holding up the rocks. They were probably sprayed when paint was blown from a person's mouth, a mist of white drifting away with the constant canyon breeze. I had seen many such paintings throughout the desert, but always they had been at functional locations, places where people could live, or at least hold an audience or build a granary. These prints were more geographic. In a place consisting of only rock and water, nowhere for a person to live, they seemed to be a recognition that this canyon is different from the rest.

I did not observe the prints one by one. Instead I stood back and looked across them, changing my vantage by sitting on a boulder or down by the water until I could see more of them. From numerous ledges they overlooked the canyon like spectators. More handprints appeared the farther I looked. It was not the sense of antiquity that was so striking, but the feeling of importance granted here. Of the thousands of canyons and side canyons within the Grand Canyon, this one became the focus of such attention.

Every other slot canyon I had seen, so carefully hewn to such depth and narrowness, had been dry, or held only the murky, stagnant water of past floods. This one cradled a clean stream, every drop of it spring-fed. It rounded inside as if it were a woman's voice singing down a stairway. Eight hundred years ago the Anasazi knew this was distinct and marked it so.

The next day I suggested entering this canyon of handprints, even though we had planned to only walk across, using this canyon as a bridge to another. Just to explore, I said. I pulled my wet suit out, so that I could last for more than five minutes in this cold spring water. Keith was in a different mood. The trek had worn on us both, but had taken particular vengeance on him. His right Achilles tendon had swollen as if filled with hot sand. The back of his left knee was red, something torn beneath his skin. He decided to stay high, to take the time to dry his gear and study these handprints. He rigged a hand line at one of the interior rims for me, anchoring it to a metal chock he inserted into a crack. "Okay, this is just a guide line," he told me. "Don't put all your weight on it. I'll be up here for an hour, then I'm coming looking for you."

"An hour," I confirmed, feeling taken care of, tugging at the line to test it. I looked up a last time to a constellation of white handprints over our heads, then climbed down on his line. The line ran out before reaching water, so I inched across a ledge and jumped in. The wet suit, a Farmer John variety, came over my shoulders to leave a circle where my chest and throat met. The water was cold, in the low fifties, so I tried not to go in over the circle, not to let the water touch my bare throat. I dog-paddled to a shallower reach, then waded into the canyon with water running nearly to my waist, pushing me along. The canyon bunched tight. I followed archways and dark, narrow tubes of rock, feeling exact hydrological values around my thighs as the water raced past.

The canyon turned into stone carvings, shapes swelling, masking the sky, marking water's passage with involute profiles. The entire canyon floor was an adaptive geometry to the motion of water; each of the shapes, the shallow cups and yawning bends, documented the curve of water's energy. Canyons this intricate are not grotesque like most active geology—the scrambled heaps of mountains, tossed boulders, and rock slides. This is the finest of geomorphology, like wing prints against snow. The stray, momentary strands of moving water leave no impression in the rock. They are too transient. But the fundamental and insistent currents leave signs, so that the bare feathers of moving water are recorded here.

I thought briefly back to Cabeza Prieta, and the recollection startled me. Water had been written all over that landscape, but very roughly, shown in shapes visible from above, in an airplane, where washes and canyons would appear orderly among the fallen blocks of mountains. To have imagined this kind of water and this kind of delicate canyon from Cabeza Prieta would have been almost a sin. It was difficult enough to imagine water there at all. The austere point that water had brought itself to in those water holes was now being traced in cursive, spelling out novels on down the canyon. But still, handprints had been painted here, just like the single handprint painted near the monumental tinaja of Cabeza Prieta. The different brands of water undoubtedly produced different cultures, but the recognition was the same.

At a waterfall dropping maybe twenty feet, I removed a coiled length of webbing I had carried around my left shoulder. The falls formed where boulders clogged the floor, forcing water to run across their roofs. I stood on a boulder's point looking down, unraveling the webbing.

The webbing reached to the frothing pool below. I anchored it to a stack of boulders and tied into it seven loops as handholds, measuring them out with my eyes, carefully tugging each one tight. As a backup, I secured an extra anchor using a small wire stopper with a metal block on the end that fit down a crack in the rock. I climbed into the waterfall, putting my full weight on the loops. The waterfall pounded at my head like fists. I sputtered, looking for air, blinking water out of my eyes. Cold water filled my wet suit, drenching the exposed flesh of my throat, causing a strong breath to leap like a ghost from my mouth. My hand groped down for the next loop. My feet searched the slick rock for something, a crack or nub or any slight imperfection. Then down to the next loop, my legs entering the concussing pool at the bottom. My feet traced the fine lips of holes and tureens in the rock, seeking different currents, finding a place to stand. Once I let go, the webbing snapped out of my hands and bucked as if being tugged by an animal. I continued from there, ducking into lower causeways.

Eventually there came a pool too long and deep to swim. I would lose my body heat. I moved to the tip of the last boulder, looking down the corridor. When I glanced upstream, I saw handprints just beside me, fingers spread just like those painted up high. For a second I was confused by these. No one would have painted anything down here, not this low in the canyon. All the other handprints were high, out of view from here. Paint could never hold against floods. The rock cannot even hold.

Then the paint faded, soaking into sandstone. It was water.

The handprints were mine. I had been moving with my wet right hand along the concave wall, using it not as a support but as a reference point.

My handprint was larger than those of the Anasazi, but it had the same configuration, spread as if meaning something: studying the shape of the rock, telling a story about a passage, announcing that the forms are all the same—water, stories, the body. The prints faded into the coffee-colored sandstone. I turned back. My hour was up.

On the sixth day we took a route across a high saddle over numerous feeder canyons. The top was a region of boulders, great red sandstone balls and disks worn from sitting out, hot in the sun. When we came to the cliff edge over one of the canyons, we heard the roar. It was the waterfall I had seen a year ago. Walking off the edge, down through crumbled boulders, we reached a point where we could see it emerging in a clean free fall, then bursting against ledges, sending a rampage of water out of sight into the descending canyon. The full length of the falls was about four hundred feet, with numerous shelves, breaking it into white explosions aside long, diaphanous skirts of water. It emerged from the cave, appearing out of a strikingly green beard of moss and other plants, an absolute anomaly up on the cliff.

We disposed of all gear except what was now needed and climbed toward the waterfall from the southwest, taking a ledge that clung to the wall. The ledge petered out, leaving a small clip of rock at eye level that could be pinched with both hands to support our bodies. We used this pinch to swing over an eighty-foot drop, blindly planting our feet across where the ledge restarted.

Gear was shuttled ahead, passed from shelf to shelf while our faces and fingertips hugged the wall. It would have been safer to bring equipment—carabiners, anchors, harnesses, rope—but the weight would have been too much. It would have stalled us long ago, so we brought what we could. After suiting up with head-lamps, webbing, and wet suits on one of the larger shelves, about a foot and a half wide, we climbed to the final spine of rock, where last year I had huddled, fearful, reaching my arm into the water.

It was quiet work here. We had fear, of course. My breathing was quick. My chest ached from nervousness in the sticky wrap of the wet suit. At the entrance, from the spine, we rigged a piece of webbing that could be grabbed in an emergency, if we lost footing and got sucked into the waterfall. Keith called it the "Oh, shit" line.

It was important to move straight into this, not to hesitate because of fear or too much caution. We would never make it in if we delayed here. For days now we had recited our mantra of *We don't have to enter the cave.* We could just get there and look through the entrance, deciding that we had seen plenty, that it was too dangerous, and walk back with clean consciences. We knew that these words were lies, becoming more and more lies as our days wore on our bodies. We came to enter the cave, to walk *inside* of a spring.

I took the line in my left hand and reached with my right foot into the brink of the waterfall, facing into the cave. Water separated around my calf, sending sprays into the air. I watched over my shoulder to see down about forty feet where the spray twisted and rejoined the falls. Once I had my next foot in, I was able to brace my hands into the entrance of the cave, swift water rising to the tops of my thighs, then bulging to my hips as I pushed forward. The water could not have been much warmer than a glass of ice water.

Keith was just getting his hands around the corner, looking toward the dark. Half in and half out, I turned to look at the daylight, to make sure we knew what we were doing, that we were making the right decision, and our eyes met once. "Pierce the veil," Keith commanded. I nodded and turned inside.

It was firehose water, charging from a crack. Nothing was soft in here. The rock, a hard limestone, was sharpened into small thorns and razors. If I were to lose my grip, I would be hamburgered before getting another hold, before getting washed out of the waterfall. Immediately my wet suit ripped where I brushed against one of the thorns. My fingers hunted out smooth places, cautiously fitting into niches, then taking some weight.

This was nothing like yesterday's sensuous, refined canyon, hugging me down through its narrows. This was absolutely raw. The water had not yet learned about daylight, about carving a path with all of its slender grace. Its knowledge was primal here. I searched ahead with my headlamp. Within a minute I left the last remnants of sunlight and turned off my light for a few seconds. Complete darkness. I waved my free hand, saw no motion at all. The boom of water stole my remaining senses.

My headlamp on, I glanced back once to see if Keith had entered. He was gripped to a wall, pulling himself ahead, making the same moves I had made. I recognized his reach, and his recoil when he tore his wet suit on a thorn.

The water did not slow as I moved farther inside. Deafening and inarticulate, the sound was terrifying. A hundred opposing currents twined up my body, to my crotch, my navel, my chest. They fumbled like mad hands demanding, racing around my legs, yanking at me, vanishing behind me toward the exit. My body hardly dented the water's boiling surface. Rivers burst from multiple corridors, pouring from crescent hallways as if bulkheads had blown in a sinking ship.

"*Choice!*" I shouted.

Keith, an arm's length behind me, yelled, "*Which is bigger?*"

I threw my arm out to a passage on the right.

"*Take it!*"

We followed these rifts for at least a hundred yards, turning back at dead ends, the cones of our headlamps shifting from water to ceiling to water. I could smell our bodies, the saporous, fertile stink of life floating aside our breath. Nothing else alive or dead in here. We came to a low archway, our lights piercing the turquoise interior. There was only enough headroom in front of us for breathing, no way to tell how far the passage led around the next bend. I looked toward Keith, shining the light at his chest so it would not strike his eyes.

The sound ahead was like wind pushed down a glass tube. "Should we keep going?" I asked.

We were spidered between knobs and walls, holding ourselves in place despite the current so that our limbs made strange angles against the rock. Keith crouched until his shoulders met the river's surface. He studied the passageway.

I did not want to drown in a cave. It was one of the more horrible ends I could imagine, pressed to the ceiling as my headlamp shorts out. So we stared at this low passage that would seal off if the water came up six inches. Keith squinted as we both trained our lights on the same spot, as far in as we could see. Mist rolled from his mouth into the beam of his light. "Looks like the way," he said.

He took a handhold on the ceiling and pulled himself in. The choice was made. I followed, studying every turn ahead with my light, taking holds in the limestone over my head, hauling myself along. My head slid underneath as I gripped my way through, my feet touching rock now and then. The passage did not widen, but after fifteen feet of travel became much taller, maybe forty feet. It was in this last passage that I passed ahead and wedged into a tight hole, with Keith shouting behind me that the cave ended here.

I kept trying ahead, but found the water only coming from the ceiling, from holes too tight to even take my hand. I turned back and looked at Keith. This was already more than I had anticipated. I had thought we would maybe venture a hundred feet into the spring, but it seemed as if we had now worked a quarter-mile back.

I pushed out my right hand like a stop sign. "This is it. No more."

Keith pointed toward dry boulders and mantles above us. "What about up?"

Our headlamps brushed the ceiling, showing a few passages. We went up. Each of us tried a different dry route, climbing through dust and pieces of rubble. I ascended a chimney, emerging into a room the size of an aircraft hangar. Perhaps seventy feet tall and over a hundred feet long, its ceiling was a lifted dome, its floor a garden of waterfalls and pools. Darkness ate my beam of light toward the back. A quarter-mile into a desert cliff, beneath two thousand feet of solid rock, inside the belly of the mother, was this: a buried grotto with the broken plumbing of a spring sending water everywhere. As I walked, my light took on altering values, passing through swift water, still water, deep water, sheeting water, plumes of mist, and shiny, wet stones. The river ran the width of a street.

When Keith arrived, we stood together, our headlamps casting about the space. Nothing was said. The water was still loud, but had more definition in here. We could hear individual waterfalls instead of the galling roar of the corridors below.

At the far end sat a broad, deep well, its surface motionless beneath a tapering ten-foot ceiling. Our lights drifted into the lagoon-blue water and to the cerulean boulders sunken beneath. Green ribs of reflected light traced the ceiling into farther chambers.

"You want to go on?" I asked.

"I'm getting really cold."

"Yeah, I'm feeling that too. You want to go on?"

He waited, studying the length of the swim, the shape of the ceiling. "Yes," he said.

We slipped into the well and swam across. In the center of my stomach I felt the drawing weight of the space below. I looked down to see if my feet might brush anything. There was no bottom within reach of my light. I did not look down again.

Now, when it touched the flesh of my throat, the water cut my blood. Sharp on the jugular, the cold moved directly into my body, pumped without reservation into my heart. Our gasping, percussive breaths came in rhythm with our strokes, as if we were trying to throw the cold from our mouths. We rounded one bend, swimming side by side as the ceiling came down to a smooth cupola five feet over our heads. We swam into one of the inside hallways.

"I can't," Keith blurted between breaths. "Too cold. I've got to go back."

We treaded for a moment, facing each other. The cold was now all the way in. "I'm keeping on," I said. "Just around this next corner."

"All right, but I'm going back."

"I'll be right behind you, in a few minutes."

"Go," he said, as he turned to swim out the way we had entered.

Cold followed the path of veins beneath my skin, into my organs. I swam ahead another several strokes before drifting into a back room, a slight wake pushing ahead of me. By now the sounds of rushing water had faded. I climbed to a shelf and stood knee-deep, flexing the muscles in my arms and legs for warmth. My mind was already faltering toward hypothermia, my thoughts becoming rudimentary, drifting away as if I were falling asleep. My face felt weak. I could not hold an expression. I would have to speak out loud to remember any of the details.

This room, I whispered. *Remember this room.*

It seemed to be the end of the cave. Water welled slowly from below. The surface quieted from my swimming until my light sank straight down, no ripples in the way. About every forty seconds a bead of water fell from the ceiling, dotting a circle into the pool. Each drip was so widely spaced that the silence between had weight. Then the weight broke with the next startling drip.

The drip seemed to be something to remember too, something that would fall every day, every year in consummate, unstirred darkness. The ripples would spread unnoticed like those of a star pulsing at the far edge of a galaxy. I whispered so that I would remember it.

I watched radiating circles disappear before the next drip fell. Then I heard my breath. I held it for a second. This was not silence like a windless field at night. It was silence like a space buried deep within the earth.

The silence, I whispered. *Remember this silence.*

I thought of the Hopi emergence story, and that before everyone was able to climb out of the sipapu, the ceremonial song ended. It could be sung only four times. The hole closed on those who had not yet reached the surface.

Those people, I thought. I looked into the pool, as far down as I could see. Were they in here? But there was nothing in here. The impossible pain of the world above, the mystery and beauty and fear, there was none of this in the far back of the cave. None of the sky and purple asters and hot winds. No emotion or desire. I reached to my headlamp and turned it off. Total darkness moved in. It was true, there was nothing. This was the beginning, so utterly still that I could not breathe. Then I heard the drop of water. It plucked the surface of the pool with a low, ripe tone. The first act of creation. I inhaled.

I swam and climbed back along our only route, aiming for the exit with fumbling, hypothermic moves. At the first sign of bluish light near the cave's mouth, I felt the soapy slickness of algae on the rock. Then moss as I waded farther with the current. Then tufts of maidenhair fern and monkeyflower with crimson blooms above the water, and a spider's web catching mist. The mouth of the cave became a green tunnel of life. I grabbed the emergency line and pulled myself from the water, out to the brightly lit spine of rock. Mayflies mobbed the air.

Keith stood on the ledge just beside me. Sunlight needled into my skin, rapidly drawing blood toward the surface. I did not know how long we had been in there. Twenty minutes at least. Half an hour maybe. Keith checked his watch. Nearly an hour and a half. The interior of the cave began washing from me like a dream. I looked down fifty feet to the ledge where we had left our gear.

"I need to get to my notebook," I said. But then I had to breathe. Each time I took a breath I forgot. By the time I climbed to my notes, the air and sunlight had turned my memory into incorporeal sensations, rendering it in an older, more arcane language. It was the same as it is with dreams. Reason was lost as I clutched at my memory. I opened the notebook and wrote what I could. *Remember this silence.*

5. THE ACTS OF
DESERT STREAMS

Southern Arizona, Northern Mexico
January, February, July

In the Pajarito Wilderness

THE NIGHT I SLEPT ABOVE THE CANYON, NO MORE THAN ten miles from Mexico, I heard coyotes. Echoes came out like floods and orgasms and things I cannot even name. I figured it was not that there were so many coyotes; rather it was that so many side canyons took the howling and twisted it into a thousand parts. This is the low end of the Pajarito Mountains in southeast Arizona, at about the point where saguaro cacti begin to flourish as the canyon drops to Mexico, then opens across a broad fan of the Sonoran Desert. Morning came when the coyotes stopped. Frost dusted the top of my sleeping bag. It was the beginning of January.

This is one of those rare places where water sings its way through the hottest of deserts. Unlike the spring-laden country within the Grand Canyon, the lower regions of Arizona often present hundreds of miles of land with hardly any surface water at all. Here, a stream emerges from springs in the Atascosa Mountains, the Pajaritos, and some other nameless battlements off to the west, meager in flow but enough to send waterfalls between boulders and to leave pools as clear and as slightly off-color as cut diamonds. Very few creeks run openly through the desert year-round, most being short-lived leftovers from heavy rains. Others, the ones that run with greater regularity, tend to get drawn through the sand to some brooding aquifer five thousand feet into the ground. The ones that stay on the surface all year, that bear the light of day, are those you can count on your fingers.

I began walking where the creek bed was dry and carpeted with oak leaves. Mustard-colored cliffs grew from the mountainside, marking where the stream, in more violent days, had cut down, peeling back the rebar and foundation pieces of the earth. Oak trees hugged the middle, crowding me to a single point where shadows dizzied the ground. At the very center, where water might be expected to run, fallen leaves were now slightly damp. My hand, pushed underneath, came up with rich, black loam. Small, stagnant pools appeared downstream. Eventually these motionless pools came together, their floors dimpled with the shadows of water striders.

When the pools converged, they began to move, giving arrhythmic but purposeful noises, like a conversation heard from another room. These were the sweet, adorned sounds of water weaving between rocks, and of small air bubbles murmuring wherever they became caught. With its ornamental and quixotic sounds, the creek washed around hopscotch boulders until arriving at the first waterfall. This was a simple waterfall, a narrow stream tipping over the edge of a moss pillow, dashing ten feet into a fat, green pool. The pool was then inset into a large room constructed between fallen boulders and a concavity of bedrock. To get inside this room, I had to place feet on one side, hands on the other, flipping back and forth as the walls changed shape over my head. I could swim, but even in the desert, winter had sunk itself too deeply into this pool. Using small fingerholds, I crept into the back of the room, pinning my boots to the curved rock just above the pool's surface. The chamber that encircled me had the architecture of crescent moons. Waterfalls of different volumes, sent at different times, had engraved deep arcs. These were not the types of marks to come from wind or simple exfoliation. This was a place of water.

Farther into the canyon there waited cauldrons, each topping off into the next. The canyon tightened, as if trying to pen the stream in. The water kept running, pouring over edges, filling everything it could as shapes became exposed from the bedrock: lone walls and graceful statues. Climbing among these obstacles became slow, picking work. I passed my pack down ledge to ledge. I searched for footholds, dropping my feet blindly for a crack, kicking away the small, ball-bearing rocks. My body stretched as I breathed into my reaching arm, looking down for the next place to plant my foot. Shapes became more refined as the water gained force, growing into tall and narrow protrusions so that the entire canyon became a gallery of Venus de Milos.

Alligator junipers grew along the slopes, and on their branches hung stars of ball moss. This is what is especially odd about the place, the ball moss, something commonly found in areas such as Florida and Costa Rica. The species, *Tillandsia recurvata,* is an epiphyte, meaning it lives on host plants but does not steal from them as would a parasite. It merely uses them for support. Related to Spanish moss, and more distantly to the pineapple, it is a tropical plant, a creature of short, grassy limbs. Some of the trees were actually buried in ball moss. Other than the ball moss in a small number of nearby canyons, and in the Chisos Mountains five hundred miles to the southeast, the next population lies several hundred miles south in Mexico.

This canyon is a museum of ecological oddities. The ball moss is simply a messenger, making it visibly obvious that this is not common territory. Once you start looking deeper than the ball moss, everything is out of place. Often within sight of one another are species belonging in low deserts, pine forests, and the tropics. A saguaro cactus stands thirty feet from an Arizona dewberry, *Rubus arizonicus,* which is closely related to raspberries and blackberries. A tropical passionflower, *Passiflora bryonioides,* sought after as an ornamental with its white petals striking against a purple corona, grows near a Virginia creeper, which is just beyond a dusty-dry mesquite tree with tiny milagro leaves. A single colony of so-called whisk ferns, *Psilotum nudum,* is found in only one place in the canyon, with the nearest other population being three hundred miles into Mexico.

These are here because of the highly prized creek, and the topographic complexities of the canyon, and the canyon's placement along the boundaries of ecological provinces. The canyon looks as if it were decorated by a mad botanist. Its drainage starts at a high oak woodland, where both water and cool air begin. Flowing with the water, cold air drops between steep walls down to the thornscrub of Mexico, brushing by certain plant species that are accustomed to cooler, wetter climates. Temperatures in these areas can come down to 9 degrees Fahrenheit in the winter. With different exposures to the sun, other sections easily reach 106 in the summer. Between these two extremes, the canyon walls twist to each cardinal direction with eighty-foot-tall spires casting shadows inside, creating a full spectrum of microclimates. With its location between the United States and Mexico, and then between Sierra Madrean mountains to the south, Sky Island mountains to the north, and desert all around, it has become a corridor of species travel from the tropics into Arizona. What is most unconventional, though, is the running water. It flows into the canyon like an invitation. The aberrant species follow.

I once came to this canyon in the spring. I arrived with a friend, an esteemed naturalist named Walt Anderson. His knowledge of birds was astoundingly complex and as bird calls drifted from the underbrush and sycamore canopies, he wrote names into his notebook in small handwriting. Bewick's wren. Bell's vireo. He pointed out the question mark at the end of a Mexican jay's call. He heard cactus wrens just behind the spotted towhees (formerly known as rufous-sided towhees) who scratched insects from beneath fallen leaves. Few of the birds were actually visible. We could hear the shuffle of towhees in the underbrush.

He told me that elegant trogons have been seen here, *Trogon elegans,* with dramatic, tropical colors in their plumage. He said he would be pleased to witness a trogon, a close cousin to the famous quetzals from the tropical forests of Guatemala. At the end of that day, as we walked up-canyon, I saw a bird flash across the west wall. A large bird, a sound of wings, and a ruby breast like a spatter of blood in the trees. "*Red,*" I said quickly. "Look there, up. It's a trogon."

Walt moved quickly to see around a sycamore trunk. "Yes, a trogon. Yes." He scrambled out his binoculars. Then he laughed out loud and reiterated that it was, indeed, a trogon.

Red was the correct word. The breast was brilliant, a color

seen in the desert only on the glossy fruits of fishhook cactus. Above the breast was a thin white band, then a nearly iridescent green body. This was a male, customarily more colorful than females. It swiveled through branches of a border piñon and landed, its tail popping once for balance. The two outermost tail feathers, hanging ornamentally below the body, angled away at their tips with slight turns like cursive serifs. Above the black stripe at the bottom of the tail feathers was a metallic sheen of polished copper, catching light in different ways.

The trogon dove away. We followed it through a labyrinth of rock, water, and sycamore trees. It paused, then flew ahead, and we kept behind it, turning corners to find it just in front of us. It stopped to return our stares from a sycamore branch, its red eye ring standing out from thirty feet away as if it had been painted on. Walt finally lowered his binoculars. Without looking away, he said that this was something, to see the passage of a trogon through here. He called the bird *regal*. It dropped from the sycamore and flew around the next turn, following this map of running water farther into the desert.

On this solitary winter walk I dropped into the vestibule of a waterfall. The pool beyond led to a broad, rounded lip that sheeted water to the next level. Columbine flowers, not yet bloomed, crowded around the edges, their cilantro-looking leaves taut over the water. These were *Aquilegia triternanta*, flowers that can be found at an elevation of ten thousand feet in the White Mountains of Arizona. The elevation of the creek was about thirty-six hundred. Around these grew border piñon pines, their needles delicate as hairs, and around them a full accompaniment of oak trees of numerous species including an Arizona white oak with convex leaves and several Toumey oaks, compact and formed like bonsai trees.

Two canyons met and the waterfalls thinned into a smooth stream flowing beneath sycamores and ashes. Exposed by floods, roots of a sycamore tree wrapped around a boulder like a starfish working open a clam. The stones along the creek bottom sat smooth and round, nicely rolled into shape by the water. Along the shaded walls grew coral bells, blood-red flowers with heads as bowed as a bishop's crosier. Among the coral bells grew wild cucumber, saxifrage, and a small, hairy-leafed *Henrya brevifolia*. The entire genus of *Henrya* is represented in the United States by this one species alone, and only in this canyon. Eleven other species make this canyon their sole home in the United States: a blue lobelia flower; a flat-bladed grass of the genus *Paspalum*; a small, tropical *Dichondra* with white petals; a couple of wild beans; an undershrub with the common name of sensitive joint-vetch; a *Lotus*; a shrubby member of the pea family called *Desmanthus bicornutus*; a strong-scented spurge; the white, hairy herb *Sida rhombifolia*; and of course the dramatic passionflower. What these all have in common is that they do not belong in the desert. Water allowed them to come.

As well as being the northernmost boundary for so many Mexican species, this creek is the southern terminus for others from the United States. The waterfall's columbine goes no farther south than here. The Utah serviceberry, Virginia creeper, and mock orange (its flowers smelling of pineapple) end here. This is also the lowest elevation for numerous species of pine, oak, and a twenty-foot-tall New Mexican locust tree that generally grows in conifer forests.

This watercourse could hardly be compared to the Grand Canyon cave with its waterfall bursting from a hole just big enough to duck through, but it indeed carried its own convoluted mysteries. Again, it is not the quantifiable aspects that matter with water. It is how it is delivered. The more I studied, the more involved water's outcome became. A water hole in bare stone, a cliff face giving birth to a waterfall, and now a desert creek responsible for a ludicrous volume and diversity of plants.

This January the sycamores, barren of leaves, showed themselves so white and heavy with hundreds of branches that they looked like ivory carvings. The stream under them was delicious with the smell of seepwillow and of honey, the source of which I could not find. I waded through narrow sections and climbed the backs of fallen trees.

In the main part of the canyon, especially beneath overhangs sheltered from rain, were signs of another wayfaring species: a meager camp with a crumpled package of Boots Light brand *cigarillos,* an empty, circus-colored bag of *animalitos* cookies, and a wrapper from a package of *Tostados de Maíz* that looked as if it had been bought off a rack in a gas station. I found a boulder rounded in just the right way, and as I sat, my back conforming to the cool rock, I noticed a spent cigarette near where my right hand rested on the ground. Another person, right-handed, had done the same, finding refuge at this one boulder out of the hundreds heaped along the canyon floor. The cigarette was Boots Light again, from Mexico.

I began hunting footprints, studying the size and style of the boots and tennis shoes and flat-soled business shoes that had come through. Like the ball moss and *Henrya* and passionflowers that have traced this thin path to the north, immigrants from Mexico cross here. These people cross without papers, walking illegally into this country as unassuming as the passing of a seed or the movement of green vine snakes following prey along the stream. Often they come from distant parts of Mexico, from as far as the rain-forest border of Guatemala and Chiapas, and often from the southern countries of Central America. Once they get this far, the canyon offers ample cover and rough terrain in which they can easily evade capture, and it shoots a direct line up from Mexico, entering the United States in one of the more remote regions below Tucson. There is water here, and relative coolness while the surrounding desert burns the back of anyone walking through.

At the low end of this canyon the walls stepped back. Saguaro cacti and mesquite reached the stream, dipping toes of their roots to the water. Floods had ripped away the barbed wire fence delineating Mexico from the United States, sending the border downstream into wrapped heaps of branches, stones, and rusted wires. Three sycamores to either side of the creek showed numerous repairs to the fence where barbed wire had been coiled around and around the trunks, each strand of a different age as if we keep returning to mark an invisible and ecologically meaningless boundary.

Those animals and plants that come through this open border become isolated as the desert closes the path behind them. These illegal immigrants also are severed from their families and communities as they cross. The desert boundary is the line that disconnects them from their homelands, severing the tropics from the rest of North America.

I slept beside the creek that night, only a mile from the border. This was a gruff little camp, set in dry grasses and winter-bare vines near the water. It was perhaps just past midnight, as the near-half moon tilted into view, when I heard steady footsteps in the loose creek gravel. Tilting my head slightly, I tried not to make a sound. They walked without flashlights, without pausing to negotiate the water, coming within seven feet of my camp. The percussion of small rocks underfoot made the sound of walnut shells being cracked open.

As the people passed, I could see their dark forms against the stars, and behind them a skyline of saguaros and tips of rock. They walked well-spaced in the chalky light, too far apart to talk, marching like a procession of intent ghosts. I could not see their faces, but I believed that they were all men, nine of them. Ahead they would wade through narrows full of clear, night-darkened water and climb hand over hand. They each carried duffels or a number of mesh and burlap bags tied into single lumps on their backs. These were broad, heavy objects, causing the men to lean slightly forward. I tried to see how their loads were hitched, ropes taut over their shoulders, some crossing at the chest. With their heads down, their eyes did not even catch moonlight. Every man carried a gallon milk jug filled with water. The jugs made sloshing sounds, and the fifth man uncapped his to drink, not slowing as he tipped his head back, then quickly replaced the cap. The pace was swift, outrunning sunrise.

I listened to their steady breathing. They did not fill the air with expectant worry—that emotion may have come during the first days of this journey, or was maybe reserved for when they would reach the first paved road and scatter into the rest of North America. All that was given to the air around them was a sense of direction and momentum. Arguments over economics or national legalities seemed feeble against the intensity of their footsteps.

The migration of plants and animals along pathways is like

water pouring through a canyon. Paths are chosen and worn down. In this canyon alone are at least 624 species, 349 genera, and 96 families of vascular plants, along with 60 species of lichens and mosses. Wild geranium. Scarlet sage. Silverleaf oak. Wild cotton. The small fish *Gila ditaenia*, commonly called Sonoran chub, comes into the United States only along this creek. The Mexican hooknosed snake, the vine snake, the barking frog, and the Tarahumara frog have entered the country through here. Along with every other organism, the species *Homo sapiens* has appeared, obeying the laws of the land, the legislature of flow. The last man passed. He walked to the side of a large, pale boulder, as each had done before him. A milk jug, half full, hung from his right fist. When his sound was gone, the night hollowed the way it does behind a train just passed. The only thing left was the sound of moving water.

Remudadero

A truck jacked up on the side of the road. Five men standing around a flat tire, the way men stand around flat tires: arms folded or hands in pockets, comments made in low voices, the slow nodding of heads. Dust. Heat. The land around looked like alligators crammed too close together. Ridges and blocks of rock and sharp skylines, the road nothing more than a drag of a knife blade across the midway point of a canyon. Sharp, angular rocks stuck up through the roadbed because the road was somewhat new and had yet to be beaten down. None of the roads in this part of northern Mexico are old, each one caving in with a landslide while someone cuts a new one somewhere else. This road could not be found on a map.

We retreated into the shade of a cliff behind the truck, letting the flat tire fend for itself, its sunbaked rubber quickly becoming too hot to touch. This morning we had driven out of Nacozari, a copper-mining town of tiered houses overlooking one another. This was in the state of Sonora, where five of us had come and turned onto this back road to head toward the base of a mountain called El Tigre. One person came with the intent of biological inventory research in the high canyons radiating from El Tigre. We would never make it that far. The rest of us came to traverse the country between here and there. An ecologist from the Mexican government had driven over from Hermosillo to join us in Nacozari on this Sunday morning. When he met us, residents had been out in fresh clothes and the town had beamed with the cordial, bright energy that permeates Mexican towns on Sunday mornings. This ecologist squeezed into the truck with us, riding with his knees crimped as we all shared sweat off our shoulders.

Now he was sitting in the shade, eating a rapidly drying piece of bread, staring over the canyon. No one talked. No one looked at the others. It was midafternoon in a region referred to as *Tierra Caliente*, Hot Land. This is distinguished by name from the low deserts of Sonora, which are simply called *Desierto*.

Between Nacozari and El Tigre is an increasing intensity of canyons, the map looking like an impossibly tangled fishnet with canyons, cañadas, and cañoncitos twisted across each other. Pieces of the map were left blank, these parts of the land having never been rendered to paper, like the Unknown Territories left by Lewis and Clark. The person with us who was supposed to be doing research was the first to say something while we sat there. Without looking away from the vista beyond the truck, he said "There's no John Wayne–ing through this country," meaning that we can't just get up and walk across it. We'll have to put the spare on and keep following the road. His voice sounded like a rock falling out of nowhere. Then quiet came again.

The canyon floor could not be seen from this part of the road. Steeper walls bore reddish minerals and stood almost entirely vacant of plant life. I could see, just barely, the tops of cottonwood trees bulging from the floor. Out of this, two common black-hawks rose in sweeping circles, not seeming to pay attention to each other, but regarding the rising wind of a heat thermal that put them in the circle together. "Common" is not a proper first name for them. Not here, at least. They are, instead, *rare*, especially here because they frequent marshes, rivers, and mangroves. They are not to be expected in Tierra Caliente.

These birds do not dive like most hawks. They hop and plunge on the ground, jabbing at frogs and fish, swerving around in dense riverside growth the same way owls haunt their forests. On a thermal they looked like any other hawk, though: wings as broad as possible to grab the rising heat, the longest feathers spread like a hand on a globe to allow the heat and wind to thread through at measured intervals. I stood and walked past the truck, past the flat tire, to the edge of the road where I could look over the backs of these birds. Sunlight sank through my hat. My hair turned hot. Still, the canyon floor was out of sight. Water might be down there. I checked the map. The place below was called *Los Alisos*, The Sycamores. That was all.

With the spare tire installed, we again pressed our shoulders together, scooted in far enough to slam the door. I had the window side in the cramped back seat. Gear pressed against the back of my neck. The truck lurched and popped over a rock, sending our shoulders forward. The bottom of Los Alisos was a jungle. I couldn't see inside. Bare rock walls came down like lava pouring into the ocean, and where they met the bottom, green boils of steam burst upward in the form of cottonwoods, willows, sycamores, and hordes of smaller, herbaceous plants. Where there was enough room on the walls, organ pipe cacti crowded the perimeter of the forest with stately, candlestick arms. Hundreds of cacti, each fifteen or twenty feet tall. Heads of palm trees showed through the cottonwoods. Palm trees, organ pipe cacti, and cottonwoods. *What kind of place is this?* I hugged my arm out the window.

One of the rarest forests in the world is the desert cottonwood-willow forest, which grows along the few and modest creeks out here. These forests cover less than 2 percent of the American Southwest, making this the most uncommon forest type in North America. The canopy below towered a hundred feet off the ground. Around good desert creeks, mature cottonwoods and willows can reach densities of five per acre, standing above fifteen submature trees of the same species, eighty saplings, and twenty thousand seedlings. The desert typically begins immediately beyond, sometimes in a line you can draw with your finger.

Within these forests are layers and hidden chambers—interfaces between the desert and the forest, and between plant assemblages and various depths of groundwater. Even from the road I could see this: variegated shades of green flowing from open patches to closed patches. The canopy, drawn along a narrow causeway, had the undulating topography of a cloud top. Floods will leave thick piles of sediment in certain areas, making the stretch longer for roots to access groundwater. In other places floods will scour right down to the water table itself, allowing for entirely different types of plants. This turns the forest into a mosaic of colors and brands of shade. The only reason any of this was here would be water, perhaps even water running on the surface—a creek. There were plenty of canyons. We had been driving around them all day. None had forests. They were all made of dry rock and cactus until here.

Each type of plant tells something about the distance to water. Whenever you see a dense, healthy cottonwood-willow grove like this, you can be assured that the water table is within ten feet of the surface. At night, when the trees no longer have access to sunlight for photosynthesis, roots let go

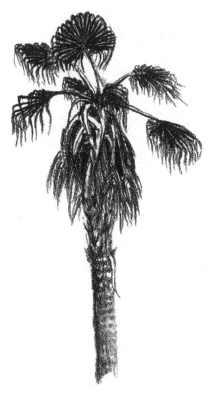

Palm along a Mexican stream

and the water table rises slightly. First-year seedlings of cottonwoods and clusters of lush seepwillow will grow only where the water table is within three feet of groundwater. Even if water is not running on the surface, you will know where to find it, by digging at night. Along these creeks, if the water table drops by one foot, about a quarter of the undergrowth will die off. Three feet will kill almost everything but the large trees. Considering that in some places human activity has sent desert water tables down by 650 feet, these riparian forests—forests associated with large water supplies—have not fared well. Many 150-year-old cottonwoods at desert washes stand barren and dead. In Arizona, nearly all of the once perennial desert streams have been robbed by the pumping of groundwater and the diversion of surface water.

From the window of the truck, the forest of Los Alisos looked healthy. Few human developments reached this far. Cattle grazing was scant and no industrial demands drew on this groundwater. What I saw below would be a subset of the cottonwood-willow forest type. It was a cottonwood-willow-palm forest surrounded by organ pipe cacti, a combination of large plants almost too exotic to be seen in one place. The rarest of the rare.

As we came down the switchbacks, I could finally see running water in Los Alisos. It looked like ice tumbling down a chute. I leaned forward to make an announcement. The driver turned, with his chin over the steering wheel, to see me in the mirror. "Listen, when we get to the bottom of this I should go on my own," I said. Everyone stayed quiet. The driver kept looking back at me. "I'll come back to the road in three days and meet you as you're driving out. I'm just thinking that this stream is where I should be. I've been looking for this."

Exactly as I finished saying this, an event occurred that would be secretly blamed on me for the remainder of the trip. I would later feel the stare of the man trying to get to El Tigre. Maybe I had wished it. A sharp hiss came out of a back tire. It oscillated as we rolled down on it, sounding like a towel slapping round and round. We got the truck to the bottom of the canyon, where the road crossed this small, clean creek. In the shade of willows we let the tire deflate all the way. We had used our one spare. No more tires.

Hitching out on this road would take some time, days. We

posted ourselves in shifts beside our display of flat tires, waiting for the unlikely passing of another vehicle on a rough road that seemed to go to nowhere. Since my shift would not be until tomorrow, I left with another man, walking up the creek, clear water flowing to my shins. We began through a tunnel of young cottonwoods, the stream path dotted with shadows each the size of a cottonwood leaf. Along the west shore was a procession of leafcutter ants, marching their scissored triangles of leaves that looked like sailboats traveling in a wobbling line. Occasionally we found a cottonwood of unusual species—the white cottonwood, called *guerigo* or *alamo blanco*, known in scientific nomenclature as *Populus alba*. With bark white like that of a birch, it stood out among the light brown trunks of the more common Fremont cottonwoods. The petioles of the guerigo leaves arched more than those of the Fremont and broadleaf cottonwoods, causing the leaves to droop. A house could be built in its shade. An ashen-colored canyon tree frog hid in the guerigo's last, slender roots that gathered at the stream bank.

The other tree of unusual nature is the palm. Its fronds cast a slightly blue shade as the sun came through. The only native, naturally grown palms you would see in the deserts of the United States would be hidden in the few slender canyons with springs in Arizona and California. I do not know what species this was. The shape and color of its leaves were not the same as the fan palms, *Washingtonia filifera*, I had seen in more familiar country. They were not the anorexic palms you might expect on a white sand beach, swaying over the water and dropping coconuts. These were stout and straight. Still, their stalks were slender compared to the sycamores and especially to the bulky, branch-laden walnut trees and cottonwoods growing all around. Willows brushed against the cylindrical trunks of the palms.

Everything near the creek had flood debris strapped all over it. Parts of trees had become stranded against the canyon walls. Mario, the federal ecologist who joined us in Nacozari, had grown up around here and earlier today told me about floods. His father had worked in the area, carving some of these roads. Once, he and his father were driving in this canyon, where a road that no longer exists crossed the floor. As they rattled up the creek they both saw the front wave of a flood coming down. It was a summer flood, one of those big thunderstorm-driven waves that shows without warning, ravaging the canyon for an hour or two before dying completely away. I asked how big. "Bigger than the truck," he said. His father popped the gears into reverse and spun the truck backward. A hundred meters in reverse, Mario said, as fast as the truck could go, jolting over rocks, throwing objects out of the bed. At a clearing his father stabbed the gears forward and lurched out of the creek bed, barely clipping the edge of the flood.

Flood history is written everywhere on creeks like this. Pieces of debris are scattered. Trees are left bent over or snapped in half. The desert is an invitation for floods. With sparse vegetation, shallow soils, exposed bedrock, intense localized rainstorms, and high relief to the land, water funnels quickly in this kind of place. Not long ago at all, a vehicle became stalled in one of these Sonoran Desert floods along an Arizona wash. A minivan full of Boy Scouts made it across the first signs of the flood, but entering just behind, a Ford Explorer stalled. It was an early spring storm, a classic slow rain that sent every wash in that part of the desert into flood. A tow truck was called in. It pulled up to the north bank and sent out a tow strap, but the strap broke. Water quickly rose around the vehicle, and the four Scouts and two adults climbed to the roof. By the time sheriff's deputies arrived, water was coursing through the windows, rising quickly. After two hours of rescuers trying to get a rope out and tossing life jackets that were swept downstream, the sport utility vehicle finally gave way. Weighing about four thousand pounds, it rolled into the flood. Rescuers managed to snare three of the people before they were swept away. The remaining three, two boys and a father, perished.

Tree rings record the passage of floods, not only by the scars of violent impact but by the ages of trees themselves. Cores taken from cottonwoods and willows on the Hassayampa River, in Arizona's Basin and Range Province, tell of cycles. About once every ten years a large number of trees establishes itself, an event that coincides with unusually large floods. The floods act as nurseries. The shedding of seeds from cottonwoods and willows matches late winter and spring floods as if the event were staged, the seeds seeking the sanctuary of large water releases. But trees cannot drop seeds on demand, whenever a storm of a certain size happens to enter the region. The event has been phylogenetically planned for, the timing of desert floods printed into the genetic strands of the plant.

Summer floods are too sudden and too furious, and vanish too quickly to adequately recharge the groundwater. Winter floods are slow and large, steadily raking over periods of days or even weeks. On a February day, a month before the death of the Scouts, I had walked to an Arizona creek bed that I usually found completely dry. Storms had been around for two weeks, and I arrived at a canyon floor that was now running thirty feet wide, probably fifteen feet deep. An actual *river* through the desert. Sediment had already been purged and the flood now ran clear. A clean flow is something you will never see in the sudden madness of summer floods. In the summer you will see only rocks, boulders, broken trees, and a thick slurry of fast mud. A fleet of canoes could be run down the smooth water of this winter river, a river that would probably be parched for the rest of the year. The seeds of cottonwoods were just preparing themselves to fly, stretching their cases on the demand of the season. Willows were only shortly behind, planning to catch the final stages of the flood, allowing them to grow closer to the center than the cottonwoods.

Floods are the key to keeping these places alive. Most desert riparian forests do not have perennial streams. They rely on groundwater, which is recharged mostly by floods. So everything living down here has got to be able to survive cataclysm because cataclysm brings life. Physical shapes in the channel are dramatically altered by floods every few years, opening and closing niches, turning the forest into ragtag scraps with different plant communities occupying different patches of fabric. The patches are constantly torn out and moved elsewhere, keeping the forest fresh and mobile.

Even the chemistry of floodwater itself is medicine. Desert streams are notorious for running nutrient-poor; then floods come like compost heaps, thick with nutrients, not only recharging the surrounding soils but also banking away new groundwater that flows beneath the creeks. These subterranean creeks of floodwater sometimes rise to the surface through gravel skylights in the bed, giving a kick of nourishment to the water up top. Wherever these zones of upwelling water appear, even months after the last flash flood, they may carry nitrogen levels 217 percent higher than those in the surface creek, and a feeding frenzy of life gathers at the hole.

This floodwater reserve itself, slowly moving beneath the creek, is one of the biologically safest, most stable regions of a desert stream. It acts as an invertebrate and plant refuge when the surface stream floods or dries—organisms will suddenly start drilling their way down as stress hits the stream surface—and each level of depth in this underworld of stored floodwater shows an entirely new arrangement of organisms, as if the place were tiered underground barracks. Inside this zone is also a store of organisms able to quickly rise to the surface and recolonize the smaller niches left vacant from a flood. It acts as a battery of reserved life and sustenance for the entire stream ecosystem. This is the same nutrient-rich water that came down in violence, probably crushing and drowning nearly every creature along the creek at the time.

With a diet of catastrophic flood, desert streams are themselves in a constant state of flux. A flood erased most of the riparian forest of Date Creek in western Arizona, a place where water flows on the surface in only a few locations. The flood came from Hurricane Nora, which downgraded to a tropical storm as it left Mexico, putting most of its punch into these desert mountains west of the town of Prescott. Arriving a month and a half after the flood, I spoke with a local rancher, Phil Knight, who had been doing conservation work on the creek for twenty-nine years. He ran six hundred head of cattle here, moving them in and out of pasture every month, or every four days, depending on the quality of the range, never letting them near the creek during the summer. For his careful treatment of the land, for allowing a bountiful forest to return to Date Creek, he had received the Conservationist of the Year award from the Arizona Game and Fish Department. He spoke as if his memory was a habitat map, describing by location a zone-tailed hawk nest, certain types of reeds, and places where lush grasses once grew so thick that they laced over the creek. "Boy, it hit this area just harder than hell," he said. "We've had some enormous floods that haven't done anything. This one took it all. I had thousands of new trees per mile out there. Thousands of them are gone now."

When I walked up the creek, it looked as if a battle had taken place. Where ash and willow trees had once been thick, and the bed had been made of sand and knotgrass, naked bedrock was now quarried waist-deep. Granite boulders four feet wide, probably twenty or thirty tons each, had stacked on top of each other, their nearest source being a mile upstream. I found one boulder the size of a file cabinet clutched in the arms of a tree. Tops of ash trees protruded from new dunes of creek sand fifteen feet deep. I walked into the open desert, and even twenty yards from the wash, mesquite trees had been pushed to the ground. If I had known a flood was coming at the time, even the flood of a century, I would have felt safe standing here. A wall of water and sand would have taken me under. Ropes of debris now wrapped the saguaros.

Phil Knight, sitting in the living room of a house 112 years old, tucked his thumbs into his belt loops and looked toward the ceiling. "This was my little beauty spot," he said. "Now it's gone." He did not cry over this. He had seen enough of how the desert operates.

At Los Alisos I picked through flood debris. The last big flood here may have been several years ago. Snags of roots and flood-driven branches hung twenty feet up in the arms of a sycamore. These were maybe from a decade or two ago. A grove of palms had once grown at the outside of a curve in the creek. Now all that was left were short husks of trunks. The palms had been top-pled and I could see that they had originally grown at the calm inside of the creek's curve. Whatever flood had last come through rearranged the creek's architecture enough to reverse the water's path through here.

About half a mile up from the decimated palm grove we found a single, large animal print in wet sand. I spread my hand beside it. Just larger than my palm, it was the track of a jaguar. Hard to tell, maybe two days old. Perhaps one day. The man with me measured the pad and the toes. At the end of this month he would be travel-ing just east of here with jaguar researchers. This was data. Of course, as soon as the creek rose, the track would be washed out. Or if the creek dried to nothing, as it would do toward the middle of summer, the track would blow away in the wind.

Nothing can be expected to remain in a place like this. Granted, many of these large trees had been here for over a cen-tury. But the reason for their presence was that floods had wetted the ground for their seeds. These are the same floods that will someday come through and level every last tree, working the creek into a new shape, erasing jaguar prints, gouging waterfalls into place, and opening new ground for the next generation of forests, which will look nothing like this.

The next day Mario and I took the hitchhiking shift. We skulked in the shade of an acacia tree. The day started hot around sunrise and we didn't feel like talking. Our two flat tires used each other as props, dusty and baking in the sun, announcing our predicament to no one. I had the map unfolded on my lap the way people spread newspapers, hands gripping either side, my head draped forward.

Unlike those I have seen in my own country, this map showed few places named for people or their deeds. This was a map of more useful terms. They were suggestions of a plant or animal, something marking the place as being different. The map showed one thousand square kilometers, and on it were nine creeks, canyons, or buttes named after the cottonwood, *el alamo*. Water is probably no more than ten feet below the surface at each of these alamos.

There were other names. *La Angostura* is the name of a canyon, meaning The Narrows. The creek of *El León* suggests the presence of mountain lions. *El Güerigal* is a grove of cottonwoods of a species other than what is usually seen, and *Las Palmitas* is a place of small palms. *Los Alamos* means cottonwoods, *Los Nogales* walnut trees, *Los Alisos* sycamores. Places like *Los Aguajes* (Watering Places) and *La Ranita* (The Little Frog) imply rich water. The mountain of *El Tigre* has jaguars.

The name that struck me was at the low end of Los Alisos, a place called *Remudadero*. This roughly translates to an act of alteration, something like a snake shedding its skin, or, literally, a spare tire replacing a flat one. The basis of the word is *change*. At Remudadero the map was missing topographic lines, as if someone had become tired of drawing them. From what I could tell, the canyon was narrow and extremely steep. That is where I would go as soon as the hitchhiking business was done.

I looked up from the map. The metal rattle of stock racks and the grumble of an eight-cylinder engine came down the road. Mario stood. A big Ford pickup with bent stock racks and no stock halted in front of our tires, dust surging forward, then settling in still air. Mario did the talking. We got a ride, and three rides later, including the back of a truck full of copper-mine workers and the back of a car filled with dogs, children, and our two tires, we reached town. One more ride got us back, returning us late at night with a sack full of beer and ice and two patched, inflated tires.

In the morning I walked alone to Remudadero. The creek burrowed into high-standing walls. As the water took a hard turn to the west, it entered and exited a cavern it had burrowed from under the cliff. Inside, water babbled over creek stones and I listened for a while, the place having the acoustics of a small performance chamber. I placed my hand in the water to make the sound change. I pulled it out to listen to it change again. In the creek outside, yellow-spotted water beetles with carapaces colored like checkerboards of cadmium yellow paint darted around my legs.

The creek changed its nature through this section. Upstream it had been a smooth run, usually the same depth all along, no major falls. Here it became much more rugged, closing down to waterfalls, pools, and rolled boulders with palm trees tucked against one another. Above stood sharp layers of cliffs interspersed with chaparral and thornscrub. The view clamped as the canyon narrowed. Armies of organ pipe cacti came to the precipices in full sunlight, while down here the creek bed darkened. Maroon-colored rock sculpted nearly into a tunnel. As the canyon deepened and narrowed, there was no more room for cottonwoods or willows, and in some places no more room for organisms that could not swim.

I had imagined it would be something like this. The creek had shed its skin, as the name *Remudadero* suggested. Everything changed. Tree tobacco grew with leaves larger than a jaguar print, larger than my spread hand. Where the canyon tilted open once more, palms crowded the floor. Cacti stood above them. The desert of Tierra Caliente stretched for a hundred miles beyond that.

Champagne waterfalls flushed the pools around my legs with oxygen. The canyon closed again, turning dark beneath stone walls. The only reason for all this change was that the creek had found a harder rock formation in which to flow. The rock resisted. The water insisted. The ground was edged open and a new breed of running water formed, while upstream, where the canyon floor was gentle, the rocks had not contested the flow. I pushed through a pool waist-deep, holding my pack over my head so it would not drag. In the dim, ambient light I followed the creek. Round, odd-shaped stones at the bottom tended my feet from one side to the other. For all the floods and all the trees that had once been uprooted and thrown through this passageway, there was peace for a moment. For all of the open desert, there was a place burrowed into shadows and water. Remudadero. The world changes.

Creeks of Galiuro

I stopped. Swallowed. Looked around my feet, my eyes burning with sweat and light. A hundred and nineteen degrees Fahrenheit, at least. This was the hottest July on record for Arizona. It was in fact the hottest single month recorded in all of North America. If I prayed for rain, the sky would laugh at me. Last time I listened to a radio I heard that forty people had died while trying to cross the border. They had all run out of water.

The creek bed on which I stood, stretching across the boundary of the Sonoran and Chihuahuan Deserts in southeast Arizona, was dry. The air carried no sound. I reached down and, among scorched white stones, picked up the shell of a turtle.

This Sonoran mud turtle had died long ago. The shell's edges flared like a conquistador's helmet. About an inch and a half long, it rested in my palm like a small creek stone, one with hardly any weight to it, as if made of balsa. Inside I could see the ribs, curved and fused to the underside the same way ribbing is built into wooden ships. I returned it to the ground and walked forward. I am never any good in this kind of heat. I lose track directions, not minding if thorns stab my legs, the same thorns I would have avoided at dawn. I crawled into the narrow shade of a cliff, watching a single cloud, waiting for it to become huge and pendulous, scratching its belly with lightning, splitting open with rain. Instead it huffed into nothing, as if exiting a boiling kettle.

I left from there and walked into the shade of cottonwoods, where I nearly stepped on a rattlesnake. It was a western diamondback stretched inconspicuously across dry leaves, not even rattling from two feet away. I made a sound—something like *whoaholycrap*—and swerved my boot the other way. The snake did not move, did not twitch, did not flick its tongue. I had seen six rattlesnakes in two days—all Arizona blacks and diamondbacks—and as always, they reacted with the firm politeness of a brief, irritated rattle, or they did not react at all. As a rule, I have been treated kindly by rattlesnakes.

Saguaro cacti stood all around the low slopes of the canyon, coming down to the edges of these deep groves of trees. I walked into the brothy darkness beneath alder trees, ducking under some of the larger, more boldly strung spider webs. Inside the shade I found a place to wait, arranging leaves behind my back and leaning against them. I waited for night, six hours away. When shadows went long at about five o'clock, I returned to a place in the bed where earlier I had detected a trace of dampness. I organized a stopwatch, a tape measure, and my notebook on the stream cobbles and watched the spot, which was still moist. At about

5:30 water came out of the ground. It did not spew up, but slowly escaped into the surrounding sand and small rocks. The wet circle grew until water became visible. Then it bubbled out like a small fountain and the creek began.

Many of the desert streams that flow through the summer emerge in this way. They come out at night, as if fearful of the sun, rising through small gravel-filled corridors that connect the stream on top to the subsurface stream flowing far beneath. By midnight, this entire creek bed would be the site of a clean, swift stream. Walking across during the day, you would find this absurd to imagine.

As soon as light strikes leaf surfaces at sunrise, the riparian forest sets its higher metabolism into motion, photosynthesizing and pumping phenomenal amounts of water up to the canopy. The thickly arranged plants along the creek are known as *phreatophytes,* meaning they have no control mechanism for water. They are not true plants of the desert. They take as much water as they can get (a day's worth for a single tree being enough for a few lifetimes of a large cactus), sending it out the leaves, into the heat, making the understory as humid as a New Orleans summer. Instead of flowing across the ground, the creek is hoisted a hundred feet into the air into the leaves of sycamores, willows, cottonwoods, alders, and Arizona walnuts. What is not taken shrinks into the ground and returns to the water table. The surface creek is sucked dry.

As light faded from the trees, the creek saturated the surrounding ground before actually taking depth. I drank it there, at its source, my lips against the rocks. Within an hour it was moving. Here and there a new channel broke forward with swift fingers, liberating the wing of a moth, the doily veins of a decomposed cottonwood leaf, a dead beetle. Then it slowed, testing the route, finding places into which it spilled. Dusk came. The creek gained speed, making sounds, pushing pieces of gravel around, sucking air from the soil. As soon as the creek had about eighty feet of ground, longfin dace, supple little fish about an inch or two long, began darting about. There must have been a hundred of them. They had spent the day in sponges of soaked algae protected under leaf piles, or in rotted pieces of wood where water had collected, surviving in a half-alive torpor as the rocks baked around them. Water beetles, who had hidden in the same fashion, spun into action.

Crouched at the water, squinting to write measurements in the coming dark, I glanced to the darker tunnel of overhanging trees upstream. Fireflies had appeared. They besieged the tall grass. Their lights were not constant or sharp but rather were ephemeral, green lanterns fading in and out, describing brief paths through the air. Eerie flickers revealed corners and closets within the canopy, and when a firefly neared the ground, a pale green circle of light cast over the twigs and leaves. They were accounted for in my notes, along with the rates of flow from the creek:

1st firefly at 7:45
many more by 7:49
dazzling by 7:54

Finally, in the dark, the gurgling sound of the creek became loud enough that the bottom of the canyon had transformed. Through a parade of fireflies and the dance of fish and diving beetles, the water had come. Tomorrow, in the sunlight, all of this would again be gone.

I should not give the impression that all the creeks here appear and disappear completely. Like the creek of the fireflies, many have surface water for twenty yards or ten feet or half a mile, with dry stretches between. At night these grow and sometimes connect, and during the day they recede, but not all of them entirely. Small waterfalls can still be found in the deepest shade during the day, and some of the creeks keep miles of water on top day and night.

I had come walking the creeks below the Galiuro Mountains, one of the more remote ranges in Arizona, northeast of Tucson and northwest of Willcox. Depending on what you count, there are well over ten good, running streams here. In the winter they run full steam, bank to bank all the way to the San Pedro River, a river that flows north out of Mexico into the Gila River, which runs south of Phoenix, curving across the state to meet the Colorado River before returning to Mexico. In the summer these small creeks are piecemeal, consisting of wet and dry sections scattered haphazardly through the canyons.

Although the Galiuros reach as high as 7,663 feet, they do not account in size for the amount of water produced in the springs and creeks below. These desert creeks, all around a 4,000-foot elevation, are too numerous. Even larger mountain ranges that feed the surrounding deserts cannot produce this volume of water. For the number of cattle historically grazing this area, about twenty-five windmills would be expected. There are only six. Much of the water is actually a remnant of Ice Age water. Stored and doled out in the increments of small streams, this Pleistocene water slowly drains from aquifers buried in the mountains, joining banks of much more recent runoff water. Radiocarbon dating on the groundwater here places it back ten thousand years, while the oldest water goes back to over fifteen thousand years. Hydrologists call it fossil water.

The Nature Conservancy in 1982 purchased forty-nine thousand acres of private land and government land leases below the Galiuros. Even as a neighboring rancher sued the Conservancy for not grazing cattle on this leased land, the conservation outfit talked the Bureau of Land Management into a five-year riparian and grassland restoration plan for the area. The plan mostly involved doing nothing, letting the place get back about its business. The boldest moves were the removal of cattle that had been grazing the area heavily since the late 1800s, and an experimental controlled burn program. The canyons at the northern boundaries of the Conservancy property are within two federal wilderness areas, which, when combined with the Conservancy's Muleshoe Ranch land, encompass the entire watershed of these desert streams.

For the most part, surrounding ranchers are complimentary of work that has been done at Muleshoe Ranch. Most of these ranches have voluntarily kept their stock below maximum numbers. Because of the ensuing quality of their ranges, after the last three years of hard drought, these ranchers were some of the few to survive without major economic losses.

The ranch manager at Muleshoe, Bob Rogers, is a congenial man in his thirties who no longer deals in livestock. He does not boom his voice, and he scratches the dirt with his work boot in the middle of a conversation. He is far less at ease in political situations than he is in repairing fences, a task that had to be done on one fence sixteen times in a single summer after a barrage of floods.

Other pieces of land belonging to the Nature Conservancy are of higher profile and have provokéd disputes: quarreling with local government or citizens over water rights or grazing or public access or hunting. Muleshoe, on the other hand, is thirty miles down a dirt road that is sometimes washed out. Scientists doing work out here usually vanish into the backcountry for the length of their research. Public visitation is minor. Rogers is pleased with all of this.

He found the only known pair of endangered Mexican spotted owls in the range. Government biologists were skeptical about his claim, saying that sycamore forests with understories of oak and juniper are no good for spotted owls, so Rogers took them there, showed them the birds. He has a good grasp of the land, how to get around. His grandmother was born beside Aravaipa Creek, which crosses the northern point of the Galiuros. Most of his family background is in the ranching business, which he considers himself to still be in. It is only that he is tending to creeks instead of cattle.

"In a canyon like Double R," he said, "cattle will get into the shade and water on a day like this and they won't move. Not for days. Not for weeks. That is why you either have old, massive trees—from before cattle grazing—or only new trees that have grown since we got the cows out." I have noticed this: one sycamore probably over a hundred years old with acres of shade below, then beneath it young, weedy sycamores shooting up everywhere. The trees of in-between age are absent, represented by the time cattle were present.

I spent some time talking with him about the creeks, getting an idea of what the different seasons are like, sorting through his records of flow measurements. We spread maps on the floor at the headquarters, got on our hands and knees. "Now *this* is some lost country," he said, scribbling his finger over a series of canyons to the north. "I don't know where this water comes from. Just doesn't make any sense to me, but it certainly is there. Right *there*," he stabbed his finger down. The creeks of Galiuro befuddle him. So much water in a place where there should be so little.

After spending a week walking the southern canyons, I traveled north, to the place Rogers had called lost country. I started in the morning in one of the canyons, taking note of whatever I saw first: a coiled Arizona black rattlesnake (coming through again later in the day, I found the bare clearing where the snake had shoved pebbles away, leaving its coiled shape on the ground) and a yellow-breasted chat scolding me through the stained-glass light of cottonwood leaves. The creek here ran steadily. It stopped in only a few places, draining into a downwelling zone to reappear elsewhere along the floor, around the next turn. These forests were the thickest I had seen. Dangling throngs of grapevines snared my ankles and I pushed through hedgelike walls of vegetation that blocked the view of the creek. A couple of times I found myself off the ground, suspended on cribs of grapevines, then stumbling out to the desert, into the light, hoping to find a shortcut. The land beyond the thin bands of forest was nude with rock. Saguaros stood here and there, along with numerous leafless ocotillos barren as fence posts. The sky was everywhere, sharp, hot, blue. A soaked bandanna stiffened in three minutes. I fell back into the forest, looking for the creek again.

The air inside was a potent marinade of humidity and heat causing my upper lip to taste like the sea. Any exposed skin became a repository for field specimens, my flesh a sticky net drawn through the brush, my forearms collecting insect wings, spiderwebs, curled bits of leaves and bark, patches of soil, and live ants. Flying insects struggled with their wings pasted to the back of my hands and to my forehead. From in here, the creek sounded like dishes being put away, a purposeful clatter in the distance. I followed the sound and ducked through to a broad pool where a small waterfall entered at the top. Fish, some of them a foot long, flashed and scattered. A rusty-orange dragonfly dodged up and down the stream corridor, its vellum wings making the rasping sound of dry garlic skins.

A spring came in from the opposite side, draining from cracks in a sheer stone wall. Shrouds of maidenhair fern and already-bloomed monkeyflower hung below the spring, dripping ten-thousand-year-old water into a natural trough, which then ran into the pool where the fish had calmed after my intrusion. I held myself up by the trunks of two young willows as I leaned toward the pool. The fish settled mostly in one place, the Sonoran suckers resting heads on each other's tails the way horses lean on one another. The smaller, more stout Gila chub kept their distance, hovering higher in the water than the suckers. The streamlined dace, both speckled and longfin species, hung everywhere, high and low, here and there.

I crouched slowly between my two willow trunks. It never seems to me that fish *swim*. Swimming seems like a mechanical process with articulated parts performing a variety of operations: the breaststroke, the butterfly, the dog paddle. There are no rigid strokes to a fish in motion. It is more like sailing. If fish had words, they would use *swim* for all of us terrestrial animals struggling through their medium, and something else for themselves.

Fish in the desert, though. It sounds like a play on words, a trick phrase. *A woman without a man is like a fish without a desert.* But these fish are not random, not accidental slips that spilled out of the mountains. They are desert fish, found nowhere else. A number of fish biologists contend that they are, along with the water they live in, holdovers from the Ice Age. There are other contentions that they even precede the last ice age. Streams are threads through time, remaining through numerous climate changes as ice ages and deserts rise and fall. The fish cannot stand up and walk to more suitable habitat, so for the hundreds of thousands of years that the desert lasts, they seek refuge in these final springs and streams, adapting to the particular rigors. I once talked with a biologist named W. L. Minckley, who had found speckled dace in a spring along the higher benches of the Grand Canyon. The only physical link between the spring and any streamflow would be during floods, and that connection consists of impassable waterfalls thousands of feet down toward the Colorado River. This, he told me, led him to believe that the fish were there *before the canyons were cut.* The fish would have lived in that one piece of water for uninterrupted millions of years.

Obviously humans have changed the course for desert fish by interfering with their insular habitats. Extinct in the desert are the likes of the First June sucker, three species of Mexican dace, the Monkey Spring pupfish, Phantom shiner, Las Vegas dace, thick-tail chub, and numerous others. In some cases, especially with the native fishes of the less-studied Mexican streams, the extirpation occurs so rapidly that there has been no time to even document extinctions, ironically similar to what is occurring in rain forests. In Arizona, 81 percent of native fish fauna is presently classified or proposed for classification as threatened or endangered.

There have been cases of native desert fishes being actively poisoned out of waterways to make way for non-native sport fish. Referred to as trash fish, most natives are not fleshy or large enough for eating or do not put up the right kind of fight against a fishing line. I once discussed poisoning with a man who had worked on one of these eradication projects, a man who went on to become the superintendent of Glen Canyon National Recreation Area on the Arizona-Utah border. In his early years he had operated a drip station, one of fifty-five stations that introduced 81,350 liters of the poison rotenone into the Green River and its tributaries in the fall of 1962. The plan was to regionally dispose of the native humpback chub, a now-endangered fish, to make way for bass for sportfishing. "That is how we saw things then," he explained with a regretful but helpless tone, as if telling of war crimes. "We didn't understand."

Minckley, one of the foremost biologists working with desert fishes, said he could not see the remaining few natives of Arizona deserts surviving the next fifty years. Minckley's words were short, gruff. I talked with him in his office at Arizona State University in Tempe, where he is a professor and researcher. His desk was a mess of books and papers. A poster of native fish species hung on the wall. "Western fishes are completely unique," he explained. "There are only a few examples left in the desert anymore. The value of a species is just . . . just . . . so hard to hold onto. These species, these fishes, are sentinels for the system. They go, and you know that the place—the larger habitat—is being decimated. One of the things that pisses me off is that it is not necessary. You don't have to introduce bass into remote streams. The biggest factor for these fishes is the competition with non-natives. Dams are not that much of a consequence. Destruction of riparian habitat is not nearly as big a factor. It's those damned non-natives."

Minckley let out a hard breath and wrenched his left hand over his forehead, having told this story before. "All a native desert fish really needs is a place where nothing preys on its young. I am really getting too old to pussyfoot around with all of this. You've got to be insane to be in this business. We are continually losing."

He lamented the lack of support for desert fishes. People fail to get excited about something so remote and unfamiliar as a fish, even if that failure draws to an end not only a large number of species but an entire form of life. Non-natives are brought into these creeks for sport, and I have been unable to argue my way through a steadfast fisherman on the topic. I started bemoaning this to Minckley, telling him that it is difficult to express the value of a fish, something called a trash fish no less. He closed his eyes, retreating to someplace far away. "I know," he said, grumbled, whispered. "I know I know I know I know."

Consider the sum of all life, the heaped arrays of adaptations flung one after the next into the abundance of forms, each possessing codes pertaining only to its ancestors and its immediate predecessors, teeming organisms hefting around history in their cells, a library of each quirk and evolutionary indecision of the past 3.5 billion years, but only a record in each species of its single divergence from the source, with no register of errors or chance events gone awry because those were discarded to extinction, leaving a peculiar animal honed to a perfect set of symbols and codices, down to the Sonoran topminnow *Poeciliopsis occidentalis*, perhaps soon to be vanquished from the planet. Protecting species is the same intrinsic gesture as preserving the original documents and constitutions of an entire civilization, or the love letters of grandparents.

Especially among biologists there is a respect for life and its uniqueness that goes almost unspoken, a reverence for the incomprehensible diversity of organisms that has woven itself into patterns across the earth. We, biologists or not, look at these creatures, including ourselves, the same way we observe stars of the night sky—with unspoken questions hanging from our mouths. To be privy to the eradication of a species and to know damn well what is going on is a shame beyond repair.

A recent government meeting was organized to discuss the preservation of certain desert fishes. One of the top policy makers announced that before anything was done that might hinder nonnative sport fish in favor of natives, they would have to assess which of the two should take priority. To keep from bursting into a rage, Minckley stood up and walked out.

Roberts at Muleshoe Ranch told me that while walking up one of the creeks he saw a bass shoot by. It was the first nonnative he had seen in that creek. Up higher is a stock tank that a family insists on keeping filled with bass for fishing. In floods the stock tank overflows and the bass tumble into the stream. Roberts swallowed and looked at the ground. It is like being told you have cancer.

To avoid the embarrassment of destroying another species, there have been mad scrambles and last-minute panics. The recovery of the Sonoran topminnow came so late that its habitat was already heavily fragmented and the species had been driven to genetic isolation. The fish that were chosen and reintroduced along numerous creeks turned out to be inbred, carrying no detectable genetic diversity at all. One of the populations in Mexico, one that was not used for reintroduction, was found to have strong genetic diversity, higher fecundity, and higher growth and survival rates. The reintroduced population from Arizona, basically engineered by humans who drove them into detached habitats, was already a dud ready for extinction.

There have also been subtle, illegal maneuvers to preserve these fish. In 1967 Minckley hauled two species out of a spring in an ice chest and transplanted them into a creek. For such a simple act, it was more consequential than many budgeted, staffed, and researched restoration attempts made since. At the spring he had found several species of native fish: the Yaqui chub, the Sonoran topminnow, and the Yaqui sucker. The Yaqui chub, *Gila purpurea*, was at the time uncomfortably near to extinction. He said, "I filled up a cooler with water, grabbed a hundred chub and female topminnows, then hauled ass up to Leslie Creek and let them loose. Somehow they took hold."

At the time there were no specific laws about transporting native fishes, but Minckley's move was somehow regarded as illegal, and a decade later government land and wildlife managers openly frowned on his actions. Ironically, his act prevented the extinction of the Yaqui chub. Shortly after he had transplanted these fish, the spring, which had become the final refuge for the species, completely dried. The fish he had transported in his ice chest became the only remaining population and are now the genetic stock of the Yaqui chub that have been reintroduced across southern Arizona.

I traveled fifteen miles north until reaching a creek directly below the crest of the Galiuro Mountains. A canyon burrowed into the desert, carrying a length of dark, fat pools and short waterfalls. The forest was no haiku, no simple arrangement. It was a mess. Flood debris and alders. Alders grew so thick that I had to place my two hands before my face, or walk backward, my backpack parting the way until the way became too tangled, and parted me. I had left the last canyon and traveled fifteen miles farther north, walking into a majesty of cliffs. Smooth walls and buttresses jetted seven hundred feet to either side, where chambers rounded into places to sit and great curves of rock. The alders thickened. Their leaves are more numerous and darker-colored than those on any other riparian tree, their branches starting near the ground and crowding each other to the oblivion of the canopy. I stopped trying to walk the edges and came down to the water, pushing my way through the stream, fish slapping my shins, water to my crotch. I pushed away vines and branches, breaking with my thighs the trapeze webs of orb weaver spiders.

The alders were so abundant due to a large flood that came through a decade earlier, spitting the remains of cottonwoods, sycamores, and willows into the San Pedro River. The alders were the first to come back. They returned with a vengeance.

Floods get rid of things, cleaning the creeks. Along with tearing out the forests, floods dispose of non-native fish. One thing natives have over these non-natives is that they can survive incredible hardship. Floods come down like rolling loads of cement. In Aravaipa Creek north of here, which carries one of the largest assortment of native fish, half of the creek's entire water output is discharged over twenty-two days of the year. A quarter of the year's water appears within three and a half days. An autumn flood on Aravaipa sent the creek fifty feet above its normal waterline, and more than half of the riparian forest was destroyed. Most aquatic insects were wiped out. Researchers returned to find that the fish had hardly even moved, that the populations kept roughly the same proportions, as if the flood had been nothing to them but a shrug.

The razorback sucker has a peculiar hump of muscle on its back, shaped like a top keel, located close to the heart to deliver immediate bursts of swimming power against overwhelming currents. As one fish biologist told me, floods mean nothing against this one muscle. While other native species—aquatic plants, invertebrates, and amphibians—must often repopulate a previously flooded stream in the form of seeds, eggs, or airborne adults, fish are often still there.

Consider the proportions. A two-inch dace and a fifty-foot wall of water, boulders, shattered cottonwood trees, and mud. The flood subsides. The dace has not moved. A researcher named Gary Meffe, working at Arizona State University, planted Sonoran topminnows and non-native mosquitofish in a Plexiglas flume. The mosquitofish has wiped out topminnows throughout most of Arizona, largely by preying on juveniles, but tends to disappear after heavy flooding in narrow canyons, while topminnows remain. This piqued Meffe's curiosity. When he sent a pulse of high water down his flume, the native topminnows quickly faced into the current, taking nearly motionless positions along the sides or near the bottom of the flume, wherever frictional drag gave the water a slight pause. Mosquitofish panicked and darted anywhere. If they oriented into the pulse it was with hesitation. They would not hold their places, flashing from side to side or turning completely around, their bodies catching different currents, their tails tucking into eddies and pulling them off course. They were flushed out of the flume. Even newborn topminnows snapped to the correct position and stayed there when a pulse came down. The mosquitofish had no genetic memory of water behaving like this, while native fish hovered in the eddies and shear zones, hunkering down, refusing to move or even twitch their fins in the wrong direction.

Few environments in the world are in such a constant state of violent expansion and contraction as this. If these streams were forests, they would vanish suddenly, understory and all, leaving nothing but hard ground, then reappear from nowhere. Devastating fires would charge through, sometimes several times in one year. The common assemblage of rabbits, elk, and bears would never do in a forest like this. An entirely new means of life would have to be invented.

On the other end of the spectrum from floods are the retreat and disappearance of the streams, sometimes daily, sometimes once a year. Rather than avoiding retreating sections of stream, some beetles and water bugs seek out these habitats in search of prey. Predator densities rise quickly. Raccoons and coatis scoop beleaguered fish out of the last pools, and black-hawks drop from the canopy to find whatever else has been stranded. The stresses and cycles of desert streams are uncountable. If not floods, then drought. At one desert stream in the last stages of drying, researchers saw eight predacious water bugs fly into two pools and consume twenty fish within a matter of a few hours.

Fish scattered ahead of me as I slid through the water. They schooled around each other, darting beneath tree roots. These were all natives. This canyon has yet to see a non-native. Dragonflies flitted and poised on the ends of twigs and snatched prey from the air. A researcher had walked into one of the nearby canyons last summer studying these insects, finding a tropical damselfly, *Palaemnema domina,* that had never been seen in the United States. In canyons west of here he captured three species of damselfly that had never been recorded anywhere in the world. Down in the rich forests along one of these Galiuro creeks he cataloged twenty-five species of damselflies and dragonflies, some with zebra-striped abdomens, others with colors scripted into their wings. With these creatures hovering in and out, the place verged on primeval.

I worked around root-strapped boulders, pushing through the water. Every few minutes I caught glimpses of the desert outside where saguaros perched across the walls. Towers of rock had pulled away, leaning out as if about to fall and bridge the canyon. These were censored views, framed by so much greenery that it seemed unlikely that there was any world beyond here at all. The sun could not get directly inside the forest, so the place became a steaming greenhouse, the air strong as horse breath.

A wind shoved through at 2:30, launching a fresh and unmistakable smell. Rain. Cold rain and hot rocks, the smell of a summer storm. There was not much of the sky to see, but there were certainly no clouds. I kept moving, trying not to wish too hard for rain, not to disappoint myself. Every summer the storms come as each desert inhabitant waits down here. We all watch the growing clouds after months of sheer heat until we are leaning toward them. Then one day they break open. The desert is deluged, flooded, reborn. The storms are insanely powerful with wind and rain. For months we wait for this.

After half an hour a thunderstorm moved over the canyon rim, lumbering in like a floating city. Thunder came through with low, gravely echoes off the walls. I looked up. *My god,* I thought, I prayed, *pummel us down here. Ravage us. Please.* This had been, in fact, the hottest July recorded across the entire Northern Hemisphere. We needed rain down here.

I found a fifty-foot boulder in the stream and climbed its back to where I had a clear view of the canyon and the heavens above. It was like standing on a glowing woodstove. The boulder sent heat straight through my body, up my raised arms to the sky. The clouds were dark with water, bulging down as if about to rip open. A few drops of rain fell. Fat drops. I closed my eyes, turned my head upward. One hit my cheek. My first rain since sometime in the late winter or the spring. But that had been a different kind of rain. So much desire in the summer desert. So much goddamned, furious desire. I was begging out loud, holding my hands up.

It did not come. The drops ended. Thunder lost its sharpness to distance. The boulder was still hot, having evaporated each drop, not letting them stain the surface for more than two seconds. I crawled off the boulder feeling self-conscious. I had made a fool of myself begging at the sky.

The sun returned, baking the roof of the forest. As I walked, spiders danced frantically in my hair and down my forehead. Grapevines unfolded around me, slinging off their host trees or their boulders. Pools turned emerald with depth and I bent over to plunge my head in, flipping my hair back so that water ran down my spine. Primrose flowers grew in the gravel, some of them a foot taller than myself.

When dusk came I unloaded gear onto rugs of fallen leaves where I would make my camp. The forest had become disturbingly dark. I glanced up, my ground pad in hand. I did not move as I looked through the offhanded crossing of branches, leaves, and vines. Dark, closed places like this make me uneasy. It is not the wild beasts or the idea of a lunatic with an ax. It is not facing my dreaded interior self. It is the informality, the thoughtlessness, the brooding wisdom, the endlessness, the closure of darkness. More than that, it is the thing in darkness I cannot name. I was once called in by an adventure travel magazine where a number of writers at a table were asked to do a piece on their fears in the wilderness. Someone said she would take spiders, and everyone laughed sympathetically. Another person said heights, and another being lost, both of which elicited noble nods and *mmm* sounds. I said dark, and not one of these outdoor folk said anything. They all looked at me to see if I was kidding. "Dark," I said. "You know. *The Dark.*" They all kept looking at me.

I stayed in the forest for a few minutes, reasoning with myself. Then I packed and climbed out. I went up only two hundred feet, scrambling in the loose rock around prickly pear cactus, before dropping my gear again. It was easier to breathe up here. Hard, definite edges and blocks replaced the boiling, fleshy shapes of the forests. It was not dusk, as I had thought. Orange sunlight embedded the cliff tops. The nest of solid green below sounded like an aviary. No matter how loud the birds became, they still seemed secretive, hidden in the trees around the water. I kicked away the larger rocks and lifted off the balls of cholla cactus. There I could sit and look down into the stirring, breathing forest. I finally stretched back, pulled off my clothes, and covered my body with a sheet.

Sometime in the night a brilliant white light branded my eyelids. I woke. There were no stars, only a black sky. The air smelled wet. The breeze, liquid. My hands were clutched over my chest and I did not move them. In fact, I tightened them, bracing for what would come next. It sounded like a block of marble cleaved open with a sledgehammer. The sky broke in two with thunder. Echoes pounded back, thrumming against my spine. Lightning shot to the southeast. The air exploded again. Lightning then fell all around, snagging on the higher terrain. Scraps of lightning showed from behind rock towers. I counted the canyons by how many echoes of thunder were returned. Four pulses of thunder: four canyons. Then I heard the tapping. Rain began to fall. Another bolt of lightning. The rain increased, dabbing my face, making the sound of bean-filled rattles. I could hear it up on the cliffs, rain sheeting against rock. Rain dimpled my sheet, then sopped the fabric against my skin. I kept my hands folded on my chest. Water ran like tears out of my eyes, into my hair, through the rocks and into the forest. The creek grew by just that much.

My prayers. I remembered my prayers.

Part Three

FIERCE
WATER

It's here! Now! Get out!

—Survivor of a flash flood in Havasu Canyon

Now come the floods. They charge down atavistic canyons drinking furiously out of thunderstorms, coming one after the next with vomited boulders and trees pounding from one side of a canyon to the other, sometimes no more than hours apart. Sometimes a hundred years apart. Sometimes a thousand. The floods always come.

As I searched for water, the floods arrived and the hunting became no longer mine. It was no longer my own longing or my own body, not some piece of knowledge I could possess. Water now had the knowledge. It dispensed with sweet sounds and the dispassionate isolation of water holes. It hammered against the earth. Floods that came around me erased all possible humanity, even in some cases the very bones of other people, turning them under where search teams could not find them, even as for months they dug as relentlessly and religiously as paleontologists.

Water becomes filthy with desire as it gains speed into flood. It cannot move in a straight line. Even in artificial flumes of cement, steel, or sandbags, it scratches its way out like a prisoner working a hole into a cell wall, steadily digging with any tool it can get. There is too much craving and energy when water moves. It wants out.

When I was younger, less experienced with floods, I brought a girlfriend into a slot canyon in Utah. We were halfway through, our bodies pressed beneath full backpacks, when a cloudburst hit the canyon. We both knew a flood would come. The ground was saturated from storms and floods over the previous week. We had been testing the canyons, pushing as hard as we could, exploring places where floods had hit hours earlier, and on this day went in even as cumulus clouds lumbered around the sky like giants.

Now it was my error. I was the one who should have known better. She was slightly less able than me with climbing over jammed boulders, wading across pools full of days-old floodwater, so I charged ahead looking for exits, then ran back to shout, *Keep moving, we need to get the hell out of here!* She never looked up, never made eye contact. She navigated each obstacle as quickly as possible, knowing as well as I that if a flood hit there would be no way out.

I had betrayed her. Out of breath, I paused and watched her, saw her determination. Her moves across the boulders were innocent. Rain poured through her flowered baseball cap, forming rivulets across her cheeks. She had no right to die here. I had no right to get her killed. Quietly, like a prayer, I said, *I would die without question to get you out of here.* She was too focused and far away to hear me.

Within fifteen minutes we succeeded to the canyon rim. The flood punched in behind us, took the canyon. She was able to smile in relief and exhilaration then, crouching under a ledge for protection from the rain. We watched the soup of red water swirl into the head of the canyon below, but I was uneasy. I had said the words. I would die without question.

When you place your hand in moving water, you will feel the curves of power looping your bones, addressing your skin with logarithmic sways. Magnify that ten or twenty thousand times and you will be killed by the force. Then your body will know. The designs of the flood will be told in nail marks left in your flesh, the rearrangement of your bones, and where your body is finally abandoned. There is something disconcerting even in seeing from a distance water that wants out this badly, that it would grapple your body if it could just touch you. It is a type of current that flips you end over end, tears away your sense of direction, your sense of control. Your arms are pulled, your frame shoved, as if a shark is punching up from below, your head jerking back. But pay attention in that moment and you will feel the intelligence of water upon you. It will tell stories of itself against your body in boils and surges and vacancies.

If you do not want to be killed looking for this secret, then the ground will tell you. Viewing the desert from a satellite, from a plane, or even from hands and knees shows the desert to be a dry, waiting map of floods. The desire of water is scribed across the desert like graffiti, until all that is left of the desert is water. Sandstone humps of the Colorado Plateau are streaked with chasms, the plateau being nothing but a dendritic fan of hundreds of thousands of miles of canyons across four states. The rolling bajadas of the Sonoran Desert consist of arroyos to the horizon. Stared at closely, each part begins to look like a math problem, decipherable into some detail about water's appetite. Rocks are eaten by sudden water, but not in clumsy, formless bites. In the scream of a flood, consummate carvings are left behind. Careful scallops are taken from the faces of canyons. This is not random work. It is artistry distilled from madness.

A small Sonoran creek, one of the more rare and lush, with nests of springs and nearly forty quiet pools, took a March flash flood twenty thousand times higher than normal flow, excavating over thirty thousand cubic feet of earth in less than an hour. The springs were destroyed. The entire geometry of the creek, with gentle descents and almost no exposed bedrock, became a ladder of boulders, waterfalls, and smoothed granite floors. Half the pools vanished. Few plants remained. Leopard frogs, Sonoran mud turtles, and black-necked garter snakes washed away with the earth beneath them. As if claiming superiority over the animal's adaptations, the flood completely wiped out a population of endangered fish, a subspecies of the Sonoran topminnow. Then, as if balancing the loss with sorcery, the flood left behind canyon tree frogs, which had never before been seen on the creek.

This give and take is never subtle. Water in flood means exactly what it says. It has no hypocrisy. Even as it murders, it leaves life behind and carves elegant, intricate passages into raw stone, all the while having no debate about its intention. It is the same water that will sit complacently in a hole for months or years, the same arrangement of atoms that flows gently, singing lullabies, the same that fiercely consumes children and tears the walls from titanic canyons.

It washes over fields beyond the canyons, soaking the earth for the planting of tepary beans or corn, depositing nutrients necessary for agriculture. But don't pray for too much water in the desert, even if the crops demand it. It will come eventually, and it will bring its desideration with it. Catholic saints are often employed to call the rain for crops or drying wells. I've heard many stories of people running to hide the small ceramic or plastic figurines they have placed, as lightning punctures the ground around them, as outbuildings are lifted away in wind, as the arroyos fill, then overflow with a raging, dun-colored water that smells of all the villages and lives upstream that have been consumed. The displayed santos are quickly clutched up, hidden away as if pulling the plug on the rain, concealing the request. At that point it is too late. The water reveals itself to the ground without reservation. And the dry ground waits, completely open with its bare rock and expectant passages like a lover who has no hesitation. The water tumbles wildly inside. The message is scrawled into the desert, a savage, but impeccable, signature.

I know a woman who has, as a forensic scientist, dealt with the bodies of flood victims. She told me of the face of a six-year-old girl. Surgically removed from the girl's head by a flood, there

were no bones or teeth attached. It was only a face, limp as a rubber mask. The rest of the body had been unharmed, *protected*,
she said. This seemed like something she had been waiting to tell
somebody. In the wrong context, it may have seemed trivial or
too grotesque for conversation, but when we talked about it, she
was enchanted by what it proposed. Something was hidden in the
water. The water *meant* whatever it had done. There was nothing
personal to the victim, no vendetta. It was just that water was too
powerful for life to withstand, and within that power was precision, as if choices were being made, she said. The final word of
water had been revealed by its own fierceness.

6. THE SACRIFICE OF CHILDREN

Tohono O'odham Reservation, Southern Arizona
February

THE STORY TOLD FROM SOUTHERN ARIZONA IS OF a Tohono O'odham man chasing a badger into a hole, intending to kill it. As the man prodded into the hole, a burst of wind shot out, as if a seal had broken, followed by rushing water. The water erupted across the ground. He backed away in fear, and when the water would not stop, he ran.

I came looking for the place where this happened, walking on the Tohono O'odham reservation west of Tucson to find a shrine. The shrine had been erected exactly where the water emerged, and where dras tic deeds had been performed to stop it, leaving the hole now completely dry. From talking to people who shared stories of such a shrine, I had heard that it was not in a wash, and not on an outcrop of rock where a spring might emerge. It was on open plains of desert, where the sudden, inexplicable appear ance of water would incite fear instead of celebration.

In one telling of the story, four villages were rapidly swallowed by the water. The people panicked and a hasty council was held among shamans. The first solution came. A small waterbird was taken to the gushing maw and shoved inside. The bird vanished below and the water dropped back slightly but did not stop, letting the people know that they had been heard but not pardoned. Then a larger bird, perhaps a crane, was forced in, which had the same result. The third attempt involved a sea turtle, probably obtained through trade and travels to the south. It, too, disappeared while the water barely flinched, consuming the offerings like smidgens of unsatisfying meals, its mouth still open, querulous.

Shamans made the next difficult demand. Two boys and two girls were to be sacrificed, even though the act was unheard of in this culture. It was decided. People protested, but the water threatened to take the entire desert, so the children were to be selected, taken from the family clans of the Coyote People and the Buzzard People, a boy and a girl from each. During the selection a grandmother hid her grandson by rolling him in a reed mat. The hidden boy was passed over.

Four children were chosen and bolstered by the grieving communities, told that they were going to a better place, that they were saving their people. It was a strong act they were doing. They walked bravely, but with tender eyes. Dressed in ceremonial clothes, faces painted, they were taken to the roaring throat of water and, like the offerings before them, forced inside. When they sank from view, the flow ceased.

Water drained back to the earth and a slab of rock was placed over the hole, sealing the children and the water forever. Another rock followed that, then another. Rocks were stacked one on top of the next until the hole was secured, and the place became an unmistakable landmark. Ocotillo stalks were cut, peeled, and erected around the rocks in certain locations so that the story would be told by their placement: four sets of ocotillo limbs marking four children, surrounded by a larger wall of hundreds of limbs with openings to the east, north, west, and south.

As I walked through the desert, I recounted the story, imagining water flushing across the ground, consuming villages, inundating forests of saguaro cacti. It was the grandmother hiding the boy that I remembered clearest. When the water subsided, she hurriedly returned to her grandchild and unrolled the mat that had protected him. The boy was not there. She found only dry scabs of algae, the kind left on rocks when water drops back.

Out looking for the shrine, I first came across an embankment of compacted, water-driven sand left far from any drainage, just out in the desert. Someone had gone at it with a bulldozer, clawing a hole and carrying away a few trips' worth of sand and gravel. I took a close look at this pile, finding behind the bulldozer scratches the fine sweeps of cross beds, common in sand deposited in quick water. I blew on a few of the cross beds, cleaning them out so that they stood more clearly, describing arcs leading east, the direction of flow. The pile would have been a notable landmark to find anywhere out here, even without this story. I was scientific about it. Some big flood from long ago. I moved on.

As I walked farther, motion showed through creosote bushes, something flashing and silver like a fish. I turned south and walked toward it, noticing that over the bushes stood a crown of crooked white dowels leaning around each other, over six feet tall. Beyond and all around was a congress of low winter clouds darkening the desert, causing the whiteness of the erect wood to stand out like chalk on slate. I watched the motion below and could hear something rustling. Too small for a person, I thought. Too redundant for an animal. The air smelled moist, the way it smells before a rain. In all of southern Arizona only two-tenths of an inch of rain had fallen in the past five months. Third-driest winter of the century. The smell was only a tease. A breeze came from the south. The scent of dampness and creosote. Creosote limbs swayed, tending to the breeze. Again came the spinning, bright flash of something in the background. I could hear quick tapping as it moved. Something plastic.

I walked into a clearing and stopped. The shrine stood before me, built from the branches of ocotillos stripped of bark and spines so that they gleamed as white as bleached bones. Several hundred of these branches, shoveled upright into the ground so that they bent and curved around one another like interlaced fingers, formed a circle over a mound of flat stones. Stuck between the stones was a glittery toy spinner, designed to catch the wind and spin like a windmill. It rattled as it spun.

When the breeze slowed, the spinner wound down and stopped. I looked around.

Bare mountains.

A road nearby.

Desert.

The stones in the center lay covered with offerings. Teddy bears and costume jewelry and beads and a plastic dinosaur. Flowers made of crepe paper had scattered like colorful little heads of lettuce, petals unfolding, faded by the sun. Feathers, worn thin by winds, hung from four entrances where the ocotillo walls parted for each cardinal direction, for each child sacrificed. Standing at the eastern entrance I waited until I could feel my

The shrine

breathing along with the rise and fall of the breeze. Until my eyes adjusted to the setting of this peculiar shrine. Until everything turned quiet.

The shrine was obviously old. Some accounts place it back over three hundred years. By the passage and work of people, the ground of the shrine had been beaten down a couple feet lower than the general terrain. Every four years the ocotillo limbs are replaced, the old ones heaped up so that they rest in massive, graying piles like haystacks, only more orderly. Rather than being thoughtlessly tossed aside, they had been stored in a routine fashion, stacked lengthwise for however many hundreds of years this shrine has been preserved. There had been no variation in the treatment. The grounds were cleared of any rock larger than an almond, leaving the sand just coarse enough to sigh beneath my boots.

Ceremonies are held here during the four-year replacements of ocotillo limbs. Little has been openly spoken of these ceremonies other than references to night processions, perhaps nine days of preparations with a tenth-day dance around children. Whatever is done, there are obviously people assigned to this place, rituals passed along.

The roads crossing this reservation are dotted with death-memorial shrines, one every couple of miles, and countless others are scattered through the country, marking drownings, horse accidents, murders, heart attacks, or suicides, showing not the burial places but the actual places of sudden death. In a region of clustered votive candles, crucifixes, Virgin Mary statues, and small plaster grottos or *nichos* filled with flowers, this desert shrine of ocotillo stood out like a piece of gallery art, its sculptor working only with natural elements. I wondered if the makers had intended it to be so visually alluring, ascending orderly from the ground, becoming playful, then delirious as the ocotillo limbs flared back toward the ground or formed corkscrews to the sky. Then the feathers dangling to the four directions. Not being in a gallery, but out among villages, roads, and open desert, it seemed even more enigmatic.

I walked toward the east entrance. Ocotillo limbs curved at their ends. To enter, I had to duck, as one should when entering a place that belongs to children, like being invited into a living-room fort made of cardboard boxes and blankets. I crouched at the rock pile and studied its offerings.

Quarters, pennies, dollar bills; numerous toy guns; hand-drilled shell beads; two fine, handwoven baskets of Tohono O'odham style; a slingshot; a plastic bag of cedar leaves brought from a far-away place; matchbox cars; paper Teddy bears made by children;

a cassette tape of rap music, its title being *Life After Death*; pens and pencils; a fuzzy, stop-sign-red elephant with a pink tongue; clutches of creosote branches; a complete miniature tea set, including four saucers, four cups, a cream pitcher, a sugar bowl, and a teapot; a Virgin Mary pendant; many shells, including a conch and an abalone; colorful barrettes; play binoculars; dolls; and pieces of coral collected from a beach.

The sense of care and order was overwhelming. These gifts were for children only, mindfully chosen. There must have been profound fear of this water, I thought. So much fear that they killed their own offspring, having to spend the remaining centuries nursing them with precious, honest gifts.

A story arose in Arizona from European influence in the 1940s, naming this not as a shrine of a flood but as one of drought. The selection of four children, a number common in Native American rites, was replaced with three, indicative of European stories. In this version, the final shaman ordered, "Take three of your youngest children, and when you have put them into a hole in the ground, the water will come again."

It was the perceived fear of drought that reflected European ignorance about people of the desert. There are, of course, Tohono O'odham ceremonies to call the rain, repeated annually with fermented juice from saguaro cactus fruit, heavy vomiting, and an invitation to the clouds, but none near as drastic as the story of sacrificed children. Drought is ordinary here, dealt with adeptly, no need to make great sacrifices. During a 1923 drought, cattle bones protruded from the sand like bedsprings. The Tohono O'odham ranchers turned around and sold the bones as fertilizer in Tucson for seven dollars a ton.

What is terrifying here is too much water. I remembered the

Hopi, how water from below brought their ancestors to the surface of this world, bringing birth. But that does not matter here at the shrine of drowned children. This is a different side of water.

As I crouched inside, I felt the ground with my hand, picturing the water beneath that had once burst through. I imagined the darkness of the space below, as if this desert were perched on a thin crust of land, floating tenuously upon the water of the underworld. One indiscretion might open a hole, allowing the water to spew up. It was not evilness that I felt from this water. It was a ravenous organism.

Purposely, I did not mull over records of local geohydrology to isolate this story of water bursting out of the ground. Even as more than 95 percent of rain and snowfall in Arizona is lost to plant leaves and evaporation, I know that water is stored beneath the desert. From the dry country of Nevada down to Mexico, in these alluvial basins pitched between barren mountains, there waits over 4.3 trillion cubic feet of water. I once spoke with a petroleum geologist who headed oil and gas exploration in the Nevada desert. One of his drill bits struck water instead of oil. He described what he thought to be a near endless fountain of water, over a thousand gallons an hour rushing from a pipe three inches wide. But the crew members were looking for oil and not water, so they capped the water by sinking concrete down the well, like heaping rocks over an unsolicited hole.

In 1912, when the first water well was drilled on the Tohono O'odham reservation by the U.S. government, some people must have watched in horror, standing far back as a drill broke through to the underworld. Children had been sacrificed to close such a hole. Did these well drillers not know this? And what did the native people surmise in the coming decades as they dug hundreds of wells for themselves and the water table dropped? First by inches, then by tens of feet, now by hundreds. The planet's mysterious interior was being sucked dry, perhaps leaving the desert to soon collapse into the gaping pit left behind.

It is true that when the earth is drained of blood, of its hidden waters, the surface will die. Crops wither. Livestock collapse on weak legs. Villages become stark. Mesquite trees, even with roots sixty feet deep, stand vacant, like concertina wire discarded among rocks.

Our offerings to water, our requests of it in the desert, must be balanced carefully. Not too much and not too little. The Tohono O'odham are famously cautious with water, their lullaby words to their children being "Don't drink too much water."

I walked out of the shrine and wandered among the stacks of old ocotillo. There were signs of recent ceremony: deliberate piles of grass bundles or sticks or small rocks. To the east sat eight stones, each larger than any of those in the shrine, each caged by two upright ocotillo limbs decorated with feathers. These, I figured, were the seats the eight shamans took, where they made the decision to sacrifice, probably singing as the children were led in. Offerings here were of a completely different nature than those at the main shrine: shells, feathers, cigarettes, a lighter. Each rock had at least one cigarette, if not an entire package, already opened but with none of the cigarettes missing. This was the adult place, where difficult judgments were made. Tobacco was to be smoked late into the night. Dark feathers tended to the breeze, tied with twine or leather to their ocotillo moorings.

Who knows water better, the children who were most recently swimming in the womb, safely inhaling liquid, or adults who have learned about terror? It would have been too easy to sacrifice adults. Adults would have died noble, civilized deaths full of symbolism and martyrdom. Children have no such impurities. Thrusting children into a womb that takes their lives was such a painful act of betrayal that there will never be enough cigarettes to ease such a decision. This is why offerings are not restricted to the children, but are also left for the adults who suffered their own responsibility. The water had no choice but to recede in the face of such a gesture.

Turning to look at the shrine, I was struck again by its image, as if I had not yet seen it. This was perhaps the most unassuming, elegant shrine I had ever seen, with its curved architecture of ocotillo arms, some of them bowing inward, their tips nearly touching the rock pile in the center. Its simple gifts, so appropriate and thoughtfully chosen, implied a disciplined understanding of the story. Cigarettes for the shamans, Teddy bears for the children. I walked back and ducked inside once more.

My emotions became raw, rising unexpectedly to the surface. It was the care taken with these offerings. It was the image I could not shake of people crying as their children bravely entered the hole, their faces soft and confused with naivete. Heat grew inside of my heart. I felt flames in my chest, pushing aside my organs. No metaphors. It was just that way.

I also came to this shrine for a young man who had been taken by the water. He drowned in a river at the age of sixteen, the youngest of a family to which I was very close. I do not know if he was sacrificed so that the world could be saved, or if he was simply stolen by water. He drowned while tubing with friends, when his tube flipped in a turbulent stretch below a boulder. A friend who made it out safely ran after him, chasing him down the river, shouting his name until he could run no farther.

The body was not found for six days.

I reached into my pocket for an offering, a fossilized clamshell I had brought from Utah, 300 million years old. I fished it out and held it forward in one hand.

"It's a fossil seashell," I said. "Very old."

Would the children play with it? Would they laugh and toss it between one another and study it, curious about its origin?

I dipped my index finger into the hollow of the shell, testing its shape. "I don't know if it's okay to say this," I whispered. "But this is for my friend too. He went into the water, just like you." I reached forward and placed it between the rocks, letting it rattle down, out of sight.

.

7. CARRYING AWAY THE LAND

Royal Arch Canyon, Grand Canyon
December

DARK.

Not the simple dark that cradles you to sleep, but dark hard as stone.

I worked a knot by hand as rainwater shoved into my coat around my neck. I had to close my eyes with the rain poking up in the wind. I couldn't see anyhow. I wore a coat, boxer shorts, and boots without socks, trying to limit what would get wet. The wind came from seven directions at once, then joined and chimed up the cliff face, making a sound that screeched out of range. I finished the knot, checked the line. It was tight. Spare climbing gear had been used to get this tarp up, and the wind strained the moorings until they buzzed. I slipped underneath into shelter, and my partner Mike Morely's headlamp came on. The light was not for finding anything, or for seeing what gear might be left out, but just a reminder that we had light, that we were still in control. Our knees pressed together. Wind came under, sprayed our faces, then went elsewhere.

We were sitting on a ledge inside the Grand Canyon, where half an hour ago the air had been still and the sky, powdered with stars, said nothing of clouds. The ledge traced one of these monolithic cliffs of Redwall limestone, its edge rounded slightly, like a bowl lip, dropping into smooth walls below. We backed against a fifteen-foot boulder, crouching as far in as we could. If the storm had come during the day it might have been different. Our options would have been clear as we scurried around, battening gear down, looking up to see which way the storm moved, where the thickest parts lay. Instead we were blind and terrified for reasons neither of us could understand. It was no longer obvious how far our ledge extended. The storm had its thumb on us, grinding us into the rock. The tarp snapped up, then bunched down on our heads. Whip cracks came from each corner.

When the tarp kept snapping furiously, I shouted, "*Jesus Christ!*"

"I know," Mike said.

"*I mean Jesus Christ!*"

He turned off his headlamp. We pushed closer together to keep as far from the edges of the tarp as possible. The first rockfall came. It sounded from the north, a series of cracks and rumbles. The rain quickly washed out its echoes. Then something to the south. This one made the sound of a train derailing into the canyon, boulders uncoupling. We could hear each part, each shatter. A section of wall had come down. It bolted down the cliff, and again the rain took away any more details.

The desert is a book of change. Right now, pages fluttered too fast to read. Rocks are always falling in the Grand Canyon. I had become used to the sound, to turning suddenly during the day to see boulders chasing each other off the edge of an outcrop, to hearing the light clatter of small stones or pebbles falling from somewhere. A few Grand Canyon geologists have kept note of rockfalls, one writing that "the weakening process is a long one, and perhaps only a little extra heating on a hot day, or a light shower or a touch of frost may be the critical factor." Tonight, everything was the critical factor. On a calm day, one of these geologists recorded thirty tons of Redwall limestone that he saw caving into the Colorado River west of here.

Boulders crumble to sand at the bottom of canyons. Intense rains wash the debris into even lower canyons. Everything is in motion. Sediment coming down the Colorado River through the Grand Canyon was once, before Glen Canyon Dam, estimated to be 27 million tons passing a single point in one day.

All of this movement began here, on this night. Hard rain wedged itself into the cracks, pouring through holes and fissures, sending mud sailing over ledges. Events known as debris flows occur here, events now heavy on my mind. Of any place on this continent, the Grand Canyon has the greatest focus of debris flows, of monumental, sudden floods that dramatically alter the landscape. I did not mention to Mike how much I was thinking of them. Weak slopes in the canyon will fail, collapsing into floods below, which turn into a boiling mess of boulders and crushed shale. Rarely do large, stable cliffs like those of the Redwall fail. Debris flows generally come from the weaker formations, but the Redwall has certainly been known to collapse. We were hearing it clearly from beneath our whipping tarp. Canyons governed by debris flows are open toward the dominant paths of weather systems, which describes our canyon. They act as precipitation traps, gathering the confined, more intense storms.

Not only is the direction of the canyons conducive to debris flows, but the actual constituents within the rock are primed to run. The sequence of formations in the Grand Canyon tends to be hard, sheer cliffs on top of weak shales on top of cliffs on top of shales. It is the shale of ancient oceans, as opposed to shale of prehistoric streams or estuaries, that best mobilizes debris flows. The shale crumbles, weakening the foundations beneath overlying walls, pulling down entire sections of cliff. The marine shales are heavy in the minerals illite and koalinite, which are basically lubricants, turning the contents of a debris flow into an oiled slurry, at the same time electrochemically bonding to increase the density of the mixture, allowing larger pieces of debris to remain afloat. Boulders become buoyant in this soup, traveling farther, quicker. Wherever these shales are exposed, debris flows are compounded. The Redwall limestone and its tiers of cliffs sit atop the Bright Angel shale, one of the heaviest in illite and koalinite. Directly overhead, barely breaching the rim of the Redwall, is the Supai Formation, a major source of boulders and weak ledges that supply the bulk in debris flows. Above that is the Hermit shale, the primary producer of lubricant minerals for these semiliquid floods. Above that, Coconino sandstone cliffs lean over the weak Hermit shale, ready to fall. In between, we crouched on a ledge, listening to the collapse.

I have spent much time in places where if I wished to find water, I had to restrict myself to nothing but thoughts of water—not planning my life, not thinking of a job, a relationship, or a destination. I have walked between water holes not letting my mind slip once, remaining vigilant to any clue that might lead to water. And now, here, all I could think about again was water,

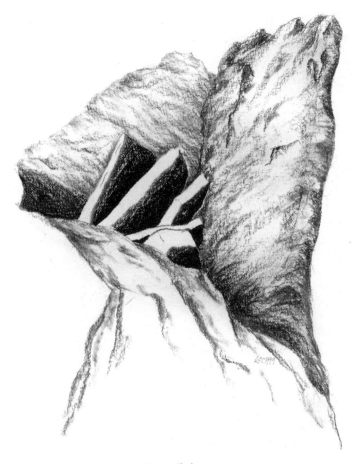

Water-piled stones

but in a different way. I could not escape it. No other thought could possibly enter my mind. I backed to the boulder in fear of water bringing down the entire cliff, turning our bodies into debris.

Most historic debris flows in the Grand Canyon are associated with the hard precipitation of convective summer thunderstorms, which tend to be isolated and influence only one or two drainages at a time. In July 1984 a debris flow descended Monument Creek, west of here. The entire side of a canyon crashed down at about 160 feet per second. When it hit the floor, debris exploded 300 feet up the opposite wall. Boulders nine feet in diameter were washed to the river, several miles away.

Mike and I were now in a December storm, not the key time for debris flows, yet in December 1966 a forty-four-foot-tall wave of boulders and slurry descended Crystal Creek, on its way into the Colorado River. Cliffs had failed in numerous places, slumping into the flood. Fifty-ton boulders bounded for miles, finally wedging into the very bottom of the Grand Canyon. On that December day in 1966 they formed one of the largest rapids along the entire length of the Colorado River. It is now called Crystal Rapids, a Class X rapids, the most difficult rating that can be given in the Grand Canyon. Before this December flood, there was hardly a riffle in the same location.

I once talked with a geologist named Bob Webb, one of the principal researchers of desert debris flows. He had encountered one in the middle of the night where Prospect Canyon opens to the Colorado River. I asked what it sounded like. "Freight train," he said. In a closet at his home he found a chart from that night's storm. He shuffled it out of its folder and pointed to a peak in a graph of rainfall. "You see that burst at the end? That's what you need to create a debris flow. And we felt that burst at camp because right around midnight our camp got blown to pieces by a high wind. Before I could get to sleep again I heard this big roaring sound." The debris flow missed the camp and the twelve members of his research team by a couple hundred feet, rumbling down the floor of the canyon into the river. In the morning he walked to the river and stared aghast at the remains of the debris flow that created a massive new waterfall in Prospect Canyon and buried in boulders the left side of a rapids called Lava Falls.

I asked him if there had been any smell to it and he tapped the side of his head with his finger, his eyes sharpening as he remembered something in vivid detail. "It was kind of a salty, musky smell that comes from those kinds of flash floods. . . . I used to go out and measure flash floods on the Santa Cruz River [in southern Arizona] and it was the same kind of decaying vegetation, muddy water smell that you get."

Mike and I were now at the source of such an event, should it come. We would be delivered to the river along with our camp and every surrounding stone. From beneath the tarp I listened to bursts of wind. They peaked and fell and peaked higher. The storm only grew. Mike told a story about an ocean voyage, then stopped talking. I prompted him to go on. He said that was all. So I asked him about climbing and about Yosemite, where he liked to travel. He started another story. This one elicited a monotone, each word given proper weight. Two summers ago he had finished a technical ascent of one of the big walls in Yosemite. Walking back with his climbing partner along a popular trail, he heard a crack and then a sound like a jet buzzing the valley. He looked up to see 170,000 tons of granite separating and falling from a cliff. I asked about the size of these pieces of cliff. He described them as a fleet of semitrailer trucks falling through the air, gently rotating as they descended.

When the boulders impacted the earth, the entire forest of pines catapulted, hurtling end over end. Mike hit the ground, held onto something. He was afraid he might asphyxiate in the blizzard of wind and granite dust that followed. He breathed through his clothes. When motion stopped, he crawled out of the dust. He and his partner were the first to arrive at the victims. One person was killed without question. Two young women were pinned beneath trees, partially crushed. He stayed with one woman, cleaning the blood, helping her with slow, calm words.

Then his story was over. He said he did not like times like this. He said that later this would make sense, in the telling of the story. But now, the earth was coming down around him. The basic footing of the planet was coming loose.

We talked our way through the storm, bolstering each other. We talked about fear and about how these things strengthen us. As we listened to rocks come down we talked about how we wished it would end, how the sun would rise and we would find ourselves alive. Eventually, amidst our talking and our silences, the wind slowed. The rain stopped abruptly, as it does when these storms suddenly change course or pass on. We both tentatively lifted our corners of the tarp and stepped into the night. Water could be heard washing down the cliffs.

We disassembled the shelter, shaking things out. Clouds left the sky as we reset our camp on the ledge. We were now gifted with a startlingly clear and calm night. I spread my bag on the flat ledge of limestone and crawled in. The night's element of consequence had been darkness. Now it was quietness. Water stopped running.

I waited with my eyes open, but there was nothing to wait for. How could I sleep? A clack of a single falling rock came from the north. I imagined it was no bigger than a drinking cup. But it was the only sound. I listened to it all the way down, each scrape and clip standing out as if speaking to me directly. It did not seem to fade as it fell hundreds of feet into the canyon.

Then silence.

Well into the 1930s it was believed that most erosion in the desert had little to do with water. Geologists cited extreme day and night temperature ranges and constant dryness, reporting that rocks must explode during the night from the pressures. They believed that it was the *absence* of water that caused desert erosion. In laboratory experiments, researchers tried to force rocks into cracking and exploding, assaulting them with temperatures and dryness far beyond what a desert could produce. The rocks did not budge. So they said that it was wind that had left deserts so chopped up with canyons and clefts. But when they hammered open these desert stones, ones gathered from the Mojave Desert in particular, they found hidden inside traces of moisture. Eventually they examined the shape of the land with increasing scrutiny. They walked the canyons. They witnessed floods and watched boulders roll away in the seething froth. Then they understood.

Desert floods come from rain. Most rain falling anywhere but in the desert comes slow enough that it is swallowed by the soil without comment. Desert rains, sporadic and powerful, tend to hit the ground, gather into floods, and disappear before the water can sink five inches into the ground. I have devised a simple experiment to explain this process. Find a curled, dried sponge under the sink and set it on the floor. Fill a glass with water and toss it, all at once, at the sponge. What you will get is water all over the kitchen floor. Now find another dry sponge. Fill the same glass with water and this time pour it slowly. The result will be obvious. The sponge is soaked, your floor relatively dry. Because of the intense nature of its storms, a desert receives rain most often as if from a tossed glass. The rain from the other night was not subtle and did not soak in. Water splashed off the desert and ran all over the surface, looking for the quickest way down. It was too swift for the ground to absorb. When water flows like this, it will not be clean tap water. It will be a gravy of debris, snatching everything it finds.

Walking alone along the canyon rim the next day, I picked through the results of these gravy flows from the night before. Agaves had been half-buried, muffled by six inches of smooth sand, while their blades poked up like birthday candles. Prickly pear cactus pads had the appearance of catcher's mitts, fielding the movement of rocks and sloughs of organic debris, straining oak leaves through their spines. Some were buried by small, square pieces of rock, remnants of Hermit shale and supai formation from above.

I gingerly lifted one of these remnant stones from a cactus pad. The rock stood white against all of the local red and maroon formations. It was Coconino sandstone, carried from several miles away. The cliffs up there are falling over each other, adding more and more material to these slopes, more sand to the river. Under certain rock formations you will sleep to the constant plucking of small rocks, pieces that whistle down and crack near your camp. The Coconino sandstone is particularly good at letting fly fractured arcs of rock, large enough to disturb you from your camp and send you elsewhere for the night.

Nearby I found in the sediment a single grayish black arrowhead. To its left, six feet away, was a small piece of broken pottery. I wheeled the potsherd between my fingers. It was not curved enough for a bowl or an actual pot. Maybe a dish, tan and glazed, seven hundred years old or so. I began counting pieces of pottery as I came to ten and then thirty of them.

A slight drainage another twenty feet away had dislodged—

along with its usual fare of seeds, rock, and sand—numerous Anasazi potsherds. They gathered with debris of like size, caught in the feathered, sandy eddies, buried to their tips, or pushed sideways against a narrowleaf yucca. These were bluish corrugated pieces, the lips of jars, painted redware, bowl concavities, sherds with angular black-on-white paintings, smooth beige pieces, gray sherds with hand-drawn burnish marks, and the handle of a mug or of a water carrier.

In this exhibition of potsherds I found some that had been broken by mule deer hooves only days ago. The trail of water-driven pottery led to the remains of a round building, eighteen feet across. Pieces of pottery had fled from the structure in every downstream direction. It was an exodus. The potsherds were steadily on their way to the interior canyons, pushed by runoff.

I crouched and set one of these painted black-on-white pieces on my left knee. Typical of this culture's attention to detail, the lines of paint were as fine as shadows of grass blades. It occurred to me that a measure of a civilization should not be how well it stands, but how well it falls. In some places the water had stacked pieces on top of each other. They could have easily been mistaken for coin-size stones, gracefully blending with every other natural object being carried away.

I held the piece up so that it cut a shape against the sky. Behind it could be seen layers upon layers of cliffs leading into canyons, dropping then to innermost chasms, eventually to the river. The thread between these landforms was water, the downhill flow, the shape that scientists could not originally understand because, they asked themselves, *how could a place defined by the absence of water be defined by the presence of it?* Each object here at the rim was fodder. We were all being fed to the passage of water.

8. CHUBASCO

The Arizona Strip
August

THIS YEAR I HAD SO MANY DREAMS ABOUT FLOODS. IN one I took a nap on a sandstone ledge and woke with my body covered in frothy, rust- colored foam, the kind that floods leave on the backs of boulders and up against cottonwood trunks. In the dream I jumped off the ledge and chased the flood. But I could not catch it. It glimmered as it entered numerous arroyos and spread beyond my reach.

There was a dream of a storm that ripped canyon walls apart, prying the cliffs until they crumbled like statues during siege. The leathery storm unraveled to the ground, and I watched it take one canyon, then the next. I was hoping not to fall under the gaze of this huge, roving creature, hoping it would not find me. But it did and it lumbered at me. I hid behind a boulder as the water surged down and exploded above my head. A protective envelope of air formed between the boulder and the fan of a waterfall, where I crouched and shivered as the flood thundered around me.

A couple of years ago I sat in a window seat of a passenger airliner. We were attempting to land among summer thunderstorms in Phoenix, banking around the city eight times as I looked down on arteries of lightning. Each time we passed the edge of a storm, the rattling of the fuselage made a sound like a box of pencils being violently shaken. Running low on fuel, we turned south for Tucson and within ten minutes of landing, a thunderstorm hit the Tucson airport, pinning us there for an hour, still in the airplane. During bursts of wind-driven rain, all conversations halted as people looked around, expecting the fuselage to buckle. After we finally took off, halfway to Phoenix I looked out the oval window from ten thousand feet and scanned the sunset earth below. Then my hands went flat against the window as I lifted from my seat, my forehead pasted against the plastic. It looked like molten gold had been loosed across the desert. Arroyos were flooding, catching sunset light, their brilliant threads working the desert, each of them advancing at the same pace, which seemed incrementally slow from up here. Tom Mix Wash, Bogard Wash, Coronado Wash, Big Wash, Rainbows End Wash, Suffering Wash, Cadillac Wash. Everything was running down there.

I turned quickly from the window. I must have looked raving because the man one seat over, a businessman from El Paso, was already tilted away from me. I blurted, *Flooding down there.* He regarded me with a kind, protective smile. *Really?* I stared at him for another three seconds. I wanted off the plane.

It was pilots coming back from Southeast Asia in the '50s and '60s who added the term *monsoon* to the Arizona lexicon. They were stationed near Tucson, and commonly referred to these summer storms as monsoons because they came on schedule each year like those of Vietnam and Korea. Monsoons are broad and slow rainstorms, liquefying the ground into mud, sweeping over entire continents like an arm brushing crumbs from a table. Arizona's "monsoons" come immediately after the harshest droughts of the year, which run right up to July. Almost half of the desert's yearly precipitation then arrives in August as if a door is flung open. Water stands against drought like light and dark.

What we have in the Southwest is more a season of *chubascos* than monsoons. If a monsoon is a big front of weather, then chubascos are needles poking through the weather map. A chubasco is a kind of storm that eats holes into the sky and the earth. It is a convective thunderstorm, the one item of weather that brings the quickest rainfall, the heaviest winds, and erodes the most land. Corrugated aluminum roofs are ripped off with horrible screeches, then sail like cotton sheets into the atmosphere. People die in chubascos when twenty minutes earlier they didn't even think there would be weather. Most of a year's precipitation can easily be unloaded in six minutes, while one mile away the ground might not even be dampened. This kind of storm is not slow, not broad, not long-lived. Often they come in groups, like packs of feral dogs bickering the winds apart in their teeth. They appear from nowhere and hurl at the ground, then evaporate as if they didn't mean anything by it.

A chubasco is an alchemy of conflict. It is superheated air forced through cold, wet air, heralding the desert's rainy season at the hottest time of the year. A low-pressure system, ripe with moisture, pushes from the Sea of Cortés and the Gulf of Mexico, colliding with the heat of an Arizona summer. Hot air rises off the sunbaked ground, shooting upward at about fifty feet a second, with low pressure leaving the sky open for heat to continue upward as long as it can. The heat pierces higher, colder layers so that rivers of air scroll backward, toward the ground. The sky becomes a sea of writhing puncture wounds. As cumulus clouds move upward, becoming cumulonimbus clouds along these rising domes of heat, enough turbulence builds to rip the wings and rudders from airplanes. Moisture caves in, driven at the earth by frantic winds. Ice churns from the sky, landing on ground that may be 150 degrees.

For over a century scientists have been trying to isolate variables out of these chubascos, tying them down to numbers for prediction. Because they bring the greatest annual rainfall to the desert, offering both water needed for crops and drinking, and disastrous floods, they have been studied down to their individual shapes, trajectories, electrical fields, and the theoretical mathematics of their frequencies. A seventeen-line equation was once composed to anticipate summer thunderstorms from a single gulch in southern Arizona. It was based on eleven years of data from forty-seven rain gauges, leading to a prediction of where and when rain is most likely to fall. After all of that, the prediction was that the rain could fall just about anywhere, and would probably do it during the summer. After seventeen lines of calculations, the mathematicians could conclude nothing more.

From canyon rims I can sit out all day just for the frank pleasure of watching these storms uncoil into the sky, their shapes as peculiar and ornate as wood carvings. Twenty thunderstorms may rise and fall, while not a single shadow crosses me all day. There are those that build into massive columns, then spread and vanish, and those that do not even catch my eye until out of nowhere they burst and steal half the sky, shrouding the ground with rain. In the evening their lighting becomes cinematic. Different storms play on each other, stealing red sunset light, giving it back orange, stretching up so that they stand on tiptoes in the last sunlight, casting shadows through the atmosphere. Then night arrives and I see their muffled lightning a hundred miles off.

This summer I sat on a rock, watching a chubasco over by the Grand Canyon. This was the Arizona Strip, a desperate piece of land stuck between the Grand Canyon, Nevada, and Utah. Hungry Valley, Poverty Mountain, Last Chance Canyon. I had started watching the storm an hour earlier when it was a cloud not much bigger than a pea from where I sat. Now it raked the planet with thunder, erasing entire landscapes inside of its rain. It looked as if someone had taken a knife and gutted the sky and, like a gift of magic, out fell a flood of purple spiderwebs. The low ceilings of clouds caught light off the richly colored sedimentary rocks below. This effect will be seen only over the naked stone of the Colorado Plateau: low, ominous clouds turned a velvet lavender by the ground beneath.

This August morning I had shaved my head until it was as bare as I could get it. The heat, like that of a truck engine, left me guzzling water, sleeping out the afternoons in juniper shade, cutting my hair off, whatever was necessary. I scattered the leftover hair into a garden of narrowleaf yuccas, and the tufts looked like the remains of a killed rabbit. So while I watched this storm, I kept running my hand over my scalp, feeling unduly naked. The storm roamed to the south once, then pivoted back to the north, and was now coming northwest, toward me. Distant thunder made the sound of something important happening somewhere else. I probed my hand over the top of my head and waited.

The edges of thunder grew curt on my eardrums. The thunder no longer sounded like someone else's. It was becoming mine. Looking into this storm was like looking into the deep colors and shapes of a huge orchid. It was *dark* in there. And being torn apart. Winds visibly shoved through the clouds, shredding the edges as if angrily ripping fabric apart, hurling some up and some down. Strands of the storm broke away and rapidly swirled into tight spirals, winding until they sprang apart. When the storm arrived, it made a vertigo wall, taking a sudden shift to the north, then west so that it swept behind me and arrived at my back. Before anything, I heard the zealous sound of rain, the ground blurring and jumping as it arrived.

I had not moved for an hour. I had been sitting on the rock feeling my skull, watching the storm come around me. At the first slap of a raindrop I jumped. I ran west, to the top of a sandstone knoll where I could get a look at the topography and quickly study the lay of drainages leading into lower canyons. Another drop hit, this one on my shoulder. The next two were on my cheek and my arm. Quarter-size prints smacked the red rock. Then the drops were everywhere, leaping all over each other. Something had opened. With the opening came an instant wind shouldering me to the side to get by. I could see it rushing through juniper trees, pushing everything out of its way. Parts of piñon cones hurled into the air. Rain came down like heavy fabric, folds of rain. It came so hard that the ground turned to smoke. Lightning struck. Three seconds later the sky split open. Fear. Sudden, instinctual fear. I ducked at the sound, threw an arm across my head.

Pockets in the sandstone immediately filled and poured one to the next. Larger pockets took several seconds, then filled and overflowed. I ran from the knoll, down its smooth dome into the start of a canyon below. Wind sprinted through, blocking me, knocking me sideways as I made quick choices, finding routes along steep rock benches, checking to see where the rain had gathered, how much of it was flowing to the floor. I was looking for a flood. Small waterfalls pirated each other, building into torrents that fumbled through fallen branches and rocks. The thunder was now sharp as billiard cracks. Rainwater ran down my legs, filling my boots. A lightning bolt struck inside the canyon ahead of me. It touched ground beside a juniper tree, so close and so bright that I involuntarily leapt in the other direction like a jackrabbit hit with headlights. No pause came between lightning and thunder. The air shrieked hysterically. Rain fell harder, signaled by the lightning.

In the past month, nineteen people had died in this state, caught in the path of water as chubascos sent floods through the desert. Bodies were still being exhumed from the mud. I figured I was safer because they had not been looking for floods, while I was. I would have just those extra seconds of lead time. I had made choices at the knoll, calculations on where water would flow, how much, how quickly. I had forgotten the seventeen lines of hard mathematics that had proven not a thing about desert rain.

The canyon walls lifted, ushering me into darker passageways until I reached a confluence of canyons and came to a churning stream. Branches, leaves, and small rocks turned over each other. In the currency exchanged by desert floods, water is the cash. The pocket change is the debris, coming in denominations of boulders, trees, rocks, sticks, sand, mud, and silt. In that order. Small change tumbled down the canyon.

I sprinted to the front of this water, leaping from side to side, trying to outrun it. It was not a terrifying bulwark of floodwater.

It was what I call an ornamental flood. Still, I kept note of places to climb out, stopping to look behind, then scanning the terrain ahead. I'll give you my categories for measuring floods: Ornamental; Powerful; and Fear of God. I have spoken with a few people who have witnessed Fear of God floods. In describing them, they often lift both hands, trying to frame something that is not there. They search all the words that they know and still cannot find the right ones. I have seen evidence of floods above the forty-five-foot mark in certain canyons and have even found pieces of driftwood a hundred feet up.

This flow on the Arizona Strip did not have the crushing force of a large flood. It was small enough so it couldn't bury its own refinement. I watched individual currents move around rocks, becoming as adorned and ornate as a Corinthian order, sending out curls and loops. The water tested the canyon floor with slender, winding fingers, pausing to fill deep holes where piñon cones and yucca pods gathered and bobbed until a route was suddenly found, funneling between boulders. I kept with this leading bore of the flood, pausing as it paused, running ahead as it rolled over itself. It swirled into depressions, building shores of foam, setting objects into motion. Seeing this first water was a blessing of details. None of the anatomical acts could be overlooked: each leaf of cliffrose or rabbitbrush pushed to life, each dune of sand disassembled.

This was unlike the running streams I had seen in the Sonoran Desert or in the Tierra Caliente of Mexico. Those free-flowing streams were long familiar with their canyons, having married themselves to every bend. Their floor cobbles had all been arranged and packed into place—*armored*, as it is called by those in the trade of fluvial geomorphology. Armored because the water knew each divot and angle it would cross every night, in some cases every day, setting rocks into place out of repetition. The water of those clean, sweet creeks had every turn memorized, sending messages up- and downstream, building entire forests like the walls and roof of a comfortable house. This flood at my feet had no such contentment. It knew nothing of the canyon ahead. Time and wind and past floods as unrelated as strangers had left barricades of unarmored debris everywhere. Every move this small flood made was original. Every stone came as news. But what impressed me was that it took up residence without deliberation. It immediately knew how to turn behind a boulder, how to run straight down a chute and then wind like a stirred pot below, as if it had been here for a thousand years. It read the world as quickly as it could move.

For whatever fluke of the storm system, this water remained relatively nonviolent and clear. Not clear enough to see through, but not like the viscous meal of a hard flash flood. I had seen the

Ornamental flood over a pour-off

insane ravage of floods before. I had watched pieces of earth cave in, stood near waterfalls of crushed boulders. Within two weeks of now I would be *inside* a Fear of God flood. But this was different. This was like seeing the pieces of creation, the first pieces that fall together, that will define everything from here on. This was the careful work. The work at the beginning, when the water first runs.

More water entered from narrow tributaries. I heard small waterfalls stammering in the dark of their chambers. They met with the stream just as I passed, one after the next adding to the flow. By then rain had gotten into every wrinkle of clothing, every crease of my skin. It came in sideways, then straight down, then whipped into circles in the enclosed canyon. Lightning girdled the sky.

The canyon tunneled into an arch, where a flat bridge of sandstone joined one wall to the next. I jumped onto the arch's roof as the stream cascaded behind me, plunging into the hole below. The stream burst against the hardpan floor and continued as I downclimbed the wall. The front of the water now traveled a couple of feet every second. The rain slowed markedly as the chubasco continued its passage to the north. But the water kept coming, already set into motion. Up higher on this land, the smallest pools continued finding and feeding each other. The stream only grew. I ran along the path of the flood, but still it would not grow to a size to topple me or drag me under.

The canyon threw itself open at an unexpected lip, falling at least six hundred feet into a much deeper series of chasms. With the stream fifteen seconds behind me, I had to look up, suddenly confronted with this enormous view. Thousands of feet of smooth towers leaned from cliffs. Between them, everywhere, were waterfalls. Waterfalls stacked on waterfalls as if a biblical flood were about to sink the earth, water rushing off the desert, over every point. One waterfall plunged eight or nine hundred feet before erupting into mist. Some were membranous and white, narrow like strings, taller than the falls of Yosemite. Others ran thick with debris. I saw one actually begin, peeling over an edge miles to the south. It sailed outward, and at an outcrop of rock shattered into ten new streamers. Each waterfall led into another gorge and into another until I could not see the bottom. Canyons within canyons, sewed together by waterfalls.

The stream came behind me. It did not pause at the edge. Did not think twice. It dashed over the rim and into open space, joining the procession. Hammering against the next ledge below, it pushed off again into five hundred feet of airspace. Wind captured the falling comet of water, spinning it into tendrils, moving the entire waterfall thirty feet to the right, twenty feet to the left. It passed from my view.

I stood over this echoing hole of canyons not sure of where I should look, what I should be hearing. The mobilized leaves and uprooted sand dunes had become canyons, had become rivers. The desert, an inert fossil of stone, had been triggered awake. All of the desert's bloodlines ran furiously, feeding off networks of precisely designed flumes, revealing the desert's sole purpose, to move water. And the water revealed its purpose, to build a land that will carry it.

Seeing this, the crust of the planet catapulting alive, revealed a depth to this landscape that could not be measured with a compass or mechanical instruments. It is measured in time, in the differences before and after storms, and in the kinetic energy that waits unaffected, then bursts like a choir. Every rock I could see out there was under the influence of water. I stood almost blinded by the animation, knowing that even when the place went dry I would be able to see it, the rocks and canyons as scrolled and driven as floodwater itself. I could only bow my head to this. This is the way things are. Always. Water flowing.

9. HAUNTED CANYON

A THUNDERSTORM CELL ARCHED ITS BACK NEATLY AROUND the curve of the North Rim of the Grand Canyon. A radio call came down in the afternoon. Heavy rain. From the interior of the Grand Canyon, 5,700 feet below, skies were partly cloudy with occasional light rain. Sprinkles really. Bryan Wisher sat in the bunkhouse, set just east of Bright Angel Creek in a cluster of small Park Service buildings. The only buildings at the floor of the Grand Canyon, they seem huddled for dear life below these huge, black, scowling faces of Vishnu schist. Screens instead of windows wrap the outside walls, the way they would on a bungalow in the tropics. For eleven years Wisher had been a ranger in this park; now he was stationed in Phantom Ranch, at the bottom of a pit where canyons run to the center, then into the Colorado River. People come here by trail. Wisher has to rescue them. Sprung muscles, dehydration, ridiculous falls from loose-rocked edges, old men who make it only halfway by sunset. It is a longer, steeper walk than most people think.

He knows weather, is familiar with quick alterations the canyon will take. He looked outside. Rain is as common to the North Rim as sweltering heat is to the floor. There were no more messages on the radio. He returned to his business.

Four o'clock. A sound of industrial motion entered the canyon, like continents grinding together. The bunkhouse shook. Wisher hit the screen door and sprinted toward Bright Angel Creek. A waist-high dam of moving tree parts and loaf-size boulders was on the move. It rolled over the crystalline water below with the hasty resolution of a book burning. It traveled about six miles an hour, just slow enough so that Wisher could jump into the lead and run, looking over his shoulder. It rumbled and broke and grabbed every rock it could, lifting it from its setting, putting it in motion. He stopped, turned, peered into the mass, then ran farther.

First, his assignment was to look for bodies and equipment. Upstream canyons are markedly more restrictive, the water much more violent. And he had no idea where this flood actually originated, which canyon was spitting it out. He squinted into the froth and debris, hoping not to see a water bottle or a backpack or the flash of someone's face gone slack in death.

Second, he was seduced by the flood. To be at the very front is like standing at the tip of creation. Only certain events have this kind of focused rage: the first breaking of ice on northern rivers, an avalanche, a flash flood; all from water. To be there at the moment is indisputable, exquisite. Wisher has pulled people from this kind of water, timing the sounds of passing boulders so he could bolt across and check an engulfed tent. During a midnight flood he once locked arms in a human chain to breach the water, rescuing five people out of Bright Angel Creek.

There was no sign that people had been captured by the water. He stepped aside and the flood passed him, kicking and shouting to the Colorado River. Even if he had seen the people, a husband and wife who had been hiking up Phantom Canyon minutes ago, there was nothing he could have done. He would have stood helpless, suddenly weak as they washed away.

The canyon of Bright Angel Creek is a hive of tributary canyons. It drops twenty-four miles to the river, agglomerating two dozen major side canyons on the way: Roaring Springs Canyon, Manzanita Creek, The Transept, Wall Creek, Phantom Creek, and the mostly unnamed canyons such as the one containing Ribbon Falls, Upper Ribbon Falls, and Upper Upper Ribbon Falls. These lesser canyons are then dissected into farther tributaries, which are again bifurcated so that the whole place looks like a kindergartner got at it with scissors.

The flood did not arrive from the usual suspect of Bright Angel Creek. It stemmed from Phantom, but not even from Phantom proper. Of all the teeming, extensive watercourses, the architect of this flood was Haunted Canyon—five and a quarter miles long. This was the discerning nature of desert cloudbursts. One and not the other. Here and not there. It began behind Widforss Point at 7,822 feet and cascaded to the desert four thousand feet below. As it entered Haunted Canyon, it ripped the world apart. New channels were excavated at the headwaters, old ones slopped over with mud. A fresh cut in the alluvium measures fifteen feet wide by six feet deep, plowed through a stately grove of cottonwood trees. Some trees bridge from side to side, felled by the flood. Others are missing entirely. Meaty, arm-wrestling roots of older cottonwoods are exposed along with the fishnet roots of everything else. Imprinted into a treeless quarry of roots is the shape of a boulder five feet tall and four feet across. The boulder is gone, carried down the canyon.

Against the still-standing trees are aprons of debris, some hurled nine feet up the trunks. They are constructed of riparian grasses, horsetails, reeds, slabs of dismembered cottonwoods measuring three feet around, roots, branches, stones, agave leaves, pieces of cactus, ponderosa pinecones, cottonwood leaves, and sodlike carpets of earth woven together by grass roots. Branches are not cleanly broken, but frayed into papery strings. The trees hosting these debris aprons are peeled of bark, as if they had been relentlessly chewed by animals trying to get out. Everything is draped with the finest material: blackened horsetail rhizomes and bits of tree bark curled like chocolate confections.

Flood-piled debris

The flood merged from Haunted Canyon into Phantom Canyon and angled southeast, mowing through thickets of coyote willow. Most are laid flat. Their topmost, lance-shaped leaves are sewn into debris on the ground. In the main channel several twenty-foot-tall willows are pressed plumb to the creek, fitting rock contours as if they had been as pliable as licked stamps.

There is a place where the canyon dumps into a hole. No debris shows here. The canyon is narrow and clean. Walls are shaped like shells and the boulders are freshly placed. Anything small enough to be carried by water was combed out. Three people had been down there, near the mouth of the canyon, when everything was scoured clean, when the wall of water came down.

They had been camping below Phantom Ranch, and had come in the afternoon to explore the waterfalls of Phantom Creek. Scattered rain did not offend them. They had no idea how long this canyon was, how many tributaries and daughters of tributaries hung above them. Still, it was the kind of deep, narrow canyon that smelled like apprehension. Most of the sky was blindfolded. Black walls crowded at the already dull light.

A terrace of waterfalls had been loud enough to mask the sound of an approaching flood. So there was no time, no warning. If there had been four seconds, they could have scuttled up the ledges. They could have found some break, but it came quick, like a car accident.

The flood buried the waterfalls above them. They had one second, maybe two. They dove behind a grayish, leaning boulder. The crease where the eight-foot boulder meets the wall, no more than nine inches wide, is now a hydraulically packed sandwich of debris. None of it can be dislodged by hand. Tamped into place are shredded agaves and the branches of every local tree species. The wood is so distressed that its pulped cellulose is downy to the touch. Resting at the top of the boulder just over their ducked heads is a twenty-pound rock tossed up here like a paperweight. Water struck the boulder with a backhanded, chin-deep slap. The wife and husband, both forty, were pulled down. They cartwheeled into the mobilized boulders. The woman's brother, in his mid-thirties, stayed on top of the flood. Likely it was luck. He pointed his feet downstream, flailed his arms. But brochure instructions cannot explain how someone lives and someone else dies in a flood. In the haystack pulses of floodwater there is no sense.

The brother hit the east shore at Bright Angel Creek. He grabbed something stable, pulled himself out. If he'd gone any farther, he would have been naked, his clothes ripped from his body. Any farther than that and he would have been dead. Badly abraded, drenched, he stumbled to the ranger station. There he found Bryan Wisher.

His words came out in a monotone, as if emerging from a cardboard box. Then he sobbed. He tried to tell the story. The flood had let him go. Now, in the safety of human company, the event was inexplicable. He had always been the better swimmer. He tried to put it in order. Sobbed again.

Wisher had no time for wasted words. He is not a callous man, but he had to know where the people were seen last. The conversation went three minutes, Wisher breaking in to reroute the story. "Where did you last see your sister and brother-in-law?"

"At the boulder."

Wisher could not find them. Helicopters and dogs could not find them. They were gone, spilled into the river miles beyond.

This was the end of the summer flood season, the final event. A month earlier fourteen illegal immigrants had been caught in a flash flood as they crawled through culverts beneath the Arizona border town of Douglas. Nine blocks into a four-foot-wide storm drain they were hit by a fist of water. Only six made it out alive, crammed beneath a manhole cover they found jammed, trapped until the flood subsided. Three days later an Amtrak train derailed into a flash flood in western Arizona. Just before sunrise, before the dining car opened with its fresh flowers and linen, the train struck a flooding arroyo at ninety miles an hour. The three engines separated while cars toppled and snapped from each other. Its manifest listed 307 passengers and 18 crew members. Over half were injured, many critically, but no one died.

The following afternoon a flash flood destroyed the village of Supai in Havasu Canyon of the Grand Canyon. A helicopter flew ahead of the flood, swerving into the narrow canyon to warn hikers, who immediately scrambled into the cliffs. When the flood reached the Colorado River, it pounded into several raft outfits docked inside the canyon. Two fully loaded twenty-two-foot snout boats, three eighteen-foot Canyon rafts, and several other large boats were hurled end over end. Deck canoes, kayaks, and trees blew out like confetti. Every rope, metal D-ring, and chock holding the boats to the rock snapped. When a Park Service crew was sent down to survey the damage, one man found a polypropylene rope and a life vest still clipped to a rock. Reaching down to cut them loose, he found that the force of the flood had actually melted them into each other. Still, no one was killed.

Two days after the Havasu flood, twelve people were struck by a flash flood in a popular northern Arizona slot called Antelope Canyon. Only one person, the hiking guide, survived, while the other eleven drowned. He was thrown onto a ledge, mud packed beneath his eyelids, completely naked. When he was found, he was delirious, asking over and over why he had lived and the others had not. A rescuer, experienced at the task of finding bodies, later told me that she was left uneasy by the implications of this flood. Each body she uncovered was stripped. Even jewelry and tightly laced boots were torn free, breaking bones to get off if they had to. Then she found the body of a man wearing only a belt and an empty camera bag. And a twenty-four-year-old woman with a handmade silver ring on the middle finger of her right hand.

The final two bodies from Antelope Canyon were never found.

Following the flood out of Haunted Canyon, Bryan Wisher finally gave up his search for the husband and wife. They were declared dead. Seven days later, well out of the search range, a raft outfit sighted the woman's body near Tapeats Creek along the Colorado River. Guides tied the body to a bush to keep it from drifting. She had floated forty-eight miles from the tilted gray boulder where she had taken shelter with her husband and brother, down Phantom Canyon into Bright Angel Creek, and finally down some distance of the Colorado River. This was farther than any drowning victim had traveled in the entire Grand Canyon. The way it was discussed among Park Service people and those who understood the circumstances, it was a sort of postmortem victory that she out-traveled even those who had drowned in the river itself. Searching for meaning in death is reflexive. Even though she had likely died before reaching the river, there was an admiration for how she was propelled through Crystal Rapids and past Elves Chasm, all the way to the clear, converging waters of Tapeats Creek. As if she had done it herself. By those well versed in this territory, she was offered a fleeting sainthood.

Twenty-one days later another raft group found her husband's body in an eddy a short distance down the river from Bright Angel Creek. Both bodies were completely naked. Bones were broken. All that remained was flesh.

The water of a flood has numbers, of course. It has clean definitions: thunderstorms, flood bores, paths of least resistance, streamflow currents. But a certain divination lies beneath, secrets that cannot be sought until the flood recedes. One canyon floods while all others remain still. A two-year-old child survived the border flood while strong, healthy adults helplessly washed away. A woman died in a flood where boulders were demolished, yet she was found naked except for her sports bra, which had not even slipped. In one case, seven bodies clogged together, almost arm in arm, while one was deposited 100 yards *up* a side canyon nowhere near the people she had died with. The Antelope Canyon flood originated from a place the Navajo call Many Ghosts Hill. This most recent flood formed in Haunted Canyon, killing the husband and wife when it hit Phantom Canyon, allowing the brother to live at Bright Angel Creek. Patterns show in the most unlikely places.

Wisher was the man sent down the Colorado River to recover the woman's well-traveled body. His voice is extremely fluid, pleasant. Even when explaining the disturbing shape of her limbs, her breasts, and her face, his words came almost as whispers, no different from when talking about being chased by the flood down the canyon. His voice conjures emotions. The sight of the woman, his first recovery of a female corpse, haunted him.

When asked what these people could have done to save themselves, he almost answered, but did not. It is a question he had been asked before, a search for a simply worded answer tying everything about death and flash floods into an unsoiled package. From his station at the bottom of the Grand Canyon, he did not give me any colorful quotes. He simply looked west. West, where Phantom Creek ran deceivingly clean, and newly ordered boulders stood like statues.

10. FLOOD AT KANAB

Kanab, Utah
September

AT ABOUT TWO O'CLOCK IN THE AFTERNOON I SNUGGED into the sticky booth seat of a Mexican restaurant in Kanab, Utah, and ordered the num ber three combination plate with a root beer. It had already started raining when I abandoned the pay phone outside and ducked in here. A good early September thunderstorm. Now hail rattled the roof. It pinged off the cars in the parking lot. In about thirty seconds the Chevron station across the street vanished into the cloudburst. People left their meals and stared out the windows, forks still in hand. Waitresses gathered at the small diamond-shaped window on the front door, a door that bore a plate that read PUSH, but was missing the SH from being pushed too often. They said things like "Oh my God" and "*Never*, I have *never* seen it like this."

Water rose hubcap-deep after only a few minutes, rushing in clean and fast, as if somebody had opened the wrong valve and couldn't get it closed. The restaurant manager, wearing a NASCAR Phoenix International Raceway T-shirt, stood under the outside awning, up to his ankles in hail and rainwater, looking serious with a mop. It was no longer a work environment in here, or a place to eat. Strangers suddenly knew each other. Waitresses no longer had to say ma'am or sir. They could lean right over the tables and look out the windows. Stories were swapped. It felt like the first snow of the year in elementary school, a sudden excitement.

A girl, nine or ten, waltzed between booths, singing to no one, "I'm from Utah and this is my first flood." Then a man stumbled through the door, shaking out his hair, and when a waitress finally addressed him he looked up as if surprised to find himself in a restaurant. "Oh, I don't know," he said. "How about coffee."

The line cook emerged from the back with an armload of dish towels. He used them to dam the bottom of the front door, to stop the stream that had appeared around the cash-register-and-pepper-mint-candy-bowl counter. Clear water bucked down the street, through the intersection, so that passenger cars foundered. Drivers' expressions could not be made out through their rippled windows.

The storm abruptly ended. A curtain opened. The rain tapered, rose, tapered, and was gone. Sunlight arrived like a father busting in on his daughter and her date making out on the couch. Fun's over. People looked back at their plates, heads shaking, and the food suddenly looked banal. One comment could be heard several times as people resettled themselves. "I thought this was a desert," they said. They were not from here.

Still, the passenger cars were stuck in the intersection, four-wheel-drive trucks plowing around them, lofting wings of water. The water in the street suddenly turned from clear to deep red, the red of the Vermilion Cliffs that surround Kanab, flowing instantly with the viscosity of milk and not water. Objects began to show. Rocks. Uprooted plants. When I saw this change, I finished my meal quickly, paid, and got out of the restaurant.

One of the pickups now swimming through the center street was mine, working toward Highway 89 on the other side of the intersection. The water that had been flowing before was just street wash, inconsequential. This red water was earth. Floodwater. It painted the town red and kept growing. I drove slow enough not to drown the engine. A river, silken with tongues and eddies, occupied the street between the Jehovah's Witnesses Kingdom Hall and the Hitch-n-Post RV Park, exceeding its sidewalk banks and consuming the RV park. People scrambled with buckets or stood stock still, dismayed. A Bureau of Land Management truck parked by the gas station was getting battered from behind as water churned over the tailgate into the bed.

Kanab Creek is the major drainage through here, gathering its water from over two thousand square miles of desert, starting in the Pink Cliffs, coming through terraced canyons of limestone and sandstone. It breaks out briefly, where the Vermilion Cliffs open onto the town of Kanab, then swirls across the border into an Arizona box that becomes part of the Grand Canyon. But this flood entered Kanab Creek from just outside of town, not from those two thousand miles of waiting canyons. It originated from a nameless canyon to the northwest that had taken the brunt of the storm. This canyon fed the flood straight through town into Kanab Creek. The narrow downstream box of Kanab Canyon was going to be a violent place in about two hours. Anyone hiking down there, or lounging on a boulder in blatant sunlight, was probably expecting the next noteworthy event to be nightfall.

An early-century flood in Kanab

If the storm had held its breath for another fifteen minutes, it would have opened over White Sage Wash to the west. The flood would have been directed elsewhere, and the BLM man could have gotten back into a dry truck and not even considered himself lucky.

A few homes showed the damage already, with mud ebbing and flowing halfway to the doorknobs. Water spilled from an open bedroom window. A man hoisted belongings away in milk crates, like a scene doctored for television news dramas. Employees at the Lumber Post fortified their front door with a black welcome mat and a couple bags of cement.

Down Highway 89, traffic backed itself into a line in both directions with the occasional car pulled askew to get a view ahead and see what was holding things up. Emergency vehicles flashed their red and blue lights at the front of each line like fingers pointing out the culprit. Between the two lines, identified by the flashing lights, ran a mile-wide swath of floodwater through a channel that had been dry for the last eight months. The flood cut the highway at a right angle. Uprooted trees sailed over the asphalt, snagging on the barbed wire fence across the way for a moment, bucking back against the force, then tearing through. I got rid of the truck on a hill and marched down to the front of the line. The sun was out, bringing the temperature to about a hundred degrees. The heat made this event seem utterly outlandish, like a trick.

A state trooper and a marshal stood with arms folded. They had brought their cameras from home. I approached them with notebook in hand, wearing shorts and sandals, asking if they minded my walking out there. I told them that I study floods. This amused them.

"Have at it," one said. He waved his arm toward the sashaying red mass occupying what was most of the time a very uneventful spot in the road, a place that usually gathers trash and hitchhikers aiming for somewhere far away. So I walked out there with permission, not getting close at all to the center of the channel where the flood crested and fell like a very long and animated Chinese dragon bounding through a crowd. Thigh-deep in mud that had the consistency and physical properties of oatmeal, I picked through the material beaching on the southern shore of Highway 89.

> *Live cottonwood leaves*
> *juniper branches*
> *willow leaves*

a battered, emptied can of Coca-Cola
rags
islands of foam made from oxygen churned into the
mud
one ground squirrel (recently drowned and still limp)
one spade-foot toad (alive and very agile)
pieces of a barbed wire fence
broken deadwood
live wood
part of a Styrofoam ice chest lid
juniper berries
an acre's worth of drifting, displaced sunflowers

Through the sheeting water an orange Department of Transportation road grader lumbered in to begin the process of getting cars through. It had difficulty navigating a busted cottonwood tree, high-siding on it for a couple of seconds, then grinding it off the road. An orange front-end loader followed. They really could not get anywhere near the flood. It was just for show, work to do. The water here, half a mile from the center of the flood, was a sheet flow exactly three feet deep. While I stood with a tape measure, scooping water samples into film canisters, mud slopping above my knees, a man stopped his beat-up van on the road. He had actually stopped at a tributary that looked too intimidating to cross, but since I was there, he rolled down his window to give me his opinion.

He was once Kanab's postmaster. He must have been the first person I met all day who was not a newcomer to Kanab. He was fascinated by the flood, but not surprised. "Not that unusual in this country," he said, his forearm fulcrumed over the steering wheel. "I'll get my backhoe. Give them a hand with this road."

Indeed, it was easy to discern who has lived in this part of the desert and who has not. Those who were born here know that deserts and floods are the same thing. When people first established the town of Kanab, they had not yet garnered generations who would grow accustomed to desert floods. The thought of flooding was the last thing on their parched minds. On August 30, 1882, about ten years after the municipality was built, an afternoon cloudburst removed most of the town. In the following five years, floods deepened Kanab Creek's channel by more than fifty feet and widened it by at least two hundred feet (partly a physical response to grazing), leaving a broad, flat-bottomed, mostly dry riverbed with steep walls where there had once been a slim finger for the creek.

At the end of July 1883, a cloudburst unleashed a flood that lasted seven to eight hours, cutting open the earth to reveal new freshwater springs. A telegram sent to Salt Lake City from Kanab read:

> Yesterday afternoon at 3:30 o'clock the heaviest flood known in this part of the country came down Kanab Canyon; the force of the water was so great that masses of earth as large as a common house floated down the stream with willows still standing upright. All the wheat in the upper field washed away. The water covered the entire field from fence to fence, the stream at that point being one mile wide. In the canyon it has washed the channel 30 to 40 feet below the former bed of the creek. A number of cattle were washed away and drowned.

W. D. Johnson, a bishop who had moved here to try the desert, had a habit of writing letters up to Salt Lake City expressing his awe at such spectacles. Of this 1883 flood he allowed that "the torrent of water in volume, rapidity, and noise resembled the whirlpool rapids of Niagara." Along with mentioning the same blocks of earth with the same "willows standing erect," he wrote that "it beat everything I ever saw. The canyon is so changed you would not know it."

Residents of Kanab would find floods coming regular as holidays. In 1886 five major floods arrived between August 18 and September 1, two of them occurring eight hours apart. The cellar of the Tithing Office filled with water, causing the building to cave in. Hailstones were said to be an inch and a half across. Sand and gravel buried several acres of adjacent land. A Kanab correspondent for Salt Lake City's *Deseret News* wrote eight days after the final September storm of 1886 that "the dams in the creek went out some time ago, but we are so used to that I had almost forgotten to mention it."

I walked back to the truck with mud and pieces of juniper covering my legs like chain mail. A pickup with its cab spilling over with teenage boys raced through far too fast. Their hollers and crazy, irreverent laughter identified them as locals, saying something about living here.

Driving through town, I saw that a mudfight had started between two young girls in the parking lot of the auto parts store, while water poured out of the building's front door. This was the grooming of the next generation. Children of Kanab would grow to understand that this is a color of the desert, not some hundred-year fluke. They would someday talk of Kanab Creek's floods with a familiarity as precise and mindfully harvested as family histories. At first it looked as if the mudfighting girls were on their knees in mud and water, but they were actually standing.

They squealed and shouted, lobbing fistfuls at each other.

This was not like floodwater you might get from the Mississippi or the Platte. It was so pure that someone from around here could tell me which rock formation it was from, how the south end of town got more Moenkopi mud than the north. You can tell by color. Or maybe even the smell, or the way it feels when rubbed between fingers. The floodwater I collected would prove to be over a tenth solid by volume, the leftover silt being fine as sifted flour. Snow shovels were brought out to get rid of the stuff in a number of parking lots.

Seven miles away, across the border in the Arizona town of Fredonia, they did not get a drop. It never even clouded over.

11. FEAR OF GOD

Grand Canyon
September

IN THE MORNING CAME THE BANGING POTS AND PANS of distant thunder. I rolled from my bag into the thin blue dawn, shuffled across the sand, and stood there naked, peeing on a broom snakeweed. All parts of the planet lay below. This was the top, four thousand feet off the floor of the Grand Canyon, between Fern Glen Canyon and Kanab Canyon. To the west an unsettled broth of storms emerged from Nevada. I ran my fingers over my head, stretched my arms into the air. It was early for this kind of weather. I would usually not see storms of this size until at least noon, when the atmosphere had a chance to embroil itself in rising late-summer thermals. The ocean must have been shedding a healthy layer of moisture in this direction. Now that I was looking, rubbing my eyes and walking to the rimrock, I saw that the storm was about the size of one of the New England states. It dragged lightning over the ground the way someone distractedly pets a cat. From here it looked like toothpicks touching ground, holding up the storm.

I had been waiting, patient, walking these canyons for weeks while sorting through flood debris, counting flood stones of different sizes, using delicate tools to measure the angles of carved bedrock. Mostly, though, I lurked in shadows, waiting for the unexpected arrival of a flood, looking up now and then to see a small cloud heading north. The late-summer storms I had been counting on had spun in every direction, ravaging Olo Canyon while I was at Shanub Point, tearing the insides out of Deer Creek while I hunted for drinking water at the rim of Tuckup Canyon. At night I sat with my knees to my chest, watching the faint blue flashes, hearing a dim rumble, ostracized by another storm heading to another place, missing me entirely.

There would not be much time before this storm arrived. I realized this and sorted through my gear. The storm wheeled east toward the Grand Canyon while I was at least a couple thousand feet too high to get into position to see a flood. No time for the big pack; it would take too long to lumber that thing down the canyon. I wrapped what I needed into a small waist pack: a bottle to hold some floodwater, a quart of drinking water, some food, tape measure, notes, binoculars, raincoat, knife, and a map. I thought of bringing the webbing to help with climbing, but figured I would avoid that kind of unpleasantness entirely. I left the rim, heading toward low ground for a flood. I felt like one of those people studying tornadoes, driving into the storm while everybody else is hell-bent to get out. But there was no one to come running the other way, calling me crazy.

The storm arrived in half an hour, combing the rims, belting out thunder that sounded like a loose aluminum roof pounding in the wind. Still another fifteen minutes before I reached the upper channel of the canyon below. This was a long, narrow catch basin of a canyon, about fifteen miles from end to end. Down inside, it dug itself into a vast chasm, sawing through the planet to the Colorado River.

Rain began as I jogged across one of the interior rims, passing the lone standing boulders that had tumbled thousands of feet to get this far. I started to run. Cloudbursts pounded into the canyon as lightning began striking open ground. I sprinted down to the channel, just above where it entered the canyon. Rain had filled my boots already.

Here the rock was basalt, a lava flow from about a million years ago. Treated with the same regard as any sandstone or limestone out here, the black basalt had been cut into a wormhole of a channel, smooth and polished. I skittered down its chutes, entering the pit of a canyon tall and narrow like a snake path through high grass. This is when I had to think, when I slowed to check every twenty feet for an escape route, some crack or ledge above the high-water mark. The old high-water mark rose as the canyon tightened—ten feet, sixteen, nineteen, twenty-five feet. From the narrow floor of the canyon I was looking for a good place to bundle up and wait out the storm, a platform as far in as possible, where I could safely sit and watch if a flood should happen through.

Built of constant steep plunges where waterfalls formed during floods, the canyon complicated navigation. One of the descents down the middle was too difficult. A small piece of Kaibab limestone had wedged into a crack over a plunge, making a chockstone, something that sat sturdy enough to use as a handhold. Twenty feet below was a plunge pool full of water, its surface jumping like popcorn from the rain. I paced a few times, looking down-canyon, up-canyon. Should have brought the webbing, I thought. I grabbed the chockstone, shook it around to see if it was stable. Good enough. So I got down there, swung my body over the stone, and held on for dear life. I wanted to see if there was a way down. I figured if there was one more hold below the chockstone, I could climb inside just that much farther.

There was not another hold. This was not going to get me anywhere. From my suspended vantage I could see plunge pools lining the canyon from here on down. I pulled myself up to climb out. But I could not get my boots on anything. The angle of the rock was wrong. All I had was this wedged stone to hang from, enough to hold me there but not enough to get me up. I grunted, cursed, squirmed around, and could not get back up. I turned quiet for a second, listening. If the flood came now, it would hit me at just about eye level. I made a trapped-animal sound and tried another position. My right arm weakened. The muscles in my chest drew tight. Then I started to kick. The waist pack wedged me in. I forced myself until something popped in my shoulder. Pain shot up my neck. It was a small strap of muscle pulled too far. I could feel my face involuntarily losing composure.

With my free left hand, I reached down and unclipped my pack. I pulled, so I could toss it up, out of my way. As I pulled, the strap wormed from my fingers. The pack fell. I saw it sail for an instant, the straps swinging out. It landed in the pool below like a sack of laundry.

My notes.

That is all I thought, *my notes.*

For two seconds I tried to find an alternative. There was nothing to hold here. I knew this already. I let go. The only thing to do to get my notes back.

Falling took longer than I thought. My legs started kicking unintentionally in the air. Then I hit the pool, chest-deep. I pawed at the gravel, sputtering juniper scales and small, wet twigs from my mouth. I pulled myself out, the pack in my right hand. The canyon echoed with my splashes.

For a moment I stood with my draining pack, listening so hard it hurt. The sound of thunder. Water running from my clothes. My heartbeat.

The world changes col-

Slot canyon flash flood

ors when you think you might die very soon. Everything stood brilliant. The purple shade of the storm had a thirsty lushness. The rock was smooth as pearl. Even as I stood panicked, listening to water pour through my pants, out of my boots, it was unmistakable that everything I believed was down here. Each part of my faith: the scalloped walls; how each sound was sharply distinguished; the smell of water on stone; the fine patterns left in sand from the last flood. Every last piece of magic and belief. I had spent my life clutched to these canyons. I had always sought this. I could feel lumps of juniper berries down my shirt.

Even if it looked feasible, I could not go downstream from here. That is definitely how people die. From desperation. Bad decisions. If a flood never came, I would be trapped in there like someone stuck down a well peering hopelessly up at a little circle of sunlight. So I turned to the place where I had fallen. I scrambled at the left side, got halfway up and scraped back down into the pool. Skin stripped from my palm like an offering. I sucked on the cut, mumbling obscenities. My flesh for an escape.

Then the right side. A couple of cracks lacing the basalt, part of the jointing that occurs in cooling lava, were exaggerated by erosion. With the pack slung over a shoulder and out of the way, I managed to reach the halfway point, just below where I had jumped. I lay back against the last handhold and rose finger by finger. I used all of my energy, a day's worth just for my fingertips. Then, just for my palms when I ran out of cracks. I used my chin, my right cheekbone, my hip. Anything I could get. It was bad rock. Too slick. My body began to shake, muscles jackhammering.

Rain plucked at my eyes. Skin started to slip, sending my heart jumping. I held to the rock with the side of my face, with my palms flat as palms can lie, the last knuckles in my fingers crimping at the rock. Water started over the edge of the canyon floor above me. It started into a waterfall. Clear water. A small, ornamental flood. *Okay,* I thought, *clear water, just clear water.* The clear water increased, spreading toward me as it ran into the plunge pool with a sluicing sound. *Oh Jesus, not now.* I could not move. If I did I would fall. I let the weight of my body settle on my flesh and the rock. I breathed. The voice of the water grew louder.

I could go down. If I could not get up, I would have to go down. I thought about the circle of sunlight, and the sad, helpless look that would be on my face. I banished the thought and went ahead with my left hand. My body would be sore tonight. Every part of it. I relished the thought. *Tonight. Out of here.* Then the right leg. My left hand drifted over, touched the bottom of the limestone chockstone at a full reach. Fingers crept up its side. I got a hold, my face still flush to the wall. I wrapped fingers around the stone. My entire weight shifted. Water ran down my arm, using my body now as a waterfall. I inched up, boots against one side, hands against the chockstone. When I got high enough, without thinking, I pushed off like a frog, thighs tight, launching my body away and landing with my torso in the gravel and water of the next higher level. My fingers dug in, keeping the dangling half of my body from yanking me off. Gravel let loose and flowed over my shoulders. As fast as I could, I scrambled away from the edge.

I bolted off to one of the walls, climbed up to the rim. Scared enough to have this crisp, anxious stare on my face, I sat in the rain watching the streamflow, which never got bigger, never muddied. It stayed ornamental. Most of the storm had hit lower in the canyon, where I would not have expected it. Big floods down there. The rain stopped. I peeled off my clothes and wrung them out so that murky water spattered the rock, then scooped water in my hands to clean the small debris from my skin and rub clean the abrasions on my palm. Scanning through binoculars (a bit foggy now), I could see water running off the Esplanade sandstone miles below.

I sat there naked for a while, thinking I would get up, dress, and walk away soon. But I did not get up. I sat. I watched. The canyon had given me back. There are certain gambles out here. A commodity of value comes into risk. I figure this is why people spend hours in casinos, tossing money down for a sense of immediacy that is often removed from civilization, a sense of wildness perhaps, where loss or gain will be simple, quick, and definitive. That would be my sense of loss at my own death—simple, quick, and definitive. I shook my head, made promises to myself. But I was here to find floods, regardless. I walked around the basalt rim, finding my way into the lower canyon.

Miles inside, the canyon floor burrowed into a corkscrew passage. Eighty-foot boulders lounged along the dry bottom, some wedged between the walls, others perched on top of each other. Walls took directly to the sky, leaving shadows to feast all over each other at the floor. This is what it must have been like, I thought, to be the first to stand beneath the Empire State Building or beside the docked *Titanic*. The canyon was enormous.

By late morning a second storm broke the canyon rim. The sky turned the color of a bruised plum. Ten minutes ago there had been no sign of clouds, straight sunlight, and now the bulk of a thunderstorm shouldered into the canyon. From a small ledge over the dry canyon floor I watched each movement in the sky, my body shifting to whip-cracks in the wind.

This second storm came erratic and elastic, leaning any direction. It was driven from the inside, from descending swells of rain that severed rising heat cells. By now it was certain; the storm had committed itself. It would land here.

I hit the stopwatch when the rain arrived like the dropping of a cement block. No pause, no first raindrops, just suddenly here. A cloudburst. These storms had been liberating forty-ton boulders lately, and I had been arriving days too late, finding only downstream carnage, falling clumsily into a pit of old floodwater, panicking even as no flood came. Storms had been swerving drunkenly across the landscape, suddenly expelling into one canyon and not the next.

Now it was here. I jumped from the ledge when a curtain of waterfalls came over me. I landed in the drainage and ran. Rain took the land. Waterfalls stirred down every cliff face. Rain beat at my head.

The flood was here, two minutes after the rain began. It filled the channel with no warning. When you hear tales of desert floods you hear about sudden waves, walls of water. These impulsive walls are deep inside the canyon, down in the menacing constrictions, or out the other side. There came no wave here at the very beginning. This was the place where the wave was constructed, the fingerprint where the storm had landed. A stream assembled, midcalf in some places, deeper behind boulders and in the plunges. And rising. Foam of released air and silt collected in eddies. I could not even track this water's origination. It was simply here, fed from every side, fed from things that were not even canyons, were not even places where water should flow.

Canyons are basically nets that catch water. Branches and fingers and tributaries scour the land above, sending everything down, so that when a storm passes, all of its rainwater is driven toward a single point. Water can run from tens of miles down hundreds of feeder canyons, spilling into deeper and deeper, fewer and fewer canyons until the volume of the flood has jumped exponentially into one final chasm where everything converges. I was in this single point. I slapped through its gathering water, running downstream to glimpse the behavior of each local tributary. Water from one side canyon choked and growled, arcing down and bursting into the main channel. A couple of tributaries added enough to triple the flood's volume, one emerging from a slim crack, ushering the curve of a waterfall. Not water, though. It was something else: half rock, half water. It ran red with Supai and Hermit shale, red like a soup of cayenne and fresh, squashed tomatoes thickened with sand and stones. It threw rocks into the air, plunking them into the flood around my legs.

There is a specific geometry to a canyon floor built by this kind of water. There will be long segments of gentle gradients interrupted by sudden drops and pools, followed by more narrow runways leading to more drops. These narrow flood canyons are built like stairways where, at critical points, the energy of increasing stream-force becomes too much. Turbulence drives water and debris until it fists a hole into the canyon. The cauldron that has now been cut into the floor is called a *hydraulic jump*. It is a method of dissipating the flood's energy into a plunge pool, some ten to twenty feet deep, before the water can resume its downstream travel. Floods spill out of these hydraulic jumps, move downstream, build force, and again reach peak turbulence, carving another bowl. This is followed by the slope, then the waterfall, then the next bowl, on and on down the canyon. The pattern is a way for the flood to shed energy, like pumping the car brakes to keep from going out of control.

Within moving water are an array of genetic instructions, which are driven into stone and passed from one flood to the next. If the water is funneled through a thick forest, say in the Olympic Mountains of Washington, it will make the same matrix of steps and pools, only out of fallen trees and woody debris, not out of bedrock. If the medium is boulders and sand, the final shape will be the same, as if sorted by hand—steps and pools in perfect order. You will see it down a steep street gutter where cigarette butts and pieces of loose asphalt have been arranged to form runs and puddles. Water is not concerned with the setting. It consistently uses this language.

This canyon sank into the Supai Formation and strangled itself with meanders and waterfalls. I found ways around, jumping between backs of boulders to keep pace with the rising water. The flood became dangerous in the constriction, boiling with mud and rocks and smaller parts of trees. Large rocks began surging up from their settings, lumbering half out of the water, then thudding downstream. I dragged my left hand on the wall, scooting far over, remembering how the desert fishes get through these floods by squeezing to the side, by keeping straight. The flood began pushing at my legs, telling me *faster, faster!* Water swelled behind my thighs, rising, causing my feet to fumble, almost knocking me over.

Maybe I had made a mistake. Maybe I shouldn't be here. It was time to get out. The first exit to higher ground within the canyon, with ledges just barely beyond reach, did not work. I ducked through a culvert of fallen boulders. Rainwater latticed my face. Where the floodwater smacked into obstacles, mud burst into the air and onto me. The rain then washed the mud from my forearms, off my neck. I turned every eight or ten seconds, wiping my face, to glance behind for the infamous wave. With the storm on top of me, I figured I was *in* the wave. The wave was building around me. At this point I could not turn around and run back up against the flow. I had to follow or I would be tumbled backward.

There are things one cannot know about canyons and floods. One Arizona flood in August 1971 came from a fairly insignificant drainage and yielded what is clearly the largest known flood for a canyon of its size. In a brief event, Bronco Creek belted out about a thousand tons of water every second. The creek, which drains nineteen square miles, was suddenly as large as the Colorado River, a river born from seven states, draining thirteen hundred times the land of Bronco Creek. You never know what you will get—where the storm will hit, how much rain will fall, or how the canyon will play it.

In general, storms travel over the Grand Canyon from southwest to northeast. For canyons like this that open into the common local path of storms, floods tend to be more numerous and more pronounced. Canyons cutting perpendicular to the path are shielded from the bulk of a thunderhead, which crosses briefly from one side to the next. The volume and frequency of storms can be read in the terraces of flood debris left at the mouths. Canyons facing into the storms have shoveled layer after layer of flood debris out, while those facing other directions have produced more scant debris. Storms happen to track along the pattern of geologic faulting in the Grand Canyon, so that many canyons, which use faults as blueprints, are open like mouths swallowing the weather. The entire Grand Canyon is thus a machine designed to capture and drive flash floods. Every last wrinkle and crack lends itself to this mechanism, showing water the quickest, most efficient way down.

A catwalk of a ledge protruded from one wall and I took it, narrow but elevated enough to be out of reach from the flood. On hands and knees I made the first moves. The canyon floor dropped around me through fallen two-story boulders. Where I had last walked, an acacia tree rattled, then bent as mud slopped through its branches. The water below grew from knee-deep to shoulder-deep. Then shoulder-deep to eye-deep. Then the references were gone.

The ledge became wide enough for me to stand as it hugged

the curving east wall. At the junction of several major tributaries, the ledge entered a four-hundred-foot-deep sanctum where floods jumped from each side, spanning well away from their cliffs. Two particular tributaries flowed with unnerving throbs, dropping from canyons that hung a hundred feet above the floor. Shapes were visible in their muddy veils, shadows of large, sailing objects. A newborn waterfall burst off one edge, throwing rocks into the air in its lead. It was as if the scaffolding of the planet was coming down, the bolts and metal sleeves of time and physical structures snapping apart, planks caving in. Wind sheeted up from the canyon floor, propelling mud and mist straight up the wall and against my face, through my soaked clothes.

You could not shout over this sound. It was like gritting teeth and clenching fists. It was the sound angels make as their wings are torn off. Occasionally a single sound stood out: the smack of a boulder, or the sucking of a thousand gallons of water finding a new path. Most individual sounds were felt only through my feet or up the bones of my arms. Breaking boulders made sharp clacks. The low-pitched sounds were those of larger rocks, and when I heard these I backed against the wall in case the earth should split open here. It is simply not possible to stand limp before something like this. The muscles in my neck stood out.

I have often thought that trapped on a shelf in a flood, a person could go insane, waiting for the flood to lift and take the ledge. I remembered a story from Havasu Canyon, when a twenty-foot wall of water came down on the village of Supai in 1910. Charles Coe, the Indian Service superintendent, was found around noon the next day with his wife and their Havasupai cook, huddled on the roof of their house. Theirs was one of only two structures left standing. The three people clung to each other, wearing nightclothes and a few blankets they had salvaged, while the flood growled around them, carrying off horses and cotton-wood trees. From the roof, they had witnessed other buildings collapsing into the flood while somehow, theirs stood. But the fear. The endless fear. During the night they had listened to the world crumble around them, to lumber splitting as roofs buckled. I imagined the fear of waiting for their house to topple beneath them. As soon as Coe was rescued and got out of the canyon, he never checked on his responsibilities to the Havasupai people he had been serving. He left Arizona and did not return.

To my back I could see the scours of old floods against the wall, over my head. How old? A hundred years? A thousand years? It became difficult to carry a thought for more than a couple of seconds. My senses jerked back and forth as if I were being dragged.

What was most remarkable in this flood was not the force or the sound, but the overwhelming smell. It was the smell of drowned pocket mice, sage, newborn canyon tree frogs and sun-heated rocks doused in ice water, the same smell as rain on a hot sidewalk. The bold, musty smell of sacred datura leaves and seep-willows. It was the smell of raw oxygen foamed into the finest silt this planet produces, and the methane of rotting cactus burped through the mud. The dissolving endosperm of acacia seeds. The damp underbelly of a red-spotted toad. Old, rank feathers of ravens, wings of cicadas, and bones of a black-tailed jackrabbit washed from the rim. It was the stench of everything living and dead.

An entire oak tree paused at the margin of a falls, then tum-bled, branches prying away as I watched. The main trunk, as thick as my chest, cantilevered over space, caught on a ledge, and shuttered down ladder rungs of exposed boulders. At the base, small rocks, most the size of kneecaps, jetted into the air. They took odd trajectories, pelting anything nearby, breaking into shrapnel. I could not count fast enough. Maybe ten rocks a second, six hundred rocks a minute, into the air. The tree was pulverized at the bottom.

Any jag or protrusion was beaten down. If I were to stick my hand in there, my bones would splinter. The flood pummeled impurities out of this canyon, ridding the place of friction and awkward shapes, taking it down to an archetypal form—that of a smooth, carved canyon. Every physical element of a canyon network is mercurial, with no hard givens, no solid obstacles. These seemingly unflagging walls of the Supai Formation were simply another moving part. This is how canyons are formed, by the sway of the earth against floods, where the shape is defined by an alertness to even the most trivial tension. If a boulder falls in, everything adjusts. Channel cobbles shift as floodwater shunts to one side, beating a hollow into the wall, while the offending boulder rapidly erodes into a hydraulic shape like the nose of a speedboat. Any interruption alters the hydraulics. The flood might change its mind and a new canyon will be built to reach a new equilibrium. The equilibrium ends up looking like a house of cards, a succession of pits and shells and sudden turns.

Flood researcher Luna Leopold called the flexible aspects of a flood *degrees of freedom*. Degrees of freedom measure the rates at which objects give way to pressure: the quick erosion of sand, the steady wearing back of stone walls, and the instant recoil of water hitting a boulder. From his technical descriptions of research sites, each item in a flood like this is a degree of freedom. Everything changes shape.

Leopold, witnessing numerous floods in New Mexico, tromping the Arroyo Caliente, Arroyo de los Frijoles, and Arroyo San

Cristobal in search of flash floods, had time in his life to decipher the motion of water through the desert, watching banks of mud caving in behind him while rocks battered his legs. In his scientific language, the relationship between a desert's geometry and its floods seems organic: "If the degrees of freedom of the [water] are reduced, the remaining factors [sand, canyon walls, cotton-wood trees, and so on] tend toward a mutual accommodation." Meaning, the more durable and deeper the canyon, the more resistance is given to a flood. The more resistance that is given, the more the canyon wears into the shape of water, and water takes on the shape of the canyon.

I stared into the melee below. The flood bounded over immov-able boulders, churning into whirlpools. It had a texture like a rapid boil, sending debris up, sucking it down, each roil a barrel rising to the surface. Nothing stayed on top for more than a cou-ple of seconds. The trunk of a cottonwood tree showed through. Smaller boulders, three feet across, stabbed and rolled against the larger ones.

About forty-five minutes after the start, the flood began reced-ing. The storm abandoned the canyon entirely, leaving the high sun to bake my head. A few more flood pulses arrived, latecomer tributaries finally sending water down, altering the flood by only a matter of inches. I climbed off the ledge and found a wide stretch in the channel where the water was not so deep. When I reached in to touch the edge of the bed, my arm quivered at the impact. There was no bed. Everything was moving. My skin stung with driven sand. A comparison of sediment loads of a desert canyon, dry all but a few hours of the year, and a year-round stream in Oregon shows that even with so much less flow time, the desert carries a million times more debris. Oregon creek beds are armored with cobblestones packed around each other, accustomed to a constant wash of water. Here, everything is angled for motion. A few of the seepwillows might stay. Half the cottonwoods in a grove may hold their ground. But everything else, the sand and boulders, is primed for momentum. You could close your eyes and run your hands across the stones in the floor of a canyon like this to tell which way the water last moved. It is called *imbrication,* the particular way water stacks objects in a downstream direction. Each rock leans against the next, placed in the position of least resistance, always the same position pointing the way down the canyon, so that if you turn and walk up-canyon, all the shapes are against you. Here and there are imbricate clusters of rocks and boulders; they look like stacked books, so uniform that you will swear someone has been emphatically arranging the local stones.

When I handled a rock large enough that it might be stationary in the water, it rotated from my hand and was dragged downstream. Large rocks actually appeared *above* the surface, tossed up for a moment as if the water had run out of room. Downstream from here, where I would not even think of going, was even more of a keyhole of a passage. The flood down there would become catastrophically huge, soon to burst onto the Colorado River like a bomb.

It would be simple enough to say that there is no grace to a flood, that it is nothing but uncooked power. That is what I saw today, the heedless battering against sandstone, against time, and against my most precious of sensibilities. But what was left behind—this entire canyon—is not graceless, not haphazard. I could see it in the camber of bedrock that the flood chose as a course. Each rock was left in a deliberate fashion. Passageways were left shaped like blown glass. The intentions of floods are expertly refined. The shape of the canyon is the shape of moving water, and the shape of water, like the canyon, will amend to the slightest bias. While resisting and accommodating each other, water and canyon both become patterns of the same intelligence.

I found a place to sit, squatting in a patch of boulder shade where I could listen to the roar come down, watching the flood dwindle. The water finally stopped. It took two minutes to arrive, then two hours and seven minutes to leave. I expected hissing, some sound of decompression. At least the isolated clatter of cobbles settling into each other. But there was nothing. I did not know how to handle the silence. The simple aspects of the environment I had admired in past days—shadows beneath a western redbud tree, the intense blue of the sky, bighorn tracks across an upper level—now seemed inappreciable. I was standing weak-limbed, uncertain of what to do. There was no evidence that it had ever happened. I picked up a cobble, something that had sailed here from miles away, an integral part of motion and violence. It was now as inert as the rest of the desert. The flood had abandoned me. I walked back to my camp to put notes together, to prove to myself that it happened.

12. FOLLOWING THE WATER DOWN

MOVING WATER HAS A WAY OF HAUNTING ME AROUND corners, out of view below. I have spent time in canyons, perching at impassable falls with useless rope in my hand as water goes on without me. It goes around the next deep, subterranean bend, talking out loud into oblivion, while I crouch, tasting the acid of desire like blood in my mouth.

When the flash flood came through this canyon yesterday, I had huddled on the ledge and stared down-canyon. I was looking at the penumbral darkness of a canyon taking a sharp turn, where water lashed and roared out of range. That is where the wild things go. Down there, in that hole.

Among those living in the village of Supai in Havasu Canyon, east of here, the tradition is to avoid the interior depths of canyons. They will not even run the river that passes down the canyon from their village. Belief is that the dead reside in these lower gorges, a belief that is probably correct. These lower gorges are the most likely areas to bring death during a flood. The belief is designed over time to prevent fatalities, beginning as a regulation (telling children never to go down there lest they be swept away) and eventually becoming a ritual. Their village has been repeatedly devastated by floods, yet few people have been killed because they do not mingle with these coarcted regions. Other tribes, with people who freely run the river and walk the narrows, live on the rims and in open country. It is the canyon dwellers who have superstitions about canyons. Floods have prompted taboos: Keep surplus food on the rim for when the village is destroyed, and never wander into the dark interior unless you are looking for death.

I am not of the Havasupai tribe. My history is more like that of a mouse exploring crevices, or of the white man crusading to nowhere. I am burned by thirst. Perhaps I am looking for death.

I tightened my full pack, tying off any extraneous straps, and placed seventy feet of climbing webbing within reach. All of my camp and my life fit neatly onto my back. I descended into the gorge where yesterday's flash flood had cast itself down. I wanted to see where it had gone.

The place steadily closed. It sent me into long chambers where boulders the size of Clydesdales had been abandoned, dropped indiscriminately. I lurked among them. The flood had recharged all the surface springs that leaked from cracks, building a stream that babbled down the passage. Once I reached the hard limestone narrows, the flow of water became constant. Walls hunched together until nearly touching, and the stream sounded like a bathtub faucet left running in a concert hall. I could see only thirty feet ahead and thirty feet behind, the canyon stealing everything each time it barely turned. These were the limestone catacombs, their roofs slivered open where light became theatrical, the blue of the limestone not even reflecting the sky. The first place that straight sunlight actually touched rock was six hundred feet over my head, and from there down light graduated into shadow, then nearly into darkness. At the bottom of a thousand feet of cliffs, the floor went from alley width to just wider than the spread of my arms.

Even with the comforting, silvery tones of running water, I could not help feeling that I was being stalked. Mauled pieces of cactus and the tangled appendages of agaves had been freshly jammed into cracks twenty feet up. The walls had the curved geometry of eggshells, too bald for the slightest handhold.

The stream quiesced into a pool extending beyond the next curve. I slung my pack onto a dry rock, removed my clothes, and swam ahead, scouting along the causeway. My feet lost touch with the floor. I swam a slow breaststroke around a turn, out of sight of my pack, then around another, a modest wake gliding off my back. Each splash sounded like a cautious rummage through a closet, which made it clear that I was the only living thing inside of here. A couple of brief, steep canyons entered from the sides, and I drifted into each of these shrines where films of water slid down their faces from an unseen source.

The pool went on—fourth turn, fifth turn. I stopped and held myself in place with hands against the wall. My heartbeat trembled the surface. This was yesterday's floodwater, still weighted with the opaque fawn color of sediments. I recounted the events of that day, the suddenness of the storm, the volume of the half-liquid mass that tore through here. I had checked the sky before entering, waiting until it was completely clear, which would maybe give me four hours of safe travel. Where floods had come the hardest, the walls were swept clean of every scratch, smooth as obsidian.

After the flood

On down the channel, as far as I could see, the walls had carved out like stacked porcelain dishes and wine glasses. This is the inside of a flood, where the only elements are water and rock honed into each other, trapped so there is no contamination by any laws of physics other than these. As if walking through the inside of a sealed nuclear accelerator, studying the scratch marks of atoms, I swam along, brushing walls with my shoulders. Each mark on the wall was a grace note where the energy of moving water had paused, dug in, and dispersed: the same principle as dimples on a golf ball, where pockmarks encourage patterns of turbulence, reducing drag, allowing the ball to travel farther. In the case of the rock face, turbulence in the water encourages the patterns of pockmarks, which then reduce the drag on a flood. A canyon is not blind stone. These cogs and wheels made of limestone are parts of a mechanism expertly designed to govern floods.

Working with the most subtle aspects of these shapes, a

sedimentology researcher named John Allen studied scallops and flutes left by moving water. He produced numerous papers, and abstract drawings of flow patterns, and inventive, official titles for the shapes he witnessed in water-scoured rock: *spindle-shaped, corkscrewed, comet-shaped, conjugate, twisted, wavelike, parabolic.* Names were given to the anatomy of simple scour marks: *leading point, dividing plane, cusped rim, principal furrow, local furrow, medial ridge, lateral ridge, rounded rim, flank.* He studied their evolution by sluicing water across partially dried beds of plaster of Paris, measuring the changing dimensions that blossomed beneath turbulent water, sometimes defacing the plaster with a trowel or the bottom of a soup can to see how the water would treat these aberrations. He watched his plaster deform into sculptures.

Shapes took on strategic development. The faster and wilder the water, the more complex the designs. Wherever a flow broke from steady to turbulent, he saw the creation of fluting marks, which is the same process that leaves steps and plunges along the length of a canyon floor, only on a much smaller scale. The stream builds force until the energy must blow out and dig a hole for itself in the rock, making a divot. The divot robs the current of its excess, turbulent energy, allowing the water to continue in an orderly fashion—until too much force is once more gained and another hole is dug. Allen saw in his experiments that the bursts are not randomly shaped. They have intrinsic forms.

By spilling dye into water that moved over his erosion marks, Allen was able to see the skeletons of ghosts. He could actually watch the structure of turbulent water as it spun into holes and wrapped around itself. The shapes revealed by the dye were the same as the shapes left in the plaster, and his drawings of the dye patterns are art. Couching the work in scientific terms, he sketched a gallery of whorled spirals, hairpin vortexes, rollers, and swirling black holes. He gave to moving water what is not visible to the eye: motifs that define the shape of a flood-worn rock. He created a dictionary for this language of water.

Straight, smooth flows and turbulent flows split from each other and reattach in orderly fashion, and the difference between the two types can be read in the rock. Smooth flows behave like diamond-bit drills moving in one direction against bedrock, while turbulent flows erode surfaces like a madman with a hatchet, betraying any impurity in the rock's structure. It can be felt with a hand. The separation from smooth to turbulent forms a palpable line on the rock face, a crest that is one of the most common, prominent shapes in a canyon: one side smooth, the other roughened.

This madman with a hatchet has a method to its blows. Researchers have been able to place tiny probes in moving water to observe the actual topography of the turbulent/smooth-water interface, a boundary so well defined that they saw calm flows—the tranquil eyes of the storm—entrained and carried away in the center of turbulent patches. In these probe tests, turbulence proved to be distinctly three-dimensional, with most turbulent zones not isolated, but connected by thin, swirling threads to other zones of turbulence. These shapes are the embryonic scallops that become embedded in canyon walls.

The best example of this order I have seen was a single western redbud tree growing toward the end of the pool in which I swam. It grew from a mound of cobbles just out of the water, and as I swam up to it, I could see that it was healthy, that its leaves had not been torn away, its yam-skin bark had not been terrorized by boulders. The trunk was only four or five inches in diameter, but firm enough that it would probably have snapped if pushed all the way to the ground. Yesterday it had been submerged in twenty feet of rampageous floodwater, deep enough to break in half cottonwoods three times its size. But even the fragile leaves remained unmolested on this tree. I had seen an oak tree yesterday, probably a stronger body than this redbud, and watched it burst into splinters in the flood. This redbud was the only plant growing down here beside a few ravaged twining snapdragons, and desert rock nettles hanging from cracks above the flood zone. It would be as likely for this tree to be found growing on freeway asphalt.

This redbud grew between the lanes of traffic. It had sprouted in one of the vortexes spun from the wall, the only place something could live in here. It came up in the center, in the detached piece of calm water that must always appear in this spot, while every object on all sides had been either destroyed or carried miles downstream. I crawled up on the cobbles and touched the tree's soft, lily-pad leaves. Soaked grasses hung high on the branches like tinsel, but otherwise the flood left no evidence of itself. No evidence other than the fact that the tree remained. Turbulence has order. It can be seen in the shapes of the walls. It can be seen in the existence of one healthy tree in a canyon that cannot even keep its fifty-ton boulders in place.

I swam farther down the corridor. As the pool descended into a flume wallpapered in carved rock, dry ledges appeared on the sides. I swam back to retrieve my backpack and ushered it down on my head to this next clearing, stopping once to rest at the redbud tree.

I set a camp within a limestone bottleneck, on a ledge as humped and gray as an elephant's back. It was high enough to be above yesterday's flood, but again, some floods had scarred the walls still higher. As I arranged my belongings on the rock, setting the cooking pot down slowly so as not to make any loud noises, I thought of the people trapped in the 1910 Havasu flood, how they clung to the roof of their house, and how they must have deliriously feared for their lives through the night as everything around them washed away. I looked to the sky. No storms that I could see, but I could see only a hundredth of the sky.

All night I listened to voices in the chortling and murmuring water. At one point I sat up. I swore I heard words being spoken up-canyon. A young man talking. A father responding. A father and son had somehow become lost and wandered in. It was dangerous to come in here at night. *What were they thinking?*

I closed my eyes and concentrated, but still could not rid myself of the voices. No one should be in here. There was no trail, no easy way to reach the rim. The dirt roads, all of them accessible only to four-wheel-drive vehicles on the most distant side of the Grand Canyon, were a two-day walk away. It was not a place where people would travel. When the voices did not come closer and they did not get farther away, I relaxed. I lay back against the rock.

The walls were flawless mirrors of severity, even in the dark, the way they cut against the stars. The stars, forming a slender ribbon, showed the only difference between dark canyon and dark sky. The voices went on the rest of the night.

⌒

Ellen Wohl, a researcher at Colorado State University, took the study of these eroding, bedrock canyons and turned it into sandbox play in order to understand the articulated carving of a channel. She designed a twelve-foot-long trough that could be tilted at different angles. Then she placed cemented material along the bottom and began running water across it at various gradients. First she found that with clear water, even at six gallons a second, erosion would not begin, so she added sand to the running water, making it more like a desert flood. The carving began. As water carried sand into specific configurations, detailed channels were engraved, offering delicate curves instead of random gouges, beginning to meander, forming a variety of shapes that she recognized from her extensive fieldwork in narrow desert canyons. Everything in her miniature canyon looked familiar.

Wohl found that as she lifted the gradient of the trough, her pretend canyons began pulsing from side to side. Instead of incising at a constant ratio between depth and width, which would leave a simple flume, they became narrow and undulating. It is what you might do if skiing down a steep slope: slaloming back and forth to slow down by way of throwing energy. At a 1 percent grade all she got was an almost straight channel. At 10 percent her canyon became broad and slightly curved. At 20 percent it narrowed and built tight, rhythmic meanders. Basically, a straight channel is unstable with water trying to get out, needing to stabilize itself with greater urgency as it moves faster. As she tilted the trough more the water quickened, complicating the dance of water as it tried to shrug its energy.

Forty-percent grades from Wohl's sandbox trough brought tortuous chutes and pools, identical to sheer desert canyons cut through solid rock. It hardly matters what type of rock is being cut. Water proves stronger than rock. Erosion from running water is not merely insipid weathering. It is a process as intricate and arithmetical as the curve of a nautilus shell.

⌒‿

I have difficulty with the numbers and abrasive calculations that come with the likes of smooth and turbulent interfaces and grade percentages. I am not stricken by the sense of violence that should take me in narrows like this. I am reminded, rather, of paintings by Mary Cassatt of women bathing children. The shapes are too sensual, too meaningful to be disgraced by numbers alone.

Walking and swimming into this flood-formed canyon, I was overwhelmed with the feeling that everything here was animated—my muscles, the rock, the water. I felt as if I were moving through a live body, taking note of the intricate organs, of the flow and pooling of blood, and of bones arched as if they had grown here. I came through valves and sockets. I swam and hoisted and inched around ledges, trying not to fall into the pools below. There came one plunge too far to scramble down. Boulders tilted far over the water. With the webbing tied to a logjam, I lowered my pack twenty feet off the cusp of a boulder. A couple of inches before it touched water, I tied it off so that the pack dangled there; then I climbed up to the edge and dove off. Once in the pool, I had to kick for a while, reaching up to untie the pack. Its weight settled on my head so that it pushed my face under. I awkwardly struggled with it across the pool like an animal unaccustomed to swimming—a giraffe or an armadillo. I climbed back up to retrieve the webbing and dove in once more with the webbing looped around my left shoulder.

Viscera of boulders and inlets blocked the path from there down. It was mostly struggle. Too much water. The canyon entered the ribbed walls of Muav limestone and again I had to suspend my pack over a pool. There was no place to dive this time. I had to climb through a waterfall, the stream thudding on my skull as I groped for handholds. Sunlight came to the bottom so that streamers of water leaping from my shoulders looked like threads of platinum. Tilting my head down, I could keep an air-space below for breathing, hearing only the garbled roar of the waterfall socked around my ears.

One last climb was necessary. I recognized the canyon below, having been here years ago, walking up one evening on the twelfth day of a summer river trip. At the time I had stopped at this rock face and cupped my hands where a small, clear stream squirreled into my palms. I had sipped this water from my hands and wondered about what was above, where this canyon might lead. I had no idea of its size then. It was evening and the climb would have been challenging, so I stayed down. I remembered standing there for a long time, looking up into the night.

Now I perched at the edge of the final boulder, looking down. I strung the full length of webbing across an angled wall, using it as a handline as I gingerly took backward steps. Reaching the bottom, I left the webbing in place for the climb back out.

Not far beyond, the floor turned to mud. The flood had met the Colorado River, backing debris into the canyon. Tree limbs stuck through. I slogged up to my thighs in a material no thicker than pudding. Around a turn, the river became audible, its rapids rumbling over the boulders that this canyon had offered up over the decades. It was a far deeper sound than anything in the canyon behind me. Beneath a sheer eight hundred feet of cliffs that spread open like French doors, I rounded to the river, climbing out of the mud onto clean beach sand.

With a custard of mud slopping off my legs, I walked out to some of the flood-thrown boulders that reached into the river.

Maybe a hundred feet across, the river's silt-heavy water passed at about eighteen thousand cubic feet every second. Eight million gallons a minute. Enough water to fill . . . what? Does it matter? Twenty thousand refrigerators every four seconds? Fifty boxcars in a blink? It was more water than I could calculate. To come upon a river like this, to walk out of the desert, even a flooded desert, and find this is like discovering an unknown ocean. The river passed with perfunctory swiftness. It is astonishing that this river flows and does not pause. Whenever I am camped at this river I wake in the night and walk to the shore, just to be certain that it is still flowing steadily, that it will never stop, never pause.

The canyon here, the Grand Canyon itself, is a cathedral of a gorge. With walls too high and steep to be accurately discussed, this is the most burrowed portion of the Grand Canyon. River guides call this stretch the refrigerator for its lack of sunlight and warmth. I washed the mud from my legs with river water, exchanging mud for a scrabbled grit of sand and ground leaves and twigs. It's not a refrigerator in the dead of summer. I sat on one of these boulders and watched the river pass.

Two hours later, after I had set a camp beneath a tamarisk bush, a twenty-two-foot snout raft pulled up and thudded against the beach. It belonged to a commercial outfit—the supply raft sent down early to capture a camp and set up the kitchen. A skull-and-crossbones flag flew from the stern. A tanned woman with strong arms jumped off the snout with a rope in her hand. At first she didn't see me. I was not sure if I should stay hidden, slink away, or wave. As she dropped a clove hitch around a half-buried piece of driftwood, she spotted me. This startled her. She scanned me for a few seconds, then looked around for my boat. Not finding one, she smiled.

She flicked her head toward the canyon I had just climbed. "Came down the canyon there?"

I walked to her, feeling suddenly awkward, aware of my limbs. "Yeah, down the canyon." My voice sounded strange, like opening an old wooden box. The first words I had spoken in nearly a month. At least the first words to somebody else.

I helped unload, figured I would get a meal out of this. "Twenty more people are coming," she told me as I helped with the big tables. "You okay with that?" She knew what she was asking. She had seen people in the bottom of the Grand Canyon before, people traveling alone on foot, appearing out of some side canyon along the river. I told her it would be all right. A change of pace. I tried to laugh, making it sound natural, but the laugh came off like I'd just tripped over my shoelaces. I still didn't know what to do with my arms when I wasn't carrying anything. I had forgotten how to act.

As she promised, within another hour twenty people arrived at the beach, piling out of eighteen-foot Canyon rafts. Once they had tents set up and clothes changed, a few came over to ask how I had arrived without a boat. After I had described to them the canyon and the route down, they looked over their shoulders, not seeing the place, which was too narrow to be visible from the beach. I could not quite explain.

That night I ate steak, beans, salad, and sautéed mushrooms. I sat in the sand and ate until I felt foolish, so one of the guides brought me a cup of rum, said I should drink it and have more steak. I did.

After dishes I sat on the soft tube of a raft. A loose oar by my leg clacked in the current. I talked with the guides late into the night, discussing floods and things wild. They told me to keep my eyes out. There should be one last body coming down the river, a man who had not been found after a flash flood in Phantom Canyon. Other raft guides, friends of theirs, found the man's wife downstream of here, tied her body to shore so she wouldn't float away. These were the two killed where the brother survived, victims of the same storm that had launched the flood down this canyon two days earlier. They had been only a short distance to the east. I told them about this flood I had seen and they all nodded, turning quietly into their own memories.

"Yeah, floods," a man said. "I've seen some floods I will never forget."

The rest of the night we told flash-flood stories: boats getting bowled over, camps split in half, people trapped on ledges. Most of the talk, though, was not about disaster. It was about the color of the water and the sensation of being near a flood. I heard some good stories that night.

When I walked back to my camp, I felt awake. Their stories had tightened my thoughts and emotions. Each person had remembered exquisite details: the weight of floodwater against the legs, a smell that could not be placed, the way water lifts as a wave comes, uncanny premonitions that led to the evacuation of each person from a canyon just before it exploded. One man explained that many of the trees in Deer Creek had been uprooted this past week. He spoke with a clear recollection of where all the trees had been. This kind of familiarity pleased me, made me feel comfortable in just hearing his voice. He never kept a notebook on Deer Creek; he simply knew because the arrangement of trees in a canyon is a thing a person should know.

I had talked to them about the language I saw written in the canyon I'd just come down, how a flood brings water to a point, forcing it to inscribe into the rock its every secret. This is the place, I said, that you would come if you wanted to know the truth about water. These canyons are like the hieroglyphic tombs of the Egyptians that we read by torchlight. The information is written here. A couple of people nodded. They had thought this too.

In the morning the river was still flowing. I sat in the sand below my camp watching, surprised as always that the river never even stopped to breathe. So much water in the desert. You see this and you imagine that you could build a city out here. But it was only water moving through, on its way out. The desert just happens to lie between here and there. This was not the desert's water. The desert's water had been in those springs, and in the floods, and in the evaporating pools in the land beyond.

I had been watching the river since before first light, with stars raining through the canyon, when the river was black, before coffee came on in the camp kitchen. Along with the sun, color came to the water. The river ran a reddish brown, its namesake color, *Colorado*, colored by the desert. And it spoke, of course, talking around its eddies, hissing up and down the beach in gracious waves, laughing behind a boulder.

Pieces of cottonwood trees and leaves of seepwillow and the crushed boulders of a thousand canyons rumbled by. Drowned beetles with decorative carapaces orbited the whirlpools. Inside this river were feathers and bones and mud and a dead man washed out of Phantom Canyon. Everything comes to the river. Water spills from seven states, traveling from hundreds and thousands of miles away. It is a pilgrimage with pathways set deeply into the land where every rock leans toward the river. It is not wind or fire or humans or gods, but water that defines this land. Could there be any doubt about the influence of water when the

Colorado River is the final say for every shape and angle of land from here to the Wind River Range in Wyoming?

The desert had made its offerings to the river, sending down its boulders and trees during the last flood. I, as well, had been sent. When people stirred in the camp and coffee started, I was asked where I would go next. A ride was offered. They could drop me downstream, at Fern Glen Canyon or Stairway Canyon, where I might find a way out. These routes had been my hope originally, but I knew little of such downstream canyons. In the light of recent floods, I was uncertain of how other canyons might have been struck. Fresh dams of boulders and mud, new waterfalls. I turned down the offer, opting for the known risk of climbing the canyon I'd just descended.

When the rafts put on the river, I left them, entering the mud again, grabbing my piece of webbing, and lurching my way up into the flooded canyon. I was immediately alone as the others continued downriver with their gear and food and laughter. Every motion I made—grabbing a handhold, pulling up—reminded me I was alone, an acute sensation now that I had seen people and eaten in their camp. The canyon was mine, the river theirs. All the way up the canyon I had the unwelcome feeling of water trying to turn me around. I kept saying *upstream*, while thrusting against my body, pushing waterfalls down on my head; water kept saying *no, downstream*. It took three extra days to again reach the canyon rim.

Epilogue
THE ARRIVAL

Kanab Canyon, Arizona
February

THE SOUTHERN MEETING OF CALIFORNIA AND ARIZONA
has a moonscape mountain range locally called *Los Chiches de
Cabrillo,* The Goat Tits. They stand a couple thousand feet
high, one sharpened pillar after the next. A saguaro cactus may
appear once every twelve miles on the Arizona side. A leafless
burst of ocotillo. Brittlebush. The rest is a tangle of mountain after mountain, and volcanic spikes so complex as to look
like a chessboard midgame, strewn with pawns, rooks, and
bishops. My grandfather tested airplanes here for the
Army Air Corps in 1943, returning every day to the base in
Yuma, Arizona. What I remember from his stories is the heat.
All he wanted to do was get his plane to a high altitude and
open the cockpit window so he could finally breathe. He said
nothing else of his time in Yuma. He never told me about seeing water from up there. Just rocks.

I know of a two-thousand-gallon water hole in a canyon

between Carrizo Wash and Bear Canyon Bluff. I know of another place, an arroyo nearby where I once dug into the sand, where a coyote and a feral burro had dug before me, and out flowed a few gallons of stored rainwater. Otherwise nothing.

Walking out here for a day, I followed crests and ducked into thin, barbed canyons. It was deranged navigation. I climbed one of the volcanic steeples so I could see around, high enough to get my grandfather's cockpit view. The desert below was bewildering, almost painful to look at. All rock, it showed no letting up, no soft places. I remembered the water on my body, the floods that had crossed me, pools in the backs of canyons. None of that here. I got about two thousand feet up there, finding a seat on a ledge below the top.

Goddamned horrible land, I thought. The land where I was born. If I had been from anywhere else it would have been easy to despise this place. It looks like a plot of half-exhumed bones—femurs and spines eight hundred feet long. The familiarity I sensed was like studying the faces of close relatives, their stories offered through expressions and scars and peculiarities in dialect. A slender, high-pitched canyon is an aunt that took care of me as a child. My father is the difficult terrain to the east, full of dark turns and revelations. I know these places. My family extends.

The blood, the connection, is water. The land begs for it, turning barren of life in many places. It also begs to be free of it, to shrug it into floods, dispelling it, dredging out canyons in the process. Caught in between, the place is broken into wild pieces, each identifiable in the desert lineage—a wash, a spire, a canyon, a bajada. I had spent two years tracing the bloodlines, meticulously studying the documents, then walking to see if it was true, if the desert was, indeed, bound by water as I had believed. From this high point I viewed the Trigo Mountains, where in the entire mountain range I had once found a green handful of water and thought that I'd made a discovery.

To say that the desert has no water is a tantalizing misstatement. It is believable. But to look over this raven land and know the truth—that there is immeasurable water tucked and hidden and cared for by bowls of rock, by sudden storms, by artwork chiseled hundreds and thousands of years ago—is by far a greater pleasure and mystery than to think of it as dry and senseless as wadded newspaper. It is not only drought that makes this a desert; it is all the water that cannot be seen. I thought of the two-thousand-gallon water hole a few miles from here. Then the big, cloistered tinajas in Cabeza Prieta, not far to the southeast. And the springs, such as Agua Dulce, and the creeks and floods beyond.

I wanted the water on my body again, to clean the wounds rocks always leave in my flesh. Looking across, I decided there was not enough here. I needed to burrow into the desert floor. I climbed down, walked about eight miles to my truck, and drove three hundred miles north to the Arizona Strip. There a canyon called Kanab carves into a limestone aquifer where an unimaginable circus of water plays down into dark corridors. It was another relative of mine, a canyon I knew.

I put on a pack and walked for eleven days into this hulking canyon. Water came out of the walls. It poured though soda-straw passageways. It filled deep holes in the backs of side canyons where the sun shines maybe a couple of times a year around the summer solstice, about three minutes each time. I got into these chilled, carved chambers, pools thirty feet deep where boulders stood through the surface like steeples of a drowned village, and I drank, I washed my skin, I doused my head and let water run down my back. A rich, dank breath ran the length of the canyon. It was the cool smell of life and water that got into my clothes and into the curling pages of my notes.

There was no quiet in the canyon floor. The orchestral tumble of water never ceased. As I walked I lost track of the simplest sounds— scratching the back of my head, swallowing, breathing. I slept in the noise, fitting my sleeping bag onto ledges out of the flood zone, my dreams frenzied and undecipherable. The water poured down the canyon and each day I followed, drugged, taken over.

All I can confirm from my walking in the desert is that water demands a simple economy of motion. If it cannot have this, if it is driven too quickly, left in a hole, or forced through the underground or through a canyon, it will imprint its surreptitious details into everything around, like shedding ballast to get free. In the desert, where it is provoked from every side, water can do nothing but shed. Its knowledge is left everywhere out here, in the fluctuating shapes of forests along the low desert creeks, and the crazy structural diversity among creatures in water holes, and the way boulders or bodies or trees pile up after a flood.

I was now reveling in these shapes and disclosures, climbing through water's exposed plumbing, my eyes drenched. No wonder our civilization is draining the aquifers and sucking each creek dry. We reach the desert and we become driven by water. A story came from back near Los Chiches de Cabrillo, slightly to the south around the sand dunes of Algodones: people returned telling of a sixteenth-century sailing ship stranded in the open desert. It is an archetype of ours, our wish for there to be so much water in such a dry place that a ship has been left aground. The ship has been reported numerous times over the past hundred years, some sightings so specific as to be eerie, such as an 1891 report that the

Sonoran desert spires

vessel appeared to be "about 80 feet in length, 18 feet breadth of beam, and of about 40 tons burden." The tale ranges from the eastern California boundary of the Sonoran Desert to the backside of the Kofa Mountains in Arizona, sixty miles away. A Tohono O'odham story tells of a tribal member waiting for the wind to blow the sand away, exposing the ship so he could board it and haul off some of its cargo before the sands returned.

This is what becomes of our minds in the desert. Water consumes us. We find abandoned ships out there. The highest human-made water fountain in the world stands in a Phoenix subdivision in the Sonoran Desert, throwing a white, liquid torch 560 feet into the sky, as preposterous a sight as a grounded ship half-buried in sand dunes. We gather and stare because water is so strong here. Never have we seen it like this. The yearning of water shows through us, the same as it does in the architecture of canyons, and in rock art at water holes, and in the swollen lips of the dead scattered across Cabeza Prieta.

My sharp longing is one of these confessions of water, embedded into me from my life here, and from the desert spring water given to me through my mother's blood. The secret knowledge of water is nothing but desire. It saturates everything in the desert.

On the eleventh day, I started back for my truck, walking up the canyon floor. Where there had been running water, now there were only dry stones. The world had changed while I was mucking around in the deeper canyon. As I walked upstream of the final springs, the creek vanished entirely where I had ten days ago been climbing on the ledges to stay out of it, shaking my head to clear the sound. Why this had happened, I could not say. A fluctuation in runoff or pressure taken off springs—there was no way to tell. The clockwork of moving water had shifted by a notch. The canyon had gone dry.

Without the splashing and the garble of deep holes, the place felt strangely vacant and unnerving. I had been abandoned. My footsteps through stranded cobbles sounded like dishes broken one by one in a monastery. As I reached the second mile of no water at the floor of Kanab, I sat to write about this phenomenon in my notebook. The pad molded perfectly to my knee with the memory of each time I wrote, worn hard on the edges. I wrote that it was a difficult silence to suddenly bear, like the space left when a diesel engine shuts down. The engine had been running for eleven days. The cogs and wheels ground to a halt. My breaths were guarded in this new quiet. As I sat on a boulder, pen scratching across paper, wind sounded from up-canyon. I kept writing and waited for the wind to reach me, to push my hair.

When it did not arrive I looked up. There was no wind.

The sound continued, occupying the canyon from wall to wall. It grew louder. *Water,* I thought. I tucked my notebook away, lifted my pack, and walked up-canyon toward the sound. I had no fear of a flood. The skies had been clear for my entire trek. I had no fear of the sound either, because I was assured it could not be water, even as I could hear the hiss and shout of voices, as if a crowd was marching toward me. I thought I was dealing with ghosts, was about to turn the corner on a circle of specters.

As I came around, I saw water bearing down. A flood. Before thinking of safety, my mind flashed onto the maps, the lay of canyons and drainages, seeking where the source might be, where an errant storm might have landed to start a small flood. Or sudden snowmelt in the mountains of southern Utah. Or a rumor sent through underground springs. I found no reason. It was not too dangerous a level, but it was at least three times larger than the creek I had originally known. It rolled over itself, tossing rocks ahead, slapping against boulders, its front line well defined with foam and woody debris. I stood still.

It was not moving quickly. Instead, it paused into plunge pools, filling them, spouting over the lips to the next pools down. Trapped in a confounded stare, I did not look for an escape route.

A researcher once took cores from trees along this canyon to read flood history in their rings. What came out was a trend as clear and succinct as tidal patterns, as the regimented drips at a seep. The tree rings, scarred at each large flood back to 1471 A.D., showed that big floods in Kanab Canyon come in swarms. On a larger scale, in the thousands of years, they do the same. As proven through layers of ancient debris piles, floods came across the entire Southwest most often from 4,800 to 3,600 years ago, about 1,000 years ago, 500 years ago, and possibly now. Long, slow inhalations waited between, during which there were no sizable floods at all. Time has been offhandedly kept everywhere water strikes. Today's flood was the pulse where the hands of the clock snapped forward. Ten days of water rushing down every slot. On the eleventh day the upper canyon dried as if in a preparatory breath; then *boom,* the flood arrived. Time was again marked.

Pebbles and rocks scratched in the lead of the flood, tumbling over one another. I crouched and dug my hand into the dry bed before me, watching the leap and dive of the approaching water. No moisture showed on my fingertips. The canyon filled with a rising sound. Eddies fell into place, currents taking over as soon as they touched rock, as if they belonged there, as if they knew exactly what they needed to do. There was no pause of indecision. The water knew right away. The creek, the flood, closed toward me. I had been studying water. I had read hundreds of scientific journal articles, taken innumerable pages of notes, produced papers, articles, treatises on the performance of water in the desert. It was all washed blank here.

Water bellowed as it neared. Complicated discussions and howls of craving. I did not step away from the flood, even as it smacked into the air ahead of me, driving down. Ever since I began my hunt for water, the scruff of my neck was grabbed and I was shoved face-first into water. The day I began my research into desert water, eight people died in a border flood, and a few days later a passenger train plunged into a flash flood. I stumbled into an empire of water holes one day. I found the route into the underworld through a waterfall. Even when I tried to rest, water came for me.

The rocks before me were static and silent. They could not be interrupted, motionless as dead faces—gaunt cheekbones and foreheads aimed upward. Suddenly they flashed alert. Water crossed them, buried them, unfurling algebraic webs of currents. I crawled onto a turtle shell of a boulder as the water arrived, encircling me. The roar rose and consumed the air. A spray of foam and mud covered my boots. I just stood there, unable to move as the flood lifted, stranding me on the back of a boulder.

BIBLIOGRAPHY

Allen, J. R. L. "Flute Marks and Flow Separation." *Nature* 219 (August 10, 1968), pp. 602–604.

Allen, J. R. L. "Transverse Erosional Marks of Mud and Rock: Their Physical Basis and Geological Significance." *Sedimentary Geology* 3, No. 4 (May, 1971), pp. 167–385.

Allen, J. R. L. *Sedimentary Structures: Their Characteristics and Physical Basis, Volume II.* Amsterdam: Elsevier Science Publishers, 1982.

Anderson, S. A. and Sitar, N. "Analysis of Rainfall-induced Debris Flows." *Journal of Geotechnical Engineering* 121, No. 7 (July, 1995), pp. 544–52.

Bajkov, A. D. "Do Fish Fall From the Sky?" *Science* 109 (1949), p. 402.

Batzer, D. P. "Aquatic Macroinvertebrate Response to Short-term Habitat Loss in Experimental Pools in Thailand." *Pan-Pacific Entomologist* 71, No. 1 (1995), pp. 61–63.

Belk, G. D. "Observations on the Clam Shrimps of Arizona." *Journal of the Arizona-Nevada Academy of Science* 26, No. 2 (1992), pp. 132–38.

Benson, M. A. "Factors Affecting the Occurrence of Floods in the Southwest." *Geological Survey Water-Supply Paper* 1580-D. Washington D.C.: U.S. Government Printing Office, 1964.

Blaustein, L. and Margalit, J. "Priority Effects in Temporary Pools: Nature and Outcome of Mosquito Larvae-toad Tadpole Interactions Depend on Order of Entrance." *Journal of Animal Ecology* 65 (1996), pp. 77–84.

Blaustein, L., Kolter, B. P., and Ward, D. "Direct and Indirect Effects of a Predatory Backswimmer *(Notonecta maculata)* on Community Structure of Desert Pools." *Ecological Entemology* 20 (1995), pp. 311–18.

Boileau, M. G. and Taylor, B. E. "Chance Events, Habitat Age, and the Genetic Structure of Pond Populations." *Archive of Hydrobiology* 132, No. 2, (December, 1994), pp. 191–202.

Bolton, H. E. *Rim of Christendom: A Biography of Eusebio Francisco Kino, Pacific Coast Pioneer.* New York: The Macmillan Company, 1936.

Bolton, H. E. *Kino's Historical Memoir of Pimería Alta: A Contemporary Account of the Beginnings of California, Sonora, and Arizona, by Father Eusebio Francisco Kino, S. J., Pioneer, Missionary, Explorer, Cartographer, and Ranchman, 1683–1711.* Cleveland, OH: The Arthur H. Clark Company, 1919.

Boulton, A. J. and Stanley, E. H. "Hyporheic Processes During Flooding and Drying in a Sonoran Desert Stream." *Archive of Hydrobiology* 134 (July, 1995), pp. 27–52.

Brown, B. T. and Johnson, R. R. "The Distribution of Bedrock Depressions (Tinajas) as Sources of Surface Water in Organ Pipe Cactus National Monument, Arizona." *Journal of the Arizona-Nevada Academy of Science* 18 (1983), pp. 61–68.

Brown, L. R. and Carpelan, L. H. "Egg Hatching and Life History of a Fairy Shrimp *Branchinecta mackini* Dexter (Crustacea: Anostraca) in a Mohave Desert Playa (Rabbit Dry Lake)." *Ecology* 52, No. 1 (1971), pp. 41–54.

Brown, L. R. *Regulation of Egg Hatching of a Fairy Shrimp* Branchinecta Mackini *Dexter (Crustacea: Branchiopoda: Anostraca) in Astiatic Desert Ponds.* Ph.D. Dissertation, University of California, Riverside, 1968.

Broyles, B. "Desert Wildlife Water Developments: Questioning Use in the Southwest." *Wildlife Society Bulletin* 23, No. 4 (1995), pp. 663–75.

Bryan, K. "Routes to Desert Watering Places in the Papago Country, Arizona." *Geological Survey Water-Supply Paper* 490-D.Washington D.C.: U.S. Government Printing Office, 1922.

Bryan, K. "The Papago Country, Arizona: A Geographic, Geologic, and Hydrologic Reconnaissance with a Guide to Desert Watering Places." *Geological Survey Water-Supply Paper* 499. Washington D.C.: U.S. Government Printing Office, 1925.

Chew, J. *Storms Above the Desert.* Albuquerque: University of New Mexico Press, 1987.

Clegg, J. S. "Do Dried Cryptobiotes have a Metabolism?" In *Anhydrobiosis,* edited by J. H. Crowe and J. S. Clegg. Stroudsburg, PA: Dowden, Hutchison & Ross, 1973.

Clegg, J. S. "Hydration-dependent Metabolic Transitions and the State of Cellular Water in *Artemia* Cysts." In *Dry Biological Systems,* edited by J. H. Crowe and J. S.Clegg. New York: Academic Press, 1978.

Clinton, S. M., Grimm, N. B., and Fisher, S. G. "Response of a Hyporheic Invertebrate Assemblage to Drying Disturbance in a Desert Stream." *Journal of the North American Benthological Society* 15, No. 4 (1996), pp. 700–12.

Coleman, S. E. and Melville, B. W. "Initiation of Bed Forms on a Flat Sand Bed." *Journal of Hydraulic Engineering* 122, No. 6 (June, 1996), pp. 301–10.

Collins, J. P., Young, C., Howell, J., and Minckley, W. L. "Impact of Flooding in a Sonoran Desert Stream, Including Elimination of an Endangered Fish Population (*Poeciliopsis occidentalis,* Poeciliidae)." *The Southwestern Naturalist* 26, No. 4 (November, 1981), pp. 415–23.

Cooke, R. U. and Warren, A. *Geomorphology in Deserts.* Berkeley: University of California Press, 1973.

Crawford, C. S. *Biology of Desert Invertebrates.* Berlin: Springer-Verlag, 1981.

Crowe, J. H. and Crowe, M. C. "Preservation of Membranes in Anhydrobiotic Organisms: The Role of Trehalose." *Science* 233 (February 17,1984), pp. 701–03.

Crowe, J. H. and Madin, K. A. C. "Anhydrobiosis in Nematodes: Evaporative Water Loss and Survival." *Journal of Experimental Zoology* 193 (1975), pp. 323–34.

Crowe, J. H., Hoekstra, F. A., and Crowe, L. M. "Anhydrobiosis." *Annual Review of Physiology* 54 (1992), pp. 579–99.

Crump, M. L. "Opportunistic Cannibalism by Amphibian Larvae in Temporary Aquatic Environments." *American Naturalist* 121 (1983), pp. 281–87.

Crump, M. L. "Effect of Habitat Drying on Developmental Time and Size at Metamorphosis in *Hyla pseudopuma.*" *Copeia* 3 (1989), pp. 794–97.

De Walsche, C., Munuswamy, N., and Dumont, H. J. "Structural Differences Between the Cyst Walls of *Streptocephalus dichotomus* (Baird), *S. torvicornis* (Waga), and *Thamnocephalus platyurus* (Packard) (Crustacea: Anostraca), and a Comparison with Other Genera and Species." *Hydrobiologia* 212 (1991), pp. 195–202.

DeMarais, B. D. and Minckley, W. L. "Genetics and Morphology of Yaqui Chub *Gila purpurea,* an Endangered Cyprinid Fish Subject to Recovery Efforts." *Biological Conservation* 66 (1993), pp. 195–206.

Dimentman, C. and Margalit, J. "Rainpools as Breeding and Dispersal Sites of Mosquitoes and other Aquatic Insects in the Central Negev Desert." *Journal of Arid Environments* 4 (1981), pp. 123–29.

Dodson, S. I. "Animal Assemblages in Temporary Desert Rock Pools: Aspects of the Ecology of *Dasyhelea sublettei* (Diptera: Ceratopogonidae)." *Journal of the North American Benthological Society* 6, No.1 (1987), pp. 65–71.

Dove, F. H. *Groundwater in the Navajo Sandstone : A Subset of "Simulation of the Effects of Coal-fired Power Developments in the Four Corners Region."* Ph.D. Dissertation, University of Arizona, 1973.

Duckson, D. W. Jr., and Duckson, L. J. "Morphology of Bedrock Step Pool Systems." *Water Resources Bulletin* 31, No. 1 (February,1995), pp. 43–51.

Dudley, W. D. *The Ecology of Temporary Waters.* Portland, OR: Timber Press, 1987.

Ebert, T. A. and Balko, M. L. "Temporary Pools as Islands in Space and in Time: The Biota of Vernal Pools in San Diego, Southern California, U. S. A." *Archive of Hydrobiology* 110, No. 1 (July, 1987), pp. 101–23.

Ely, L. L., Enzel, Y., Baker, V. R., and Cayan, D. R. "A 5000-Year Record of Extreme Floods and Climate Change in the Southwestern United States." *Science* 262 (October 15, 1993), pp. 410–12.

Evans, D. D. and Thames, J. L. *Water in Desert Ecosystems.* Stroudsburg, PA: Dowden, Hutchison & Ross, 1981.

Fisher, S. G. and Minckley, W. L. "Chemical Characteristics of a Desert Stream in Flash Flood." *Journal of Arid Environments* 1 (1978), pp. 25–33.

Fisher, Stuart G. *Hydrologic and Bimnologic Features of Quitobaquito Pond and Springs, Organ Pipe Cactus National Monument.* Cooperative National Park Resource Studies Unit Technical Report, No. 22. Tucson: University of Arizona, 1989.

Fry, L. L. and Mulla, M. S. "Effect of Drying Period and Soil Moisture on Egg Hatch of the Tadpole Shrimp (Notostraca: Triopsidae)." *Journal of Economic Entomology* 85, No. 1 (1992), pp. 65–69.

Garrett, J. M. and Gellenbeck, D. J. "Basin Characteristics and Streamflow Statistics in Arizona as of 1989." *U.S. Geological Survey Water Resources Investigations Report* 91–4041 (1989).

Gerson, R. "Sediment Transport for Desert Watersheds in Erodible Materials." *Earth Surface Processes and Landforms* 2 (1977), pp. 342–61.

Glennon, R. J and Maddock, T., III. "In Search of Subflow: Arizona's Futile Effort to Separate Groundwater From Surface Water." *Arizona Law Review* 36, No. 567 (1994), pp. 567–610.

Godwin, H. "Evidence for Longevity of Seeds." In *Anhydrobiosis,* edited by J. H. Crowe and J. S. Clegg. Stroudsburg, PA: Dowden, Hutchison & Ross, 1973.

Graf, J. B., Webb, R. H., and Hereford, R. "Relation of Sediment Load and Flood-Plain Formation to Climatic Variability, Paria River Drainage Basin, Utah and Arizona." *Geological Society of America Bulletin* 103 (1991), pp. 1405–15.

Grimm, N. B. and Fisher, S. G. "Stability of Periphyton and Macroinvertebrates to Disturbance by Flash Floods in a Desert Stream." *Journal of the North American Benthological Society* 8, No. 4 (1989), pp. 293–307.

Hallet, B. "Spatial Self-Organization in Geomorphology: From Periodic Bedforms and Patterned Ground to Scale-Invariant Topography." *Earth-Science Reviews* 29 (1990), pp. 57–75.

Hand, S. C. and Gnaiger, E. "Anearobic Dormancy Quantified in *Artemia* Embryos: A Calorimetric Test of the Control Mechanism." *Science* 239 (March 18,1988). pp. 1425–27.

Harvey, A. M. "The Occurrence and Role of Arid Zone Alluvial Fans." In *Arid Zone Geomorphology,* edited by D. S. G. Thomas. London: Belhaven Press, 1989.

Hassan, M. A. "Observations of Desert Flood Bores." *Earth Surface Processes and Landforms* 15 (1990), pp. 481–85.

Hathaway, S. A., Sheehan, D. P., and Simovich, M. A. "Vulnerability of Branchiopod Cysts to Crushing." *Journal of Crustacean Biology* 16, No. 3 (1996), pp. 448–52.

Hayden, J. "Ground Figures of the Sierra Pinacate, Sonora, Mexico." In *Hohokam and Patayan Prehistory of Southwestern Arizona*, edited by R. H. McGuire and M. B. Schiffer. New York: Academic Press, 1982.

Hereford, R. and Huntoon, P. W. "Rock Movement and Mass Wastage in the Grand Canyon." In *Grand Canyon Geology*, edited by S. S. Beus and M. Morales. New York: Oxford University Press, 1990, pp. 443–59.

Hereford, R. and Webb, R. H. "Historic Variation of Warm-Season Rainfall, Southern Colorado Plateau, Southwestern U. S. A." *Climatic Change* 22 (November, 1992), pp. 239–56.

Hereford, R. "The Short Term: Fluvial Processes Since 1940." In *Geomorphic Systems of North America*, edited by William L. Graf. Geologic Society of America, Centennial Special 2 (1987), pp. 276–88.

Higa, L. E. and Womersley, C. Z. "New Insights into the Anhydrobiotic Phenomenon: The Effects of Trehalose Content and Differential Rates of Evaporative Water Loss on the Survival of *Aphelenchis avenae*." *The Journal of Experimental Zoology* 267 (1993), pp. 120–29.

Hirst, S. *Havasuw 'Baaja*. Supai, AZ: Havasupai Tribe, 1985.

Hjalmarson, H. W. and Kemma, S. P. "1991 Flood Hazards of Distributary-Flow Areas in Southwestern Arizona." *U.S. Geological Survey Water Resources Investigations Report* 91–1471 (1991).

Hochachka, P. W. and Guppy, M. *Metabolic Arrest and the Control of Biological Time*. Cambridge: Harvard University Press, 1987.

Holden, P. B. "Ghosts of the Green River: Impacts of Green River Poisoning on Management of Native Fishes." In *Battle Against Extinction: Native Fish Management in the American West*, edited by W. L. Minckley and J. E. Deacon. Tucson: University of Arizona Press, 1991, pp. 43–54.

House, P. K. "Hydraulic and Geomorphic Re-evaluation of an Extraordinary Flood Discharge Estimate: Bronco Creek, Arizona." *Geological Society of America Abstracts with Programs* 26, No. 7 (1994), p. A-235.

Howard, A. D. "Case Study: Model Studies of Groundwater Sapping." In *Groundwater Geomorphology: The Role of Subsurface Water in Earth-Surface Processes and Landforms*, Geological Society of America Special Paper 252, edited by C. G. Higgins and D. R. Coates. Boulder, CO, 1990.

Inbar, M. "Rates of Fluvial Erosion in Basins with a Mediterranean Climate Type." *Catena* 19 (1992), pp. 393–409.

Jackson, J. K. and Fisher, S. G. "Secondary Production, Emergence, and Export of Aquatic Insects of a Sonoran Desert Stream, *Ecology* 67, No. 3 (1986), pp. 629–38.

Jain, S. C. and Kennedy, J. F. "The Spectral Evolution of Sedimentary Bed Forms." *Journal of Fluid Mechanics* 63, No. 2 (April, 1974), pp. 310–14.

Juliano, S. A. and Stoffregen, T. L. "Effects of Habitat Drying on Size at and Time to Metamorphosis in the Tree Hole Mosquito *Aedes triseriatus*." *Oecologia* 97 (1994), pp. 369–76.

Kam, W. "Geology and Ground-Water Resources of McMullen Valley, Maricopa, Yavapai, and Yuma Counties, Arizona." *Geological Survey Water-Supply Paper* 1665. Washington D.C.: U.S. Government Printing Office, 1964.

Karcz, I. "Possible Significance of Transition Flow Patterns in Interpretation of Origin of Some Natural Bed Forms." *Journal of Geophysical Research*, 75, No. 15 (May, 1970), pp. 2869–73.

Kieffer, S. W. "The 1983 Hydraulic Jump in Crystal Rapid: Implications for River-Running and Geomorphic Evolution in the Grand Canyon." *The Journal of Geology* 93 (1985), pp. 385–406.

King, J. L., Simovich, M. A., and Brusca, R. C. "Species Richness, Endemism and Ecology of Crustacean Assemblages in Northern California Vernal Pools." *Hydrobiologia* 328 (1996), pp. 85–116.

Kingsley, K. J. "*Eretes sticticis* (L.) (Coleoptera: Dytiscidae): Life History Observations and an Account of a Remarkable Event of Synchronous Emigration from a Temporary Desert Pond." *The Coleopterists Bulletin* 39, No. 1 (1985), pp. 1–10.

Koons, D. "Cliff Retreat in the Southwestern United States." *American Journal of Science* 253 (January, 1955), pp. 44–52.

Kubly, D. M. "Aquatic Invertebrates in Desert Mountain Rock Pools: The White Tank Mountains, Maricopa County, Arizona." *Journal of the Arizona-Nevada Academy of Science* 26, No. 2 (1992), pp. 55–67.

Laity, J. E. "Case Study: Theater-Headed Valleys of the Colorado Plateau." In *Groundwater Geomorphology: The Role of Subsurface Water in Earth-Surface Processes and Landforms, Geological Society of America Special Paper 252*, edited by C. G. Higgins and D. R. Coates. Boulder, CO, 1990.

Langbein, W. B. and Schumm, S. A. "Yield of Sediment in Relation to Mean Annual Precipitation." *Transactions American Geophysical Union* 39 (1958), pp. 1076–84.

Laronne, J. B. and Reid, I. "Very High Rates of Bedload Sediment Transport by Ephemeral Desert Rivers." *Nature* 366 (November, 1993), pp. 148–50.

Leopold, L. B. and Miller, J. P. "Ephemeral Streams—Hydraulic Factors and Their Relation to the Drainage Net." *Geological Survey Professional Paper* 282-A. Washington, D.C., 1956.

Linde, K. "Grand Canyon—A Quantitative Approach to the Erosion and Weathering of a Stratified Bedrock." *Earth Surface Processes and Landforms* 7 (1982), pp. 589–99.

Liu, B., Phillips, F., Hoines, S., Campbell, A. R., and Sharma, P. "Water Movement in Desert Soil Traced by Hydrogen and Oxygen Isotopes, Chloride, and Chlorine-36, Southern Arizona." *Journal of Hydrology* 168 (1995), pp. 91–110.

Loaiciga, H. A. "Flash Floods in Desert Rivers: Studying the Unexpected." *Eos, Transactions, American Geophysical Union* 75, No. 39 (September 27, 1994), p. 452.

Low, B. S. "The Evolution of Amphibian Life Histories in the Desert. In *Evolution of Desert Biota*, edited by D. W. Goodall. Austin: University of Texas Press, 1976.

Lowndes, A. G. "Living Ostracods in the Rectum of a Frog." *Nature* 126 (1930), p. 958.

MacKay, W. P., Loring, S. J., Frost, T. M., and Whitford, W. G. "Population Dynamics of a Playa Community in the Chihuahuan Desert." *The Southwestern Naturalist* 35, No. 4 (December, 1990), pp. 393–402.

Maguire, B. Jr., "The Passive Dispersal of Small Aquatic Organisms and their Colonization of Isolated Bodies of Water." *Ecological Monographs* 33, No. 2 (1963), pp. 161–85.

March, F. and Bass, D. "Application of Island Biogeography Theory to Temporal Pools." *Journal of Freshwater Ecology* 10, No. 1 (March, 1995), pp. 83–85.

Maxson, J. H. and Campbell, I. "Stream Fluting and Stream Erosion." *Journal of Geology* 43 (1935), pp. 729–44.

McGrady-Steed, J. and Morin, P. J. "Disturbance and the Species Composition of Rain Pool Microbial Communities." *Oikos* 76 (1996), pp. 93–102.

McGuire, R. H. and Schiffer, M. B., eds. *Hohokam and Patayan Prehistory of Southwestern Arizona.* New York: Academic Press, 1982.

McLachlan, A. "Life History Tactics of Rain-Pool Dwellers." *Journal of Animal Ecology* 52 (1983), pp. 545–61.

McLachlan, A. "Habitat Distribution and Body Size in Rain-Pool Dwellers." *Zoological Journal of the Linnean Society* 79 (1983), pp. 399–407.

McLachlan, A. J. "What Determines the Species Present in a Rain-Pool?" *Oikos* 45 (1985), pp. 1–7.

McLay, C. L. "Comparative Observations on the Ecology of Four Species of Ostracods Living in a Temporary Freshwater Puddle." *Canadian Journal of Zoology* 56, No. 4 (1978), pp. 663–75.

McNamee, G. ed. *The Sierra Club Desert Reader.* San Francisco: Sierra Club Books, 1995.

Meffe, G. K. and Minckley, W. L. "Persistence and Stability of Fish and Invertebrate Assemblages in a Repeatedly Disturbed Sonoran Desert Stream." *American Midland Naturalist* 117, No. 1 (1987), pp. 177–91.

Meffe, G. K. "Effect of Abiotic Disturbance on Coexistence of Predator-Prey Fish Species." *Ecology* 65, No. 5 (1984), pp. 1525–34.

Melis, T. S., Phillips, W. M., Webb, R. H., and Bills, D. J. *When the Blue-Green Waters Turn Red: Historic Flooding in Havasu Creek, Arizona.* U.S. Geological Survey Water Resources Investigations Report 96–405. Tucson, AZ, 1996.

Melis, T. S, Webb, B. H., Griffiths, P. G., and Wise, T. W. *Magnitude and Frequency Data for Historic Debris Flows in Grand Canyon National Park and Vicinity, Arizona.* U.S. Geological Survey Water Resources Investigations Report 94-4214. Tucson, AZ, 1995.

Milber, P. "Hur Länge Kan Ett Frö Leva?" ["What is the Maximum Longevity of Seeds?"]. *Svensk Botanisk Tidskr* 84 (1990), pp. 323–52.

Minckley, W. L. and Deacon, J. E., eds. *Battle Against Extinction: Native Fish Management in the American West.* Tucson: University of Arizona Press, 1991.

Moore, C. B, Vonnegut, B., and Botka A. T. "Results of an Experiment to Determine Initial Precedence of Organized Electrification and Precipitation in Thunderstorms." In *Recent Advances in Atmospheric Electricity.* London: Pergamon Press, 1958–59.

Morton, R. A. and McGowen, J. H. "Large-Scale Bed Forms and Sedimentary Structures Developed Under Supercritical Flow During Hurricane Flooding." *The American Association of Petroleum Geologists Bulletin* 60, No. 4 (April, 1976), p. 700.

Nagay, K. A. "Seasonal Patterns of Water and Energy Balance in Desert Vertebrates." *Journal of Arid Environments* 14 (1988), pp. 201–10.

Naiman, R. J., Décamps, H., and Pollock, M. "The Role of Riparian Corridors in Maintaining Regional Biodiversity." *Ecological Applications* 3, No. 2 (1993), pp. 209–12.

Nakayama, Y. *Visualized Flow: Fluid Motion in Basic and Engineering Situations Revealed by Flow Visualization*. Oxford: Pergamon Press, 1988.

Newman, R. A. "Genetic Variation for Larval Anuran (*Scaphiopus couchii*) Development Time in an Uncertain Environment." *Evolution* 42, No. 4 (1988), pp. 763–73.

Newman, R. A. "Adaptive Plasticity in Development of *Scaphiopus couchii* Tadpoles in Desert Ponds. *Evolution* 42, No. 4 (1988), pp. 774–83.

Paizis, S. T. and Schwarz, W. H. "An Investigation of the Topography and Motion of the Turbulent Interface." *Journal of Fluid Mechanics* 63, No. 2 (1974), pp. 315–43.

Paylore, P. P., DeGrazia, T., and Powell, D. M. *Kino...A Commemoration*. Tucson: Arizona Pioneers' Historical Society, 1961.

Peel, R. F. "Water Action in Desert Landscapes." In *Processes in Physical and Human Geography*, edited by R. F. Peel, M. Chisholm, and P. Haggett. London: Heinemann Educational Books, 1975, pp. 110–29.

Pewe, T. L. "Land Subsidence and Earth-Fissure Formation Caused by Groundwater Withdrawal in Arizona: A Review." In *Groundwater Geomorphology: The Role of Subsurface Water in Earth-Surface Processes and Landforms, Geological Society of America Special Paper 252*, edited by C. G. Higgins and D. R. Coates. Boulder, CO: 1990.

Potochnik, A. R. and Reynolds, S. J. "Side Canyons of the Colorado River, Grand Canyon." In *Grand Canyon Geology*, edited by S. S. Beus and M. Morales. New York: Oxford University Press, 1990, pp. 461–81.

Priestley, D. A. and Posthumus, M. A. "Extreme Longevity of Lotus Seeds From Pulantein." *Nature* 299 (September 9, 1982), pp. 148–49.

Proctor, V. W. and Malone, C. R. "Further Evidence of the Passive Dispersal of Small Aquatic Organisms Via the Intestinal Tract of Birds." *Ecology* 46 (1965), pp. 728–29.

Proctor, V. W. "Viability of Crustacean Eggs Recovered From Ducks." *Ecology* 45 (1964), pp. 656–57.

Quattro, J. M., Leberg, P. L., Douglas, M. E., and Vrijenhoek, R. C. "Molecular Evidence for a Unique Evolutionary Lineage of Endangered Sonoran Desert Fish (Genus *Poeciliopsis*)." *Conservation Biology* 10, No. 1 (1996), pp. 128–35.

Quisca, A., Aguirre-Pe, J., and Plachca, F. P. "Newtonian Fluid Mechanics Treatment of Debris Flows and Avalanches." *Journal of Hydraulic Engineering* 122, No. 6 (June, 1996), pp. 262–63.

Raudkivi, A. J. *Loose Boundary Hydraulics*, 3rd edition. New York: Pergamon Press, 1990.

Reid, I. and Frostick, L. E. "Channel Form, Flows and Sediments in Deserts."In *Arid Zone Geomorphology*, edited by D. S. G. Thomas. London: Belhaven Press, 1989, pp. 117–35.

Ricci, C., Vaghi, L., and Manzini, M. L. "Desiccation of Rotifers (*Macrotrachela quadricornifera*): Survival and Reproduction." *Ecology* 68, No. 5 (1987), pp. 1488–94.

Riggs, H. C. *Developments in Water Science: Streamflow Characteristics*. Amsterdam: Elsevier Science Publishers, 1985.

Robinson, J. V. and Dickerson, J. E., Jr. "Does Invasion Sequence Affect Community Structure?" *Ecology* 68, No. 3 (1987), pp. 587–95.

Rolston, H. III. "Fishes in the Desert: Paradox and Responsibility." In *Battle Against Extinction: Native Fish Management in the American West*, edited by W. L. Minckley and J. E. Deacon. Tucson: University of Arizona Press, 1991, pp. 93–108.

Schär, C. and Smith, R. B. "Shallow-Water Flow Past Isolated Topography Part II: Transition to Vortex Shedding." *Journal of the Atmospheric Sciences* 50, No. 10 (May, 1993), pp. 1401–12.

Schlesinger, W. H., Fonteyn, P. J., and Reiners, W. A. "Effects of Overland Flow on Plant Water Relations, Erosion, and Soil Water Percolation on a Mojave Desert Landscape." *Soil Science Society of America Journal* 53 (1989), pp. 1567–72.

Schmidt, K. H. "Talus and Pediment Flatirons—Indicators of Climatic Change on Scarp Slopes on the Colorado Plateau, U. S. A." *Zeitschrift für Geomorphologie Supplementband* 103 (1996), pp. 135–58.

Schmidt-Nielsen, K. *Desert Animals: Physiological Problems of Heat and Water.* Oxford: Oxford University Press, 1964.

Scholnick, D. A. "Seasonal Variation and Diurnal Fluctuations in Ephemeral Desert Pools." *Hydrobiologia* 294 (1994), pp. 111–16.

Scogin, H. "Runoff Generation and Sediment Mobilisation by Water." In *Arid Zone Geomorphology*, edited by D. S. G. Thomas. London: Belhaven Press, 1989, pp. 88–135.

Sharma, K. D., Murthy, J. S. R. "Sediment Transport in Arid Drainage Basins." *Journal of Environmental Hydrology* (1993), pp. 20–27.

Shaw, J. "Hairpin Erosional Marks, Horseshoe Vortices and Subglacial Erosion." *Sedimentary Geology* 91 (1994), pp. 269–83.

Shepherd, R. G. and Schumm, S. A. "Experimental Study of River Incision." *Geological Society of America Bulletin* 85 (February, 1974), pp. 257–68.

Simons, L. H. and Papoulias D. "Recovery of the Gila Topminnow: A Success Story?" *Conservation Biology* 3, No. 1 (1989), pp. 10–15.

Smith, Z. A. *Groundwater In the West*. San Diego: Academic Press, 1989.

Sohn, I. G. "Possible Passive Distribution of Ostracodes By High-Altitude Winds." *Micropaleontology* 42, No. 4 (1996), pp. 390–91.

Spangler, L. E., Naftz, D. L., and Peterman, Z. E. "Hydrology, Chemical Quality, and Characterization of Salinity in the Navajo Aquifer in and Near the Greater Aneth Oil Field, San Juan County, Utah." *U.S. Geological Survey Water Resources Investigations Report 96–4155*, 1996.

Spence, J. R. and Henderson, N. R. "Tinaja and Hanging Garden Vegetation of Capitol Reef National Park, Southern Utah, U. S. A." *Journal of Arid Environments* 24 (1993), pp. 21–36.

Stanley, E. H. and Boulton, A. J. "Hyporheic Processes During Flooding and Drying in a Sonoran Desert Stream: Hydrological and Chemical Dynamics." *Archive of Hydrobiology* 134 (July, 1995), pp. 1–26.

Stanley, E. H. and Fisher, S. G. "Intermittency, Disturbance, and Stability In Stream Ecosystems." In *Aquatic Ecosystems in Semi-Arid Regions: Implications for Resource Management*, edited by R. D. Robarts and M. L. Bothwell. Saskatoon: N.H.R.I. Symposium Series 7, Environment Canada, 1992.

Stanley, E. H., Buschman, D. L., Boulton, A. J., Grimm, N. B., and Fisher, S. G. "Invertebrate Resistance and Resilience To Intermittency in a Desert Stream." *American Midland Naturalist* 131 (1994), pp. 288–300.

Stanley, E. H., Fisher, S. G., and Grimm, N. B. "Ecosystem Expansion and Contraction in Streams: Desert Streams Vary in Both Space and Time and Fluctuate Dramatically in Size." *BioScience* 47, No. 7 (July/August, 1997), pp. 427–35.

Storey, K. B. and Storey, J. M. "Metabolic Rate Depression and Biochemical Adaptation in Anaerobiosis, Hibernation and Estivation." *The Quarterly Review of Biology* 65, No. 2 (June, 1990), pp. 145–74.

Stromberg, J. C. "Frémont Cottonwood-Goodding Willow Riparian Forests: A Review of Their Ecology, Threats, and Recovery Potential." *Journal of the Arizona-Nevada Academy of Sciences* 27, No. 3 (1993), pp. 97–110.

Stromberg, J. C. "Growth and Survivorship of Fremont Cottonwood Seedlings, Goodding Willow, and Salt Cedar Seedlings After Large Floods in Central Arizona." *Great Basin Naturalist* 57, No. 3 (1997), pp. 198–208.

Stromberg, J. C., Richter, B. D., Patten, D. T., and Wolden, L. G. "Response of a Sonoran Riparian Forest to a 10-Year Return Flood. *Great Basin Naturalist* 53, No. 2 (1993), pp. 118–30.

Stromberg, J. C., Wilkins, S. D., and Tress, J. A. "Vegetation-Hydrology Models: Implications for Management of *Prosopis velutina* (Velvet Mesquite) Riparian Ecosystems." *Ecological Applications* 3, No. 2 (1993), pp. 307–14.

Stromberg, J. C., Tiller, R., and Richter, B. "Effects of Groundwater Decline on Riparian Vegetation of Semiarid Regions: The San Pedro, Arizona." *Ecological Applications* 6, No. 1 (1996), pp. 113–31.

Toolin, L. J., Van Devender, T. R., and Kaiser, J. M. "The Flora of Sycamore Canyon, Pajarito Mountains, Santa Cruz County, Arizona." *Journal of Arizona-Nevada Academy of Science* 14 (October, 1979), pp. 66–74.

Valett, M. H., Fisher, S. G., Grimm, N. B., and Camill, P. "Vertical Hydrologic Exchange and Ecological Stability of a Desert Stream Ecosystem." *Ecology* 75, No. 2 (1994), pp. 548–60.

Van Haverbeke, D. R. *Physico-Chemical Characteristics and Ecology of Ephemeral Rock Pools in Northern Arizona*. Masters Thesis, Northern Arizona University, 1990.

Vassilicos, J. C. "Turbulence and Intermittency." *Nature* 374 (March 30, 1995), pp. 408–09.

Ward, D. and Blaustein, L. "The Overriding Influence of Flash Floods on Species-Area Curves in Ephemeral Negev Desert Pools: A Consideration of the Value of Island Biogeography Theory." *Journal of Biogeography* 21 (1994), pp. 595–603.

Warren, P. L. and Anderson, L. S. "Gradient Analysis of a Sonoran Desert wash." In *Riparian Ecosystems and Their Management: Reconciling Conflicting Uses*, technical coordinator R. R. Johnson. Tucson, AZ: First North American Riparian Conference, April 16–18, 1985, pp. 150–55.

Webb, R. H., Smith, S. S., and McCord, V. A. S. *Historic Channel Change of Kanab Creek, Southern Utah and Northern Arizona*. Grand Canyon Natural History Association Monograph Number 9, 1991.

Webb, R. H. "Occurrence and Geomorphic Effects of Streamflow and Debris Flow Floods in Northern Arizona and Southern Utah." In *Catastrophic Flooding*, edited by L. Mayer and D. Nash, Boston: Allen and Unwin, 1987.

Webb, R. H., Pringle, P. T., and Rink, G. R. "Debris Flows From Tributaries of the Colorado River, Grand Canyon National Park, Arizona." *U.S. Geological Survey Professional Paper* 1492. Washington, D. C., 1989.

Weiss, E. "Ground-Water Flow in the Navajo Sandstone in Parts of Emery, Grand, Carbon, Wayne, Garfield, and Kane Counties, Southeast Utah." *U.S. Geological Survey Water Resources Investigations Report* 86-4012(1987).

Wells, S. G. "Geomorphic Controls of Alluvial Fan Deposition in the Sonoran Desert, Southwestern Arizona." In *Geomorphology in Arid Regions,* edited by D. O. Doehring. Proceedings Volume of the Eighth Annual Geomorphology Symposium, State University of New York at Binghamton, September 23–24, 1977. London: Allen and Unwin, 1977, pp. 27–50.

Wharton, D. A. "Water Loss and Morphological Changes During Desiccation of the Anhydrobiotic Nematode *Ditylenchus dipsaci.*" *The Journal of Experimental Biology* 199 (1996), pp. 1085–93.

Whitford, W. G., Freckman, D. W., Elkins, N. Z., Parker, L. W., Parmalee, R., Phillips, J., and Tucker, S. "Diurnal Migration and Responses To Simulated Rainfall in Desert Soil Microarthropods and Nematodes." *Soil Biology and Biochemistry* 13 (1981), pp. 417–25.

Wiggins, G. B., MacKay, R. J., and Smith, I. M. "Evolutionary and Ecological Strategies of Animals in Annual Temporary Pools." *Archive für Hydrobiologie/Supplimenteband* 58, Nos. 1–2 (September, 1980), pp. 97–206.

Williams, W. D. "Biotic Adaptations in Temporary Lentic Waters, With Special Reference To Those in Semi-Arid and Arid Regions." *Hydrobiologia* 125 (1985), pp. 85–100.

Williams, W. D. *The Ecology of Temporary Waters.* Portland, OR: Timber Press, 1987.

Wohl, E. and Ikeda, H. "Experimental Simulation of Channel Incision Into a Cohesive Substrate At Varying Gradients." *Geology* 25, No. 4 (April,1997), pp. 295–98.

Wohl, E. "Bedrock Channel Incision Along Piccaninny Creek, Australia." *The Journal of Geology* 101 (1993), pp. 749–61.

Wohl, E. E., Greenbaum, N., Schick, A. P., and Baker, V. "Controls on Bedrock Channel Incision Along Nahal Paran, Israel." *Earth Surface Processes and Landforms* 19 (1994), pp. 1–13.

Wondzell, S. M., Cunningham, G. L., and Bachelet, D. "Relationships Between Landforms, Geomorphic Processes, and Plant Communities on a Watershed in the Northern Chihuahuan Desert." *Landscape Ecology* 11, No. 6 (1996), pp. 351–62.

Woodward, B. D. "Predator-Prey Interactions and Breeding-Pond Use of Temporary-Pond Species in a Desert Anuran Community." *Ecology* 64, No. 6 (1983), pp. 1459–55.

Wyllys, R. K. *Pioneer padre: The Life and Times of Eusebio Francisco Kino.* Dallas, TX: The Southwest Press, 1935.

Young, R. W. "Waterfalls: Form and Process." *Zeitschrift für Geomorphologie Supplementband* 55 (September, 1985), pp. 81–85.